Praise for *Spare the Kids*

"*Spare the Kids* is a necessary book. Drawing from history, popular culture, and cutting-edge research, Stacey Patton makes a careful and persuasive argument against the practice of hitting children. Without condescension or unnecessary moralizing, this book will challenge your most deeply held assumptions and refute your strongest arguments. More importantly, it challenges us to develop a healthier and more humane approach to raising and loving our children."

—Marc Lamont Hill, author of *Nobody: Casualties of America's War on the Vulnerable, from Ferguson to Flint and Beyond*

"The impact on child-rearing among so many black families of Stacey Patton's *Spare the Kids* may well prove as powerfully corrective as Harriet Beecher Stowe's *Uncle Tom's Cabin* was upon the acceptance of chattel slavery."

—David Levering Lewis, two-time Pulitzer Prize winner for biographies on W. E. B. Du Bois

"In a nation where violence is so readily offered as the answer to one or another problem, Stacey Patton's bold and uncompromising dismantling of the logic behind corporal punishment is a much-needed corrective. Though aimed specifically at support for the practice in the black community, this is far from a simple scolding of black America. Indeed, Patton brilliantly demonstrates the ways that corporal punishment is indelibly linked to white supremacy, and a continuation of the systemic logic that undergirds it. In that sense, her work is less moralizing—something we already have more than enough of—than a structural analysis of systemic injustice and how that injustice has been transmitted directly, and often brutally, onto the bodies of children. Though Patton aims her words directly at the black community, to the extent that corporal punishment is far too common among American families generally, this book has the potential to impact a broad and diverse audience."

—Tim Wise, author of *White Like Me: Reflections on Race from a Privileged Son*

"Patton's book is the most forceful case against corporal punishment ever made—rooted in a deep understanding of the historical devaluation of black life, informed by the best science on trauma and violence exposure as predictors of future violence, and written in a fierce, urgent tone. If you turn these pages, you will stop beating your child. Ending the legacy of the master's lash in our schools and rejecting the preacher's admonition against sparing the rod in our homes may be the surest way for parents to show black children that their lives matter."

—Khalil Muhammad, author of *The Condemnation of Blackness: Race, Crime, and the Making of Modern America* and professor at Harvard Kennedy School

"*Spare the Kids* is a heartbreaking—and important—book that addresses the nightmarish reality that black parents devoted to bringing up their children with love and respect may engage in punishment that hurts their families and reinforces ideas of white superiority and black inferiority. Skillfully weaving together history, the experiences of black families, the reports of researchers, and the work of child advocates, Stacey Patton is leading a call for change that will transform child-rearing forever."

—Jorja Leap, author of *Project Fatherhood: A Story of Courage and Healing in One of America's Toughest Communities*

"As a writer who had my daughter in my middle thirties and my son in my forties, I had thought a lot about how I wanted to raise them. I decided before they were born that I would not spank them. Stacey Patton's *Spare the Kids* confirmed my instinct that it couldn't be a way to build the kind of loving, trusting relationship I wanted to have with my kids. Being a parent is hard, no doubt. We make decisions all day, every day, small ones and big that impact our children's daily lives and ones that have long-range consequences. Patton's book reminds us that by respecting black children, their thoughts, their gifts, and their humanity, we show them that we love them."

—Benilde Little, national best-selling author of *Good Hair, The Itch,* and *Welcome to My Breakdown*

Spare the Kids

WHY WHUPPING CHILDREN
WON'T SAVE BLACK AMERICA

———

Stacey Patton, PhD

BEACON PRESS
BOSTON

Beacon Press
Boston, Massachusetts
www.beacon.org

Beacon Press books
are published under the auspices of
the Unitarian Universalist Association of Congregations.

20 19 18 17   8 7 6 5 4 3 2 1

This book is printed on acid-free paper that meets the uncoated paper
ANSI/NISO specifications for permanence as revised in 1992.

Text design and composition by Kim Arney

Library of Congress Cataloging-in-Publication Data
Names: Patton, Stacey, author.
Title: Spare the kids : why whupping children won't save Black America /
Stacey Patton, PhD.
Description: Boston : Beacon Press, [2017] | Includes bibliographical references.
Identifiers: LCCN 2016036845 (print) | LCCN 2016050249 (ebook) |
ISBN 9780807061046 (pbk. : alk. paper) | ISBN 9780807061053 (e-book)
Subjects: LCSH: African American families. | Corporal punishment of
children—United States. | African American children—Abuse of. | African
American parents—Attitudes. | Children and violence—United States.
Classification: LCC E185.86 .P336 2017 (print) | LCC E185.86 (ebook) |
DDC 305.23089/96073—dc23
LC record available at https://lccn.loc.gov/2016036845

The chart entitled "Major Influences on Parenting Among Key Subgroups"
on page 53 is courtesy of Hart Research/Zero to Three National Center for Infants,
Toddlers, and Families, L. H. Hudson, Overview of Day and Goals of Meeting,
presented at the Safe Babies Court Teams Project Expert Advisory
Committee Meeting, Washington, DC, May 2012.

The data in the "Paddling and Lynching" map on page 118
is courtesy of the Charles Chesnutt Digital Archive.

Both images on page 168 are courtesy of the Curt Teich Postcard Archive.

"Oh - I is not!," on page 169, is courtesy of the Curt Teich Postcard Archive.

"With My Love," on page 169, is from the author's personal collection.

The image on page 170 is from the author's personal collection.

To my village parents: Pamela Newkirk, Faith Hampton Childs, David Levering Lewis and Ruth Ann Stewart, Lillian Rhyme, Dorothy Hayes, Pamela Fleeks, Virginia Yans, Edna and Damon Williams, Maureen and Joseph Pallotto, David and Marina Ottaway, Donna Garcia and Scott Albert, TaRessa Stovall, Janice Walker, Kevin and Cheryl Brown

———

To the loving memory of Bonzal "Bunny" Hamilton and Rosalind Donna Jefferson

In the treatment of the child the world foreshadows
its own future and faith. All words and all thinking lead
to the child—to that vast immortality and wide sweep of
infinite possibility which the child represents.

—W. E. B. DU BOIS

Contents

1

A FAMILY CONVERSATION

This book isn't just about hitting children. It is about black children and *freedom*. It is also a book about black America and our pain. It is an examination of history, racism, trauma, crime and policing, media, child welfare policy, science and medicine, popular culture, religion, humor, schooling, sexuality, and who gets to be a child in America.

At a historical moment when young people around this country are declaring to the world that black lives matter, that black girls rock and that they are magical, it is clear that the tides have changed. Our children want to breathe. Their hands are up; don't shoot. They don't want to be stopped. They don't want to be frisked. They don't want to be told to police their bodies in public spaces or to hold their tongues. They don't want to be forced to lie down on filthy sidewalks and submit to the injustice of the moment. They don't want to be the next Freddie Gray or Sandra Bland, portrayed as a "thug" in the news or turned into yet another heartbreaking hashtag on social media.

They are not alone.

Their parents and loved ones don't want them to experience such injustices either. They want their children to have opportunities to grow up to become healthy, thriving adults. This has been the cry of generations of black parents since slavery. These fears and the illusiveness of these simple hopes have been central to the struggle of black lives for all that time. But over the past few years, we've been caught in an endless cycle of grieving. The killings of unarmed black people by cops, and the senseless street murders of our young people by other blacks in cities across this country, have elevated parents' fears and left them wondering how to protect their children. The body count has also intensified debates over physical punishment.

We live in a country where pregnant black women still have to ask the same ethical questions that the civil rights activist W. E. B. Du Bois posed a little more than a century ago: *"Is it worthwhile? Ought children be born to us? Have we any right to make human souls face what we face today?"*[1] These days, even white parents have written about the fears they have for the black children they are raising. They share black parents' frustrations over their inability to protect their adopted and biological children from the racial harms outside their homes.[2]

The cold, hard truth is that we live in a country where black children don't get to be children. They face a culture that questions their intellectual abilities and slanders their humanity at every turn, and a criminal justice system that subjects them to adult penalties, even for first-time offenses. Black four- and five-year-olds are 18 percent of the country's preschoolers but make up nearly half of out-of-school suspensions for toilet mishaps, crying, and throwing tantrums.[3] By age ten, black children are considered less innocent than young white children and are perceived to be older than they actually are, especially by police officers.[4] And the darker their complexion, the more likely they are to receive harsh punishment (including paddling with wooden boards from schoolteachers and administrators) and longer sentences from the courts.[5]

We live in a society where black children who end up in the emergency room are less likely to receive pain medications because white people do not believe black people experience physical pain in the same way.[6] Where a teenage boy can't walk to the store to buy iced tea and candy without being stalked and shot by a neighborhood watchman. Where a black girl can be yanked out of her seat by her neck and tossed across a classroom by a school resource officer.

We live in a society where a twelve-year-old boy playing in the park gets mistaken as a twenty-year-old man and is shot dead by the police within two seconds. Where a teenage boy can't hang out with his friends playing rap music in a car without being killed by a white man irritated by the loud beats. Where a black teen's dead body can lie in the street, baking in the sun for four hours in front of his parents and a traumatized community. Where the legal system insists time and again that black children are responsible for their own deaths. Where adults debate whether unarmed children deserved to die because of their size, because they stole something, because they got suspended from school or smoked marijuana in the past.

We live in a country where the suicide rates among elementary-age black children have nearly doubled since the 1990s, while suicide rates among white children have fallen, according to a 2015 report from the *Journal of the American Medical Association*. Researchers pinpoint exposure to violence and traumatic stress, as well as aggressive school discipline and a higher likelihood of early-onset puberty as possible risk factors. This trend should not be surprising given this country's treatment of black people. On top of their own pain, our children are receptive to what their parents and elders are feeling, displaying, discussing, and experiencing.[7]

There are so many traps for our young: drugs, mass incarceration, neighborhood and gang violence, racist teachers, the school-to-prison pipeline, sex traffickers, trigger-happy cops, a predatory foster care system, the George Zimmermans and Darren Wilsons of the world, poisoned tap water—the list goes on and on. There's a lot to be afraid of.

Given these ugly realities, it's not a surprise that black parents are telling their children whatever they need to in order to keep them safe. Work twice as hard. Be three times as good. Pull up your pants. Take off that hoodie. Cut those dreadlocks. Act right around white folks. Don't make sudden movements. Keep your hands out of your pockets. Don't mouth off at the cops and don't run from them even if you're afraid. Black parents have always searched for armor to protect their children from people who instinctively see them as threats.

Another way black parents try to protect and love their children is by physically punishing them. Whether we call it whupping, beating, spanking, or "loving" discipline, for many, not to hit is considered neglectful and irresponsible black parenting. Our religious leaders preach this. Neighbors enforce it. Comedians and radio personalities joke about it. Political leaders claim it will save our communities, lead to peace in our streets, and keep young black bodies out of jail and the morgue. Millions of people give a virtual thumb's up on social media when they see viral videos of parents physically punishing or shaming their kids. And far too many of us will even argue that whupping kids is "a black thing," as if it's behavior we are genetically predisposed to and can't change.

But corporal punishment is not a black thing. Between 70 and 80 percent of all Americans hit their children. National surveys have varied over the years. Still, this book is solely focused on corporal punishment within the black community. It is an effort to understand how whupping children became so deeply embedded in our culture as good parenting. I ask: Why do so many black people have faith that whuppings will keep our children safe? Why do we consider our physical and emotional pain—and the scars left behind—to be signs of strength, even though our security and health in this country remain precarious? Why do so many of us believe that our personal achievements, or the fact that we haven't been jailed or killed, should be attributed to painful whuppings? Although we have been making these arguments for generations, black children should not have to feel the burning sting of a centuries-old whip to learn or to be kept safe.

My big assertion is this: the violence our children face from the police, school systems, the streets, *and* from their parents is all interconnected. It is what one of my Facebook friends calls "strange and bitter fruit from the same tree." The belief that we need to whup our kids to keep them in line is deeply grounded in our collective psyche, in much the same way that racists believe black folks are culturally deficient and police officers disproportionately see us reaching for guns when we're actually reaching for IDs.

I've heard too many black mothers say, for example, "If I don't whup my son's behind now, he will knock me down later." These mothers were usually talking about toddlers or young adolescent boys. Their words demonstrate how racist ideas about the potential criminality and violence of black males seeps into black parents' thinking about their own children.

This book is going to challenge some of our long-held beliefs about physically punishing children. It makes a private conversation public. I realize that I am committing a cultural taboo by airing our dirty laundry. I am also fully aware that black parents, especially black mothers, are already publically, routinely criticized and blamed for our poverty, crime, and countless other issues. I'm not trying to add to the chorus of stereotyping hate that sees black parenting as the source of society's problems. But the deification of black mothers is just as damaging as white racist stereotypes against them. Thanks, in part, to the late rap artist Tupac Shakur, the black mother is the only woman in our community who can be a crackhead and a "black queen" at the same time. We put Mama on a pedestal and hesitate to call her out because she's holding up our families, often by herself. But that doesn't make it okay for her to beat the black off us. That kind of celebration excuses accountability for parenting practices that are damaging to the overall well-being of black children. We have to talk about this.

This book may also bring up some old wounds. It gets to the very foundation of what many of us have been taught by family, church, and society. But when it comes to discussions about hurting children's bodies, my number one concern is *not* hurting children's bodies. The only empathy I have for the adults who hit children comes from the fact that many of them are doing the only thing they know to do. After all, most American parents were hit as children, and there is no universal parenting program designed to educate parents about the harms of hitting or nonphysical alternatives. It's unrealistic to expect that people whose brains have been wired to hit children and not see it as an act of violence will intuitively do the opposite.

If you have children and hit them, you might feel discomforted by the fact that your actions are connected to the trauma of the whuppings you got as a child. It might piss you off to hear me say that you didn't "turn out fine" because of the whuppings, but that you either turned out fine *in spite of* the pain or that you are a survivor of unrecognized trauma. It might tick you off to hear me say that there are lots of folks walking around who may have been abused and don't even know it. My hope is that this book will be so disturbing that it will make it difficult for people to continue hitting children in peace.

I have an idea of where resistance will come from, though. Everybody is always up in black folks' business trying to tell us how to handle our lives. And we put up with this everywhere. But our homes belong to *us*. They may not be perfect, but they're ours. We're not going to have anybody coming into the only space we have and telling us what to do with the bodies of children we created, feed, clothe, pray for, and worry about all day every day. It doesn't matter if it's our neighbors; our teachers; medical, legal, or psychological experts; child protective services; the government; or even somebody like me, a young black woman who doesn't have children at all.

No matter what, we believe it's our *right* to teach and discipline our children the way we see fit. But there's little acknowledgment that the world is much more open today than at any other point in human history. We know a lot more now thanks to science. But instead of adapting our parenting approach to meet the challenges of our current world, there are still many of us who long for the "good ole days" when kids didn't act so bad and knew their place. We believe that the "good ole days" were safer. The family unit was intact. There was no War on Drugs, and schools didn't need metal detectors. People could get a good-paying job and a house with only a high school diploma. Men settled scores with their fists, not guns. With so much going on in the world, there are lots of reasons why kids seem different today. Is it really because we're not whupping them enough?

"Tough love" is often cited as the reason for this more idyllic era. In the good ole days, if you got out of line at home, you went to the backyard and picked your own switch. Lots of us had to do this. I had to do it myself. Switches, belts, extension cords, wire hangers, shoes, and basically any object within reach was fair game for my married, black, middle-class adoptive mother who whupped me. I wasn't always beaten this way, of course. Sometimes it was a milder pop with her hand. But it all hurt. It all made me cry. It all made me afraid of her. Which was the point, to hear my elders tell it. They said that if my adoptive mother didn't nip my behavior in the bud, bad things were doomed to happen: I'd try to "rule" over her; flunk out of school; become a teen mom; do jail time; or end up in an early grave.

This is a situation we all recognize. But it was not unusual for my adoptive mother to take things much further. I still have the physical scars from all those whuppings, and I spent the bulk of my childhood in New Jersey's foster care system until I aged out at eighteen.

It is my experience with physical, verbal, and emotional abuse in my adoptive parents' home that sparked my interest in the historical treatment of black children during and after slavery. I had a suspicion that my whuppings, though meted out solely by my adoptive mother, had something to do with history. She whupped me like her parents whupped her, and like her grandparents whupped her parents, and like her great-grandparents whupped her grandparents, and like "massa" whupped her great-great-grandparents.

When I was a doctoral student in African American history at Rutgers University, I learned that the larger cultural devaluation of black adults and children informs the way black parents discipline their children. The lingering effects from the trauma of centuries of slavery and post-Emancipation racism has produced what acclaimed author Joy DeGruy has described as multigenerational maladaptive behaviors that continue to be passed on from black parents. These parents suffer from chronic stress and from what's known as post-traumatic slave syndrome, which we inherited from our enslaved ancestors.[8] DeGruy's theory is similar to the results of research by doctors at New York's Mount Sinai Hospital, who discovered that the Jewish descendants of Holocaust survivors have undergone changes in their genes as a result of their parents' trauma.[9]

Those inherited stress-related genes can shape the way people cope with their environment and manifests in poor physical and mental health and in social dysfunction. This passed-on trauma has not only led to the adoption of whuppings as a parenting method. It has also indoctrinated this same behavior in people's children and their children's children, long after this kind of punishment lost its relevance as a survival tactic on plantations and during the racial terror of Jim Crow. The white culture that traumatized generations of black people and taught them to fear the whip now continues to blame and criminalize us for the results.

In my child advocacy work and during my career as a journalist over the past decade, I have interviewed scores of scientists, parents, children, child abuse survivors, and child welfare experts all around the country. Then, during the 2014 Adrian Peterson child abuse controversy and debates over the actions of Toya Graham, the infamous "Baltimore Mom" who went upside her son's head during a race riot in April 2015, I took a lot of heat when I appeared on national television and said these parents, regardless of their intentions, were wrong for hurting their children's bodies. I was adamant that a parent's intent does not trump the impact of violence against a child. In our media moment, we quickly reacted to those controversies but then the country moved on from those stories without the necessary reflection, analysis, and solutions. And so here I am, continuing the conversation with this book.

Some of you may dismiss this book as biased, assuming that the abuse I endured during my childhood clouds my opinion about "reasonable" corporal punishment. Guilty as charged. My whuppings and my scars shape the person I am today and the book in front of you. But I'm not alone in my thinking. My views are equally shaped by data and ample research, which demonstrate the destructiveness of *any level* of hitting children. I see all forms of hitting as acts of violence, and I believe that children should enjoy the same right to bodily integrity as adults.

Experts in the business of understanding child development and parenting practices universally affirm that there's no solid science to suggest that hitting children, to any extent and regardless of race or ethnic background, is good for them or for society. There is plenty of scientific evidence, however, demonstrating the long-term damage resulting from these types of punishment. This is true even when spankings don't leave marks or other serious physical injuries. The effects might not be apparent for years—until after puberty or early adulthood.

Studies by researchers at a number of universities have shown that corporal punishment and chronic stress can have a negative impact on children's brain development.[10] As a child grows, certain parts of the brain are particularly vulnerable to stress. Constant hollering, belittling, threatening, and hitting sets off biochemical responses that can change the architecture of a child's brain and lay the groundwork for a low IQ, a quick temper, aggressiveness, hypervigilance, delinquency, depression, suicide, drug and alcohol abuse, future domestic violence, an inability to regulate impulses, dysfunctional relationships, and early intrusive sexual thoughts and activities.[11] This abundance of research has not changed public opinion or practice.

So why don't we listen to the evidence? Why do we continue hitting our children when we remain on the bottom rung of every measurement of health and progress? We're the most locked up, unhealthy, stressed out, demonized group of people in America. Whupping children hasn't saved us from any of this! We have been whupping for centuries and we have not turned out fine as a people. Could it be that all that violence is one of the root causes of our problems? How committed are we to passing on trauma to future generations? Are we devoted to pain and suffering and being victims?

I understand the immediate urge to defend black spaces, black parents, and black culture and identity. But we should consider that maybe—*just maybe*—white supremacy has done a masterful job of getting its victims of centuries of racial oppression to continue its trauma work and convinced us to call it "love." If we insist on continuing this whupping tradition, let's at least acknowledge what we're really doing, where this errant programming really comes from, and what the real long-term consequences are.

I also recognize that we understandably have a profound distrust of white "experts." After all, these are the same professionals who use science, medicine, statistics, and the media to call us inferior and pathological, and to shore up their own sense of identity and mythical sense of superiority. How do you trust the people who tell you to stop beating your kids when they're constantly creating and sustaining the conditions that compel us to do whatever we feel we need to maintain our kids' safety? It's a cruel, double-edged sword.

And yet . . .

Yearly statistics gathered by the National Child Abuse and Neglect Data System consistently show that black children are mistreated and killed by their family members at significantly higher rates than white and Latino kids. Social workers and district attorneys will tell you that most of these family members aren't monsters. They see a slap across the face or a seemingly innocuous pop sometimes result in a serious injury, or even a fatality. Other cases escalate slowly. Parents don't start off with extension cords. It gets to that point when they believe a belt or a hand no longer works. In fact, many district attorneys I've talked to over the years say it's not "bad" parents intentionally hurting their kids who end up with convictions for child abuse or homicide; it's those who started spanking and amped up as the child got bigger.

We tell ourselves that what we're doing is different, saying, "Well, I wouldn't whup my child with a switch or an extension cord." "I wouldn't leave welts and bruises or break bones." "I wouldn't make my child bleed." "I wouldn't whup them when I'm angry. I would sit them down and explain to them why they're being punished."

But I'm here to tell you—I've read hundreds of case files. Those parents who got that knock on the door from child protective services and who found themselves standing in front of a judge being convicted for abuse said the same things. They were genuinely shocked when they were told that their parenting practices were against the law. Until that moment, they, too, had been told that this was the right way to raise a black child. It was the way they were raised. They didn't end up in the emergency room, their mama and 'nem didn't go to jail, and getting whupped and scarred with weapons wasn't called abuse.

Black people, we must rethink our approach.

In 2014 black children, who made up around 14 percent of the total child population, accounted for 24 percent of children in foster care, according to the most recent annual report published by the Children's Bureau.[12] Factors such as low birth weight, crushing poverty, having a young mother, low education, and having no father listed on a birth certificate place children at a higher risk for being reported to child protective services, which are highly concentrated in poor black neighborhoods. If we're honest, the child welfare industry in this country is about policing poverty and reinforcing the powerlessness of people of color.

When we hit our children, we put them at risk of becoming among the thousands of black children who enter the foster care system every year and have a 50 percent longer stay than children of other races, which is the express lane to the juvenile justice system and ultimately to adult prison. Our youth, who are often bounced from home to home and placed in facilities far away from their parents and everything they know, often fail to get adopted or returned home, which puts them more at risk for not graduating from high school or transitioning into independent living. When we hit black children, we put them at risk for being suspended and expelled from school and becoming yet another victim in the "school-to-prison pipeline." When we hit black children, we put them at risk for entering a foster care system that forces disempowered young people to take psychotropic medications against their will.

Seriously.

A 2015 report from the Franklin Law Group, a child advocacy organization based in Baltimore, found that since the 1990s, when I was in the foster care system, there has been a 55 percent increase in the prescribing of psychotropic medications to foster kids. Foster kids, including infants, are prescribed mind-altering drugs at rates nine times higher than children not in foster care. I have met kids in care who were taking four or five psychotropic medications at a time, even though there was no real medical evidence to support their regimens. Black children, especially girls, are diagnosed with higher rates and prescribed off-label medications with black box warnings indicating that the US Food and Drug Administration does not sanction the drug for children.[13]

The ramifications of this are staggering.

Numerous reports on the unregulated medication of children have found that long-term use of these drugs causes serious side effects and long-term consequences. Taking these medications can "suppress and disrupt normal brain development and function, alters chemical levels in the brain, and impacts mood and behavior," according to a Baltimore Law Group report. They have also been found to cause neurological disorders, the development of breasts in boys, brain shrinkage, obesity, cardiovascular issues, violent behavior, suicidal ideations, restlessness, low energy, aggression, diabetes, insomnia, memory loss, and shortening of the lifespan by twenty-five years. The drugs are often prescribed for traumatized and grieving children as a way to control their behavior in lieu of counseling services, which are often not available because they are more expensive than drugs.[14] Kids labeled violent, explosive, or difficult become easier to manage when they are chemically sedated.

Knowing this, it should be no surprise that black children are stereotyped as being angry or overly aggressive. Intentionally or not, it becomes a self-fulfilling prophecy. This explains why a largely white social services system and psychiatric community misdiagnose and overmedicate our youth.

When we whup our children, we also put them at risk of joining tens of thousands of young people who "age out" of a foster care system and then often struggle badly, with more than one in five becoming homeless after age eighteen. Instead of making a successful transition into productive adulthood, one national study found that 38 percent of former foster youth had emotional problems and chronic health conditions. Fifty percent had used illegal drugs; only 48 percent had graduated from high school by the time they left the system; fewer than 3 percent had earned a college degree; and 71 percent of young women had gotten pregnant. They also faced higher rates of unemployment and public assistance, and their own children were more likely to need foster care. And one in four ended up in prison within two years of leaving the foster care system.[15]

With all this data, I find it shocking that hitting children is still actually legal, while hitting between adults is considered a crime and hitting an animal is defined as "cruelty." While theoretical and rarely enforced, laws even protect people in prison from corporal punishment. But with children, state laws actually define how to strike a child's body *appropriately.* Why don't we extend the same courtesy to children that we extend to prisoners or dogs?

A 2008 study by Elizabeth Gershoff, a University of Texas developmental psychologist, found that a whopping 85 percent of children have been physically punished by their parents by the time they reach high school?[16] The late Murray Straus, a former sociology professor and an expert on corporal punishment who passed away during the writing of this book, examined numerous surveys taken over several decades. He found that the number of parents who spank their children, or admitted that spankings are sometimes necessary, slowly dropped from around 90 percent in 1968 to about 70 percent in 1994. This number has remained fairly steady in recent years. These findings cut across racial and class lines. Still, a number of researchers across the country have found that black families report using physical punishment 10 percent more than parents from other communities.[17]

I often hear black folks complain that the problems we face in our communities are a result of a generation of "bad" children who are disrespectful, spoiled, entitled, and aren't being spanked enough. You've probably heard the popular complaint: "They made it a crime to discipline your kids." But while the numbers show a decrease in spanking, America is still a country that hits its young. If the majority of Americans are slapping, spanking, popping, whupping, or beating their kids, then is it really true that the smaller proportion of kids who aren't being hit are responsible for the violence and crime in our society?

As parenting expert L. R. Knost notes in *Jesus, the Gentle Parent*, it is more likely that when children learn to hit and hurt, that "might is right," and that violence is the answer to their problems and an outlet to stress, they take those lessons out into the world. The problem isn't "kids today," Knost argues, but rather the problem is with "parents who repeat the patterns their own parents set or with societies who view normal stages of [child] development as somehow abnormal."[18]

Meanwhile, children are still being hit at school. Every state except Iowa and New Jersey allows teachers and administrators in private and parochial schools to paddle students, and nineteen states still allow public school students to be hit with wooden boards. A disproportionate number of students disciplined this way are black. Unlike their white counterparts, black parents overwhelmingly sign opt-in forms in support of the practice.[19]

The reasons black folks hit their children are supremely complex. Black Americans have been allowed to legally parent their children for only 150 years. Slave parents whupped their young to prepare them for the harsh realities of plantation life and to protect them from abuse at the hands of masters, overseers, and other whites who only valued black life as a means to profit.

During Jim Crow, whupping was used as a survival tactic to teach black children proper racial etiquette so they would not risk being beaten or lynched by whites. The practice is now a trusted form of resistance to racism because we're convinced it does more to help than to harm. However, no reputable research has ever supported this. In fact, what fifty years of research around the world has shown is that when we hit children, we are often sowing the seeds for the very behaviors and negative outcomes that whuppings are supposed to prevent—namely, disobedience, aggression, dishonesty, antisocial behavior, mental health problems, poor educational achievement, low self-esteem, early puberty, risky sex, and a host of other issues. Whuppings are literally changing brain chemistry and the brain's physical architecture. The stress our children face is putting them at risk for chronic health problems over their lifespan, and the trauma is even being passed on to future generations through their DNA.

We can decrease these risk factors for our children if we would consider parenting practices that avoid hitting. But I know that even if

Jesus Christ himself came down and said, "Stop whupping your kids," there would be a lot of folks who'd do it anyway. I expect skeptics. I know some of you don't think I have a leg to stand on because I'm not a parent. I am humble enough to admit that I don't know what it's like to wake up in the middle of the night to a screaming child. I don't know what it's like to have a child I birthed disrespect me to the point where I want to slap her into next week. I don't know what it's like for my heart to be on edge each time my son walks out the door to go to school, or to the store, fearing he might return in a body bag. I get why people have been quick to dismiss the information I share because they believe a childless person cannot possibly understand this reality. Parenting is damn hard. Though I may not have children, unlike a lot of people who do have them, I haven't forgotten what it feels like to be a child.

Choosing a nonhitting option will take a lot of work and a lot of creativity, self-control, and patience. But we must call all forms of hitting children by their real name: *violence.* This means we have to do some deep reflection and wrestle with the contradictions of our families, upbringings, and religions. It means that we have to dare to imagine what it means to raise intellectually, spiritually, and socially free black children. I mean absolutely free.

Just as whuppings won't save black America, nor will our silence. Let me be clear: I don't want to talk about what's *wrong* with black people, but rather how racist systems and policies have created a hostile environment that has caused levels of trauma that have resulted in our hurting one another. While black parents and caretakers may perpetuate cycles of pain and trauma when they whup their children, white America—the grand Yoda of violence, despite positioning itself as a source of civility—is always supplying the ingredients for our problems.

My hope is that this book will help my people enter into a conscious awareness of how whupping children is part of an unhealthy social conditioning rooted in the history of racial trauma and plays a role in preventing us from healing and thriving as a people. If we really believe that whupping is a black thing or that we have some innate predisposition to pain and suffering, then where is there room for change, for growth, and for us to create new possibilities?

We have a saying in our culture, "what goes on in this house, stays in this house." But whupping your child is not just an individual event that takes place between you and your child within the privacy of your home. Humiliating or inflicting pain onto your child's body is a social experience that reinforces society's oppressive power structures. Whupping our children encourages them to accept violence as normal and natural and to demand respect through violence. When black folks participate in this kind of ritualized violence under the guise of teaching, love, and protection we are colluding in the continued subordination of our race.

We have a responsibility to ensure that we prepare the next generations of black children to continue the struggle for racial equality. We cannot achieve this with children who are physically, intellectually, emotionally, and spiritually broken. We cannot save our communities and achieve peace and prosperity with young, fearful people who grow up believing obedience is their greatest virtue. We should work to nurture our children to become curious, resourceful young people who endlessly push the boundaries and become the kinds of adults who change the world instead of being changed or victimized by it— including a racist one.

I firmly believe that sparing the rod and restructuring the black family as a liberated, violence-free zone is one of the strategies we cannot live without. I don't pretend to have easy or definitive answers and interventions for the remarkably complex issues this book explores. But here's what I do know about our brilliance: African Americans are the descendants of the survivors of the Middle Passage, centuries of American slavery, and Jim Crow–era genocidal violence. After all that black folks have been through in this country for almost 400 years, now is not the time for more self-inflicted pain and trauma.

We can raise resistance, or we can raise order. The hard truth is that every time we whup our kids, it says we believe America's racist messages about our humanity—that the only way to make us healthy, responsible, law-abiding, moral, and loving people is through a good whupping.

Do we really believe this?

2

"A LOVE WHUPPING"

Reflections on the Adrian Peterson and "Baltimore Mom" Controversies

"Whupping—we do that all the time."

Back in September 2015, the ever-outspoken NBA Hall of Famer Charles Barkley made this statement during a debate with Jim Rome on the CBS sports show *The NFL Today*. Barkley, who is often celebrated for defying political correctness and speaking without fear, appeared on the show in the wake of Adrian Peterson's arrest and indictment for child abuse.

The 6-foot-1, 217-pound star running back for the Minnesota Vikings had punished his four-year-old son after the child pushed one of his siblings. Peterson sought to teach him about violence by stuffing leaves in his mouth and repeatedly hitting his bare skin with a switch from a tree. Hospital photographs showed lacerations covering the boy's legs. A police report said he also sustained defensive wounds on his hands, and cuts and bruises on his back, buttocks, legs, ankles, and scrotum.

"Got him in the nuts once I noticed. But I felt so bad, n I'm all tearing that butt up when needed!" Peterson said in a text message to the boy's mother.

In a follow-up text he wrote, "Never do I go overboard! But all my kids will know, hey daddy has the biggest heart but don't play no games when it comes to acting right."[1]

Peterson's attorney, Rusty Hardin, said his client was not a child abuser. "Adrian is a loving father who used his judgment as a parent to discipline his son. He used the same kind of discipline with his child that he experienced as a child growing up in east Texas. . . . It is important to remember that Adrian never intended to harm his son and deeply regrets the unintentional injury."[2]

During the CBS segment, when Rome asked if it was ever appropriate to hit a child, Barkley responded by saying that it is a culturally acceptable practice in black communities. When Rome pushed back by calling Peterson's parenting abusive, Barkley cautioned against telling parents living in "different environments" how to discipline their kids. He then suggested that if whupping children became illegal then "every black parent in my neighborhood in the South would be in trouble or in jail under those circumstances."

Let's be real: Barkley is right. His comments represent a routine understanding of how to discipline children inside the black community. He simply articulated what the overwhelming majority of black Americans believe when it comes to disciplining children. This belief isn't grounded in research or widespread discussions of best practices, but rather in the purported benefits in their own lives.

So many people defend whupping kids by citing their own scars as beneficial and positively transformative, believing "I was whupped and I turned out fine." Barkley cited his own physical injuries sustained during his grandmother's whuppings and shrugged them off as a typical experience for black children.

"I've got beat with switches. I've had many welts on my legs and lacerations," he told a visibly disturbed Rome.

Barkley's matter-of-fact comment reveals that getting cut and bruised during a whupping is so common that many black people don't recognize those types of injuries as evidence of abuse. When Rome argued that the open wounds and bruises on Peterson's son constituted "a beating," Barkley suggested that Peterson may have gone overboard, but then he took issue with the semantics.

"I don't like the term 'beat.' We call it 'spanking' or 'whupping' our kids," Barkley said.

"Beat," "break," "spank," "pop," "wear that ass out," "tear that butt up," "whup." Changing the word or the spelling is often a defensive maneuver that tries to downplay the level of violence. Not to mention, there's no consensus among black people about the meaning of each one of those terms, nor is there an agreed-upon working definition of what constitutes abuse. In my travels across the country doing child advocacy work, I've talked to folks who've told me that their parents whupped them with switches, belts, and extension cords, but they didn't feel that those punishments were abusive. If we put ten people in a room and asked them what it means to "beat" versus "spank" or "whup" a child, we won't get a consensus.

Most times what people choose to call physical discipline is representative of the cultural or regional vernacular they grew up in. For example, my adoptive mother never said she was going to "spank" me because she thought that was a "soft" approach that white folks used on their kids. The threatening language she used—from *"I'll slap the black off you"* to *"I'll knock your head off"*—often bordered on the homicidal.

While folks split hairs over terminology, what binds them together is that each euphemism is about hitting a child, each involves pain, and each poses the risk of seriously injuring or killing a child in a moment of anger. Added to these varying cultural and generational definitions, even the law doesn't reflect consensus. The legal line distinguishing physical discipline from child abuse varies widely from state to state, with no clear, across-the-board definition.

According to the American Bar Association's Center on Children and the Law in Washington, DC, some states allow spanking, paddling, and switching "if administered in a reasonable manner," while others, such as Texas, allow "reasonable physical force" when and to the extent believed necessary "to maintain discipline." Other states don't "specifically prohibit corporal punishment, even where it results in a serious injury to the child, as long as deadly force was not utilized."[3]

But how do you determine whether a child is acceptably bruised or not? Who gets to define "reasonable"? Leaving it to angry and frustrated parents caught up in the heat of the moment results in parents such as Adrian Peterson being arrested or, worse, children being killed.

The day after his CBS interview with Jim Rome, Charles Barkley appeared on the Dan Patrick radio show and didn't back down from his stance. He also admitted to punishing his daughter, who is now an adult. "I hope I never crossed the line. . . . She was spanked pretty good a few times, and she probably deserved it," Barkley said.

Reflecting on his own childhood whuppings again, he said, "I'm pretty sure my grandmother, who was the greatest woman who ever lived, may have crossed the line at times, but you know what? I feel pretty good about the person I am today." This kind of celebration of our elders whupping us is too often viewed as a sign that the wounds have healed, that the scars are calloused, and the pain has resulted in strength and good character that we might not have developed without the violence.

Barkley wasn't alone in his sympathy for Peterson and defense and celebration of whupping kids. On a different segment, the retired NFL running back Ricky Williams, who just a few years earlier was often cited as an example of what is wrong with today's professional athletes, also told Rome that whupping children is status quo in the black community. Williams said his mother beat him and he turned out fine. If such discipline were considered illegal, Williams said, "My mom would be under the prison," he said.

Rome noted that Peterson hit his son in the testicles and asked Williams, "You don't have a problem with that?"

"I don't," Williams replied.

Meanwhile, Detroit Lions running back Reggie Bush appeared on the *Boomer & Carton* show on WFAN in New York and said he had been punished the same way that Peterson whupped his son. "I know a lot of my friends and a lot of guys I played with, they were punished the same way, too. I got what we call whuppings." Bush went further by saying that he planned to discipline his infant daughter similarly. "I definitely will try to—will obviously not leave bruises or anything like that on her. But I definitely will discipline her harshly depending on what the situation is."

After his comment drew outrage, Bush said he misspoke about using a switch on his daughter. "Spanking is different than a branch or stick," he said. "I believe in spanking a child if needed, not beating them."

A chorus of black male athletes also used Twitter to voice their support for Peterson and to reflect on how whuppings had made them better people. Utah Jazz power forward Trevor Booker recalled having to pick his own switch. New Orleans Saints running back Mark Ingram Jr. and Arizona Cardinals defensive end Darnell Dockett implied that "love" validated the countless whuppings they received. Phoenix Suns forward Anthony Tolliver credited being beaten with switches and belts with saving his life.

A few people used their platforms to speak out against what Peterson did and the broader culture of accepted abuse. Most notable was Cris Carter, a Hall of Fame football receiver and sports analyst, who spoke emotionally about his own upbringing during an appearance on ESPN's *Sunday NFL Countdown*. He recalled how his single mom raised seven children by herself and used physical discipline as a parenting tool.

"My mom did the best that she could do. . . . But there are thousands of things I have learned since then that my mom was wrong," he said. "This is the twenty-first century. My mom was wrong. . . . And I promise my kids I won't teach that mess to them. You can't beat a kid to make them do what you want them to do."

But for the most part, the comments by Barkley and many other black athletes hit home for millions of black Americans. That's because the majority of black parents in America, not just in the South, view hitting children as synonymous with good, responsible parenting. Researchers have consistently found that more black parents spank their children than those of other ethnic groups.[4] For example, in 2014 the Maryland-based nonprofit research organization Child Trends found that 81 percent of black women, as opposed to 62 percent of Latino and white women, agreed that a child sometimes needs a "good hard spanking." Asian women were the least likely to agree. The research also found no significant difference for men along racial lines. And while many people assume that poor, uneducated, single black moms are most likely to agree with spanking, surveys conducted by Child Trends for more than three decades have found that a greater percentage of black women who are childless, married, and have attended college agree that children need to be physically punished.[5]

Sadly, hitting children who can't protect themselves has become part of our cultural DNA and identity. For many black parents, not spanking is viewed as selling out or acting white. We mock parents who use "time-outs," who take away phones and iPads as punishment, and who employ verbal reasoning with children. We scoff at their privilege and how nice it must be to have the luxury to ignore the misdoings of your children in public spaces. Only those with privilege have the time to read parenting blogs and books about positive discipline. Only those who don't have to worry about being seen as another bad black parent can think that no TV time for little Connor and Becky will lead to them knowing how to act right in the world. This kind of racialized mockery has become part of how we rationalize hurting black children's bodies.

The embrace of whuppings isn't only about affirming our blackness, like celebrating Kwanzaa and knowing the words to the Black National Anthem. The decision whether to physically discipline our children is seen as one of life or death. Embracing alternative parenting styles is viewed as risky, one that might lead to unruly children who don't "know how to act," or worse, invite the violence of American racism. Meanwhile, as increasing numbers of white folks continue to explore nonviolent methods of child-rearing, black folks have convinced ourselves that we must whup our children because if we don't then the police will beat them, lock them up, or kill them.

Well, how is that parenting strategy working for us?

Not well. Just look at the weekly murders of black children across this country and the epidemic of locking up our adolescent kids. If whupping our children kept them from being killed by the police, then why are activists in the streets protesting police brutality? If whupping our children has been so successful at keeping black people out of prisons, then why are we having a national conversation over mass incarceration?

Black parents are taught, and teach one another, that the only way to protect kids from the violence of white racism is to mimic the methods and logic of society, but they become vilified and punished for doing that, as well. And as black parents perpetuate this culture of physical discipline against their children, white America argues that violence, including whupping children, is exceptional and unique to blackness even though white people taught us to whup and break the will of our children during slavery.

Part of this logic also embraces racist beliefs that we are inherently criminal, that we are destined to be menaces to society, that the only way to break the cycle of crime and poverty in our communities is to beat it out of our children. We keep whupping our children, yet the US Department of Education has reported that half of all preschoolers suspended more than once are black. We keep whupping our children even as students of color face harsher punishments in school than their white peers even though they are less likely to engage in bad behavior. This leads to a higher number of youth of color being incarcerated.[6] We continue to use a negative to prevent future negatives. Our fear that saying no to whupping kids will lead to a life of crime and pathology is without any basis. None whatsoever.

We keep telling ourselves that whupping our children will protect them even though research at Villanova University in 2013 found that darker-skinned black students were more likely to be suspended than black students with light skin.

We keep whupping our children even though researchers have found no evidence that they are more likely to misbehave than other groups of children, even though they are suspended and expelled at higher rates.[7]

We keep whupping our children even as they remain overrepresented in the nation's foster care system, which has become a feeder for the juvenile justice and adult prison systems. In some states, such as California and Illinois, up to 80 percent of adult prisoners have had contact with the foster care system as a result of child abuse, and in Connecticut 70 percent of juveniles in confinement have histories with foster care.[8]

We keep whupping our children even though, according to data from the US Department of Health and Human Services, in the past ten years alone, whupping children has resulted in nearly 280,000 reports of physical abuse against black children, with more than 758,000 of our young entering foster care because of physical and other types of abuse and neglect. Even more horrifying is that during that same time period, 3,839 black children died as a result of maltreatment, with about 40 percent being victims of physical abuse. That's an average of about 380 fatalities per year![9]

It is true that children of other races also lose their lives as a result of abuse, but the rate of fatalities is consistently three times higher for blacks. When we look at these awful statistics, a disturbing truth emerges: in addition to the threats from the trigger-happy police and gun-toting men "standing their ground," the safety of black children is under peril from a culture of whuppings.

This is a public health crisis. And yet many black folks continue to loudly and proudly describe the pain of their own childhood whuppings as a sign of strength, a source of humor, and essential to shaping them into the successful people they are today.

On top of our cultural attachment to hitting our children, America's complicated history has conditioned us to accept that pain is a *necessary* part of learning and growing up black. Too many people across the color line believe that black children are inherently problematic and disrespectful thugs, the root of society's problems, and are in need of punitive forms of control.

Truth be told, if whupping black children were a prerequisite for white recognition of our humanity and civil rights, and for good black citizenship and success, then black Americans ought to be ruling this country right now. Parenting based on beatings has not led our people to the Promise Land.

But we continue with the status quo. As we wage war on the bodies of our children and their emotional well-being, all the measures of health, wealth, educational achievement, and general progress tell a much starker story. The truth is that racist America is determined to keep black communities under siege by locking up and even killing our future leaders. To keep on living King's dream and embrace some *After School Special* idea of colorblindness, far too many black Americans cosign the dehumanization of our children. We do this every time we hit them.

The entrenched belief in whupping children is driven by black parents' very real fears about the safety and well-being of their children in contemporary America. A Pew Research Center survey published in December 2015 found that black parents worried more than white parents that their children might get shot at some point, either on the streets of unsafe neighborhoods or by the police.[10] The concern is justified, of course.

The most troubling example of this happened in 2014 when a Cleveland police officer mistook twelve-year-old Tamir Rice for a twenty-year-old man and instantly shot him dead when he and his partner saw Tamir playing in a park with a toy gun. No wonder "the talk" is as much a part of child rearing as the "birds and the bees" conversation and teaching kids to drive. It instills reminders of how to act around white people and how to stay alive if approached by a cop.

- Do not ever run. They will shoot you.
- Say "yes, sir" and "no, sir." Do not mouth off.
- When asked to retrieve anything, move your hands slowly and narrate your movements.
- If told to get out of the car, again, move slowly.
- You and your vehicle may be searched with no explanation. Do not protest.
- If police backup arrives, definitely do not protest.
- Be prepared to turn your pockets inside out and lie down on the ground.
- You may be handcuffed.
- Accept any injustice that arises. You can file a complaint later.

The goal of these lessons is to keep our young people alive. Black parents would rather pick their child up from the police station than the morgue.

The debates about physical discipline that we witnessed during the Peterson controversy are not new. But the spate of killings of young, unarmed black people (John Crawford, Rekia Boyd, Mike Brown Jr., Jordan Davis, Shantel Davis, Freddie Gray, Darnisha Harris, Kendra James, Trayvon Martin, Renisha McBride, VonDerrit Myers Jr., Tamir Rice, Cameron Tillman, Laquan McDonald, and others who will be killed) has elevated black people's questions about "how to protect" our children to a new level.

The connective tissue between the Peterson case, whuppings, "the talk," and the epidemic of police shootings was on full display in Baltimore in April 2015. Toya Graham, the infamous "Baltimore Mom," snatched her son out of a riot that erupted after the death of twenty-five-year-old Freddie Gray, who suffered a severed spinal cord while in police custody. Hours after Gray was laid to rest, Graham, a single mother of six, arrived at Mondawmin Mall and saw her sixteen-year-old son, Michael Singleton, dressed in black clothes and a mask, poised to throw rocks at police officers in angry protest. After a rumor spread on social media of a "purge," dozens of police in full riot gear and a heavily armored BearCat tactical vehicle greeted students as they left Frederick Douglass High School and headed toward the mall.

Officers prevented the students from boarding school buses and the local subway, leaving them with no way to get home. According to eyewitnesses, the police escalated the situation by marching aggressively toward groups of stranded, angry students. Students threw bricks and water bottles at police. Police officers maced students and hurled rocks and bricks back at the children.[11]

A Baltimore teacher told *Gawker*, "Those kids were set up, they were treated like criminals before the first brick was thrown."[12]

"These kids are just angry. These are the same kids [the cops] pull up on the corner for no reason," Sandra Almond-Cooper, the president of the Mondawmin Neighborhood Improvement Association, told the *Baltimore Sun*.[13]

By the time Graham appeared on the scene, cameras were rolling but she didn't care. Her goal was to get her son out of the chaos and back home safely. When she made eye contact with him, she went ballistic.

"Get the fuck over here!" Graham screamed as she repeatedly hit Singleton upside the head.

Once unmasked, young Michael backed away from his mother, subdued, with a look of humiliation in his eyes. The fifty-second video of the incident was viewed millions of times. The mother and son suddenly became media darlings, appearing on CNN, *The View*, and the *Today* show. As Graham paraded her son on the media circuit, it was akin to giving a child a whupping and making him come out to say hello to company. And America ate it up. Oprah Winfrey gave Graham a thumbs-up seal of approval to drive home the narrative that good mothering requires physical force. The *New York Post* encouraged more black mothers to beat the protest out of their kids with the headline: "Forget the National Guard . . . Send In the Moms."

MSNBC's Joe Scarborough, who called Ferguson teen Mike Brown Jr. a "thug" and blamed him for his own death, jubilantly called Graham "a good, strong mother." The Reverend Al Sharpton cosigned by saying Graham should be praised for her actions. Former NAACP president Kweisi Mfume called her slapfest "necessary violence." During an interview on CNN, he dismissed critics who noted the contradiction of a mother using violence to show her son that violence is wrong.

"Yes, she hit 'em. She was trying to make him understand that she loves him," Mfume said.

Even the White House weighed in, seemingly giving her parenting choices presidential approval. Press secretary Josh Earnest channeled his inner Mr. Rogers, calling Graham's actions a powerful expression of love. "That same kind of passion and concern, and love for the well-being of one's child, is the kind of thing that can contribute to a young man or woman having the type of opportunity to succeed that a lot of other kids don't get," he said during a televised press conference.

The Obama administration's endorsement isn't surprising given that this same president had previously articulated his support for whupping children. In 2013, Obama delivered a "tough love" speech at the NAACP's one hundredth anniversary gathering where he, yet again, lectured black folks on the importance of good parenting. He advised that in addition to spending quality time with children, making them put away the Xbox, showing up for parent-teacher meetings, helping them with homework, and getting kids to bed at a decent hour, "We need to go back to the time when parents saw some kid fooling around, it wasn't your child but they'd whup you anyway. Or they'd tell your parents, and they'd, you know . . ."

The president's comments before the NAACP audience, the epitome of old-school Negro-ness, were met with huge applause and laughter. But the fact is, our biracial president grew up around Asians and white people and was not shaped by black adults during his childhood. One has to wonder if his white mother and white grandparents embraced such parenting choices. And surely we cannot assume that they called it "whupping," unless Southern black vernacular has taken root in Hawaii. Instead, Obama, who has admitted that he had to teach himself how to be a black man in America, has learned to reinforce his credibility within the black community by reminiscing nostalgically about corporal punishment. It was his way of saying, "I'm black. I'm one of you."

Given the power of his perch, his past experience as a community organizer in the violent city of Chicago, and the fact that his words carry a lot of weight, it was irresponsible for Obama to promote whupping children. Not to mention, it's not a practice in his home. In an interview, the First Lady, Michelle Obama, said she tried spanking her daughter Malia once or twice and found it unproductive. "I did it one or two times and just found it to be completely ineffective because it was less about teaching a lesson and more about my own [feelings]."[14]

It is clear that from Oprah to Obama, Charles Barkley to Al Sharpton, and Joe Scarborough to racist police, everyone appears to be in agreement that the bodies of black children need to be whupped, especially those like Toya Graham's son, who was railing against his own oppression.

At the height of the "Baltimore Mom" controversy, I appeared on a CNN segment with Illinois congressman Bobby Rush, a former Black Panther who took to the House floor with a large photo of Graham hitting her son and made a "special appeal to African American mothers." He described the picture as an "image of a strong black mother" giving her son "a love whupping—to snatch him back from the senseless violence that's currently plaguing the city of Baltimore." Rush added, "As this picture demonstrates, mothers can and mothers must be the mobilizing force to take back our streets." He then asked mothers across the country to show solidarity with Graham by wearing yellow.

Since slavery, black women have taken their racial duty to keep black men alive very seriously. When the choice is survival versus revolt, we mostly choose whatever action will keep our children and husbands and brothers alive. And so it is with Graham. The public's view is that she saved her son's life that day. I, however, was adamant that her tough-love approach and literal preemptive strikes against Michael do nothing to break the cycles of violence in our homes and communities. The widespread celebration, in fact, had little to do with what was good for Graham, her son, and the black community as a whole. The reason she was being worshiped by the news media was not because of a genuine understanding of her fear and motivation for hitting her son, but because she symbolized the tradition of keeping black male bodies in check. Never mind that her violence against her son may only incite his anger and frustration because it prevented him from resisting the systems of oppression in his community.

Six months after she made headlines, CBS News caught up with Graham and found her not living the life of a hero. She and her children were in danger of losing their home. They were struggling to put food on the table and the mother and son still lived in fear of the violence ravaging their neighborhood.

Before Freddie Gray's death, between January and April 2015, Baltimore had seen more than one hundred shootings and forty homicides, earning the city the nickname Bodymore, Murdaland. While law enforcement, black political figures, the media, and racist trolls online were busy portraying the young people who took to the streets of Baltimore to fight for their rights as hooligans, I cheered for them. They were doing exactly what they were supposed to be doing: embracing a longstanding American tradition of resistance, all in the name of democracy and freedom. They did what generations of young people from Soweto to Palestine have done to fight for their own lives when their country devalues and demonizes them, when no one else will stand in solidarity with them.

The media complained that the vandalism, arson, and looting were just opportunistic violence and those young people had no real political agenda, as if black people living in poverty don't have the ability to be organized and intentional. Lawlessness and "thugs" threatened "peace," the pundits argued. Never mind that peace was defined by the killing of unarmed black youth, systemic harassment by the criminal injustice system, mass poverty, unemployment, divestment in schools, poor housing, and inadequate health care. But I saw young people living out Dr. Martin Luther King Jr.'s words, spoken three years after his famous "I Have a Dream" speech: "The riot is the language of the unheard."

I have great compassion for parents like Toya Graham who are doing the best they can to raise up children under enormous stress while barely scraping by. This is a mom who was so afraid for her son's life that she admitted trying to shield him from the police and Baltimore's dangerous streets by keeping him in the house. Ultimately, parents like her just want their children to live, even if that means enacting violence against their bodies and spirits to keep them in their place.

I have compassion because she is parenting in an environment where the powers that be make sure that average black parents, especially single moms, are embedded in circumstances where their needs for the bare essentials of life for themselves and their children remain unmet. Racist aggression, disenfranchisement, discrimination, incarceration, and generational theft of black wealth have ensured that most black folks are constantly in survival mode.

Moreover, whupping our kids creates a false sense of protection that actually plays on white racist narratives that locate antiblackness at the feet of black children's bodies and behavior. In other words, we believe that stop-and-frisks, school suspensions and expulsions, mass incarceration, and death-by-police are rooted in the black child's body that needs more whuppings. What's so disturbing is that racism is let off the hook. A militarized police force is not the problem. Systemic racism, from the War on Drugs to racial profiling, from hypersegregation to community divestment, is not the issue. The message is simple but extremely dangerous: more than rampant poverty, more than overzealous police, more than entrenched racism, the behavior of black children becomes the true enemy of peace. The distracting conversation turns the spotlight back on to black youth and the shared belief across racial lines that the only way to keep black children safe from racism and out of trouble is to hurt their bodies.

Given the celebration of Graham, it's no surprise that countless black parents are now using their cell phones to broadcast their tough-love parenting all over social media. At one level, these public displays of humiliation reflect black parents' sense of insecurity and inadequacy in rearing their children, as they seek applause for projecting strong values and a no-nonsense approach. These public displays of extreme discipline are an overcorrection and a declaration to the world: "Look what we're doing! We're parenting! We don't let our kids run wild. We're demanding discipline. So, hey, America, shut the hell up!"

At another level, the public whuppings reveal how there's nothing easy about parenting a black child today. Adults keep arguing in circles about the appropriate ways to discipline children's bodies into safety and achieve the peace we've been longing for in our communities. Meanwhile, black children all over this country continue bearing the brunt of racist devaluation on top of the pain of being hit by their loved ones. Irrespective of the reasons—rage induced by racism or a yearning to protect and ward off death—the hitting still hurts.

But let's be clear: contrary to popular belief and decades of surveys, studies, and racial stereotypes, whupping children didn't begin as "a black thing." It's not even native to us. There's no evidence that our ancestors in West Africa embraced this kind of child-rearing. It was introduced with the arrival of Europeans on the African continent centuries ago. We've just kept the tradition going.

3

EXTENDING THE MASTER'S LASH

The Historical Roots of Whupping Children in Black Communities

One of the saddest untold stories in American history is the ways that its victims of racial oppression and violence have hurt the bodies of their own children in an effort to protect them from a hostile society.

While physical punishment is so deeply rooted in the American way of raising kids, history provides a clear explanation for why so many black people embrace this harsh form of discipline while falsely believing that whupping children is something uniquely black. Looking to the past can help us understand how and why this society, which intentionally chips away at the vitality of black life, continues to demand this vicious cycle of abuse against black children even as it disproportionately criminalizes us for doing it. The fact is, white America has long derived power from assuring that black children are victims of physical, intellectual, psychological, and spiritual violence and that the people raising them are complicit in their abuse. This is what white supremacy requires.

Indeed, black folks have imported violence into our culture by embracing the idea that whupping our children will garner freedom and acceptance from white America and usher our communities into safety and prosperity. It's never worked.

So then how did this violent child-rearing practice become so deeply implanted in our culture? Why do so many of us believe that if we "spare the rod," then all hell will break loose? Or that we will lose our "black card" or dishonor the legacy of our loving elders who whupped us so we wouldn't grow up to smoke crack, be a welfare queen, go to jail, or worse?

We must journey through a few historical time periods to lay the foundation for understanding why whupping children is a practice that did not begin with us but got etched into the DNA of our bodies, memory, and culture even as white America gradually moves away from this kind of violence when it comes to their own children.

Hitting and abusing children has a long history that's been part of virtually every culture and society dating back to biblical times. The Bible itself is full of scriptures sanctifying child abuse. Think about Abraham, who nearly sacrificed his only son as a test of his faith in God. King Herod massacred innocent babies in a failed attempt to kill Jesus. Lott had drunken sex with his daughters. Young female sex abuse victims were required to marry their rapists. God sent two bears to murder forty-two kids who made fun of Elijah's baldness. Let's not forget Psalm 137:9, which praises bashing the heads of babies to prevent the rise of a new generation of Babylonians.

For 2000 years of European history, going all the way back to the Greeks, whose worldview can be seen within modern Christianity, adults deliberately exploited, tortured, raped, and killed their own children. Lloyd deMause, the controversial psychologist and historian, wrote, "The history of childhood is a nightmare from which we have only begun to awaken. The further back in history one goes, the lower the level of child care, and the more likely children are to be killed, abandoned, beaten, terrorized, and sexually abused."[1]

For the most part, deMause and other scholars have painted a dark and horrifying picture of childhood in western societies. European parents beat their young with cat-o'-nine-tails, shovels, canes, iron rods, and sticks. Infanticide was common and unpunished due to poverty, the need to limit family size or to eliminate political rivals, and because people believed that physically or mentality disabled children were the handiwork of the devil. During antiquity and the Middle Ages, about half of babies born were killed by their caretakers, and not just by poor parents; the ruling-elites had just as high rates of child killings.[2] Children were burned, shaken, tossed about, and flung into rivers, trenches, and heaps of animal manure. They were also intentionally starved; castrated; thrown into fires by their parents as sacrifices to gods; cooked and eaten as part of fertility rites; fed poisons that plastered their insides; rolled in snow until they froze to death; sealed into the walls and foundations of bridges and buildings; and abandoned on hillsides and roads where birds, dogs, and wild beasts scavenged and devoured unlucky waifs.[3]

In ancient Greece, a disobedient son could lose his tongue, eye, or fingers. Greek infants born with deformities were considered unfit to be raised and thus killed in order to preserve "ideal" racial characteristics. Young boys and girls suffered routine sexual molestation by older men. A young person could be kept as a "pet-child" for entertainment and pedophilic gratification, or sold into slavery or hard labor by a parent as payment or collateral for debts. Even as late as the nineteenth century, American medical journals reported regular findings of sexually transmitted diseases on children's anuses, genitals, and mouths when their parents had the disease.[4]

From royals to regular folks, centuries of Europeans grew up with severe beatings being a regular part of a child's life. This is of little surprise given the dominant beliefs. According to some historians, the modern vision of childhood as a distinct and bound phase of life, one of innocence and insulation from violence, did not begin to significantly take root in Europe until the early 1600s. Before that, many children generally did not have the right to be free from violence. That right was granted only to adults because adults defined themselves as free and moral against the unfree, immoral, and criminal young. Countless diaries, letters, autobiographies, and medical reports detail routine mistreatment of children throughout history.

Don't get me wrong; I'm not saying that *all* European children suffered abuse or that *all* European mothers and fathers from the past parented with hardened, sadistic hearts. Parents across different cultures and times, whether they were German or British, French or Greek, loved their children, displayed tenderness, worried about them, and showed interest in the stages of their development. Some even advocated for humane treatment of the young.[5] At the same time, many

European parents also lacked the capacity to respond to their children's developmental behaviors with empathy. As deMause explained, "It is, of course, not love which the parent of the past lacked, but rather the emotional maturity needed to see the child as a person separate from himself."[6]

Naturally, this harsh treatment of children—along with the desire for land, profit, fame, and a religious zeal to civilize and convert the "poisoned" souls of native people to Christianity—bred a culture of adult violence, which drove conquests, colonization, slavery, and genocide. In fact, these practices were rationalized through seeing Africans and indigenous peoples as "children" whom they felt free to brutalize, rape, and kill.

As a result, for white kids, a different worldview developed. By the seventeenth century, white children were slowly categorized as innocent and therefore entitled to claim rights against the violent treatment that was endemic to childhood before that period. By the nineteenth century, with changing attitudes about children's welfare, beatings gradually decreased for white children, although it did not disappear; it turned into a milder form of punishment called spanking.[7]

For centuries, childhood for Europeans was a period of systemic violence, labor exploitation, enslavement, and sexual abuse. But when Europeans sought to enslave Africans, they imposed the category of "child" on them and modeled their racist system of exploiting black bodies on the longstanding ideologies of childhood and the brutal treatment of children in order to justify their enslavement. By the seventeenth century, a separate and unequal definition of childhood gained traction, with a childlike status encapsulating the permanent inferiority and savagery of blackness. In other words, white people began to recognize the vulnerability of their own children and had to rescue them, if only partially, from this unthinkable close proximity to blackness and the brutality of childhood.

White adults began to reconceptualize white childhood as a newly developed space of innocence, promise, and security. As such, white children were imagined as partial adults who could be gradually guided out of savagery and into whiteness by being educated and perfected to their highest potential, and afforded special protections because they would mature into future beneficiaries of white "civilization."

Black slaves, on the other hand, even in adulthood were by definition irredeemable, wild animals and eternal children whose bodies were always ready sites for exploitation, control, and brutal treatment.

The only people who are fully categorized as "children" today are also racialized. In other words, there's no such thing as a "white child." There's only whiteness, which is always a form of privileged adulthood. Likewise, there's no such thing as a "black adult." There's only blackness, which is always a form of dehumanized childhood. And so the bodies of underage and adult blacks occupy the same unprotected space of childhood and continue to be subjected to the same racist violence. In other words, black children are exempt from the protections young people should be granted—to play, run, get dirty, and make mistakes. Their innocence is denied and negated, as they are viewed as stereotyped black adults. And they are treated accordingly in schools, in public spaces, and, sadly, within their own families.

Long before the first Europeans landed on this continent to build a "model" Christian nation, they had grown accustomed to doling out sexual and physical violence against their own children, whom they regarded as savages. That brutality cascaded across generations and continents, and got transferred into other cultures through slavery and colonialism, while white people gradually began sparing their own children from brutality. It shouldn't be surprising, then, that traumatized black people in America eventually inherited their oppressor's violence and carried it forward, in much the same way, to their own children.

When the Puritans sailed from Great Britain and arrived in the forests of New England in the early 1600s, they not only were survivors of religious persecution, but also a culture of profound child abuse that isn't part of our Thanksgiving narratives. This history of abuse may explain why they were also violent with one another, with indigenous communities, and with enslaved Africans. This group of separatists from the Church of England came to America to begin new lives and to establish new colonies and cultures. They sailed the ocean blue with their generationally inherited traumas, Christian and white supremacist worldviews, and a strong belief that children were potential threats to the social order. Beatings rather than nurturing parenting were needed in preparation for citizenship and salvation.

Ambitious and self-righteous in ways that would make Donald Trump proud, the Puritans brought disease, love of warfare, and a delusional belief that God had chosen *them* to inherent an already occupied land. They initially regarded the millions of indigenous peoples already living on this land as the "lost children" of God who could be brought out of ignorance to benefit from a "higher civilization." They believed they had been touched by God to create "a city upon a hill" founded on biblical teachings. This preordained "manifest destiny" of theirs and of other European settlers and their descendants was to be achieved by stealing the continent and bringing the so-called "gifts" of democracy, civilization, and Christianity to people of color.

For these early colonists, the New World was a violent and terrifying wilderness where they faced brutal life-or-death struggles. In their new environment, the Puritans endured harsh winters, horrible plagues, poor harvests, hunger, imperial warfare, frontier vigilantism, rape, child abuse, and the ever-present hand of the Grim Reaper, which snatched the lives of the young and old alike. Indigenous peoples initially rescued white settlers from some of these calamities by feeding and teaching them how to use the land. But as the Puritans and other waves of European settlers acquired more experience in the New World, the Native Americans were seen more and more as obstacles standing in the way of "progress" and civilization.

Heretics, witches, and those who had the nerve to question authority were also threats to Puritan visions of a godly life. Religious dissenters and sexual fornicators were publicly whipped, branded with hot irons, beheaded, hanged, and burned at the stake. So despite stories of turkeys and funny hats, it shouldn't be surprising that a people who suffered such profound child abuse and witnessed public displays of sadism spent the next century engaging in genocidal terrorism that decimated native communities.

If the Puritan's so-called "model" Christian community was to succeed, everybody had to assume an assigned place within the family, church, and society. White male supremacy reigned and people were expected to accept authority and rigidly defined limitations of their positions in life. Individuals belonged to society, not to themselves, so it was crucial to have strict child rearing that produced orderly adults who respected authority and didn't breach the peace. The Puritans took the Bible literally and they were serious about raising obedient kids. It was the sacred duty of parents to keep tight reins on them and teach them respect in order to save them from a life of sin and their souls from hellfire.

Ruling children through shame and harsh punishment was necessary because their "wicked" behaviors could bring the wrath of God down upon the entire colony. They believed that harsh correction in this life by a parent was certainly nowhere near as bad as God's punishment. Spoiling children was discouraged even during infancy because, like their counterparts in Europe, the Puritans believed that children were "born evil" with the stain of Adam's "original sin" on their souls, and so they had to be broken and civilized by "beating the devil out of them" when they misbehaved. I should note that this Christian concept that children were born innately wicked and shameful creatures was *not* part of the broad cultural thinking of Native American or West African societies before direct contact with Europeans and European Americans.

In the eighteenth century, missionaries observed that Indian parents viewed their children as "sacred gifts from the creator." Hitting a child was atypical. One missionary wrote that Indian parents fostered independence by letting their children "follow their own inclinations" and "do what they like and no one prevents them." Since the goal was to foster pride, independence, and courage, children were not hit, "only reproved with gentle words." Indian parents feared that threats, coercion, and physical punishment would make children timid and submissive."[8]

Popular fundamentalist preachers of the era railed against sinful children, who needed to be beaten into adulthood. Preachers told their congregations that children were sinful by nature and they backed up their sermons by citing scriptures such as Proverbs 22:15: "Folly is bound up in the heart of a child, but the rod of discipline will drive it far away."

The fiery Pilgrim minister John Robinson's 1623 treatise "Of Children and Their Education" urged parents to break the wills of their sons and daughters. "Surely there is in all children, though not alike, a stubbornness and stoutness of mind arising from natural pride, which must be broken and beaten down."[9]

"Better whipped than damned," warned the Reverend Cotton Mather, a Boston minister who was involved in the Salem witch trials during the 1690s.[10]

In a sermon on parenting, Mather's contemporary, the Reverend Benjamin Wadsworth, said of newborns: "Their hearts naturally are a mere nest, root, fountain of sin and wickedness; an evil treasure from whence proceed evil things. . . . Their hearts are unspeakably wicked, estranged from God."[11]

Not surprisingly, there was little concern in colonial America about child maltreatment, which meant that many abused children went without protection. As children were considered "property," their parents were allowed to treat them as they saw fit and prosecutions for abuse were rare and mostly involved servants who beat their apprentices. There were a few cases of children who were removed from their homes not because of abuse, but because parents were not instilling proper religious training and a strong work ethic in their offspring.[12]

Unlike many Native American children who were not physically punished by their parents and were encouraged to be autonomous, misbehaving Puritan kids were branded, sentenced to hard labor, tied to wooden posts and beaten with whips, canes, switches, and paddles in the town center or outside the court, church, or schoolyard. Sometimes a child's head and hands were placed in a wooden pillory, or "stretch-neck," where they were left standing in a bent position while passersby teased them and threw trash and rotten food at them. In the 1640s, Connecticut and Massachusetts passed "Stubborn Child" laws, which required the death penalty for children over age sixteen who disobeyed, cursed, or hit their parents, or denied that the Bible was the absolute word of God.[13]

This abusive treatment of white children was symptomatic of a broader culture of control and violence in a colonial America that exploited the many to produce wealth for the elite propertied class. How else to keep the anger and resentment of the masses in check but through coercion and sadistic, ritualistic forms of violence? In colonial America, punishment of indentured white servants and convicts included fines, imprisonment, banishment, tarring and feathering, servitude, whipping, pillorying, boring tongues with hot irons, cropping ears, and hanging.[14]

By the 1680s, the escalation of the British slave trade brought increasing numbers of Africans to the colonies. The enslavement of Africans on plantations in various parts of the South would dominate America's labor system. Torn from their homelands, those Africans were thrust into a new kind of violent culture where they were introduced to the most barbaric dimensions of a European Christian worldview and its practices that didn't come from an authentically spiritual place but were designed to ensure the profitability of the slavery enterprise. Before our ancestors arrived in America, white men were slaughtering Indians, and beating their servants, wives, and children. Slaves were brutally "seasoned" by overseers and masters, and soon our ancestors saw beating as an essential feature of child rearing and crucial to equipping children with the skills they would need to survive the harsh realities of plantation life.

The European approach to child discipline was quite different from what was common in precolonial West African cultures. There's no one generalized, pancontinental statement that can be made about child discipline practices in Africa prior to the arrival of Europeans during colonization, after, or even today. That's because Africa is a vast continent with diverse religious practices and thousands of cultural traditions, ethnic groups, and languages.

In precolonial Africa, oral traditions such as songs, tribal legends, proverbs, tales, and fables were used in place of written records to relate important facets of history and to pass on information from one generation to the next. Before Europeans introduced Western education and literacy in order to more easily convert Africans to Christianity, families, clans, or tribes used games and riddles to teach children their heritage, good manners, respect for elders, the value of cooperation, and allegiance to ancestral spirits. Elders sometimes incorporated fear into the education process by telling children that if they disobeyed then they'd grow hair on their neck, witches would get them, or the earth would open up and swallow them.[15]

Because Africans relied so heavily on oral traditions, we lack written historical documentation about the firsthand experiences of growing up or parenting practices prior to the Atlantic slave trade and European colonization. We are left to rely heavily on the writings of

European voyagers, missionaries, anthropologists, and ethnologists. But we must look at these accounts with a skeptical side eye given how Europeans' views of Africans were colored by racist thinking, Eurocentric schooling, and paternalistic prejudices that saw Africans as a less advanced people who needed to be guided into the light of civilization. And, of course, many of those European observations were used to legitimize the slave trade, colonialism, and missionary campaigns.

Despite the lack of historical documentation on precolonial African parenting practices, in 1941 the noted white anthropologist Melville Herskovits wrote a book titled *The Myth of the Negro Past*, in which he rejected the idea that black people adopted whupping kids from their slave masters. He claimed that whupping children was an integral part of child training in West Africa.

"When we turn to data from Negro cultures concerning whupping as a form of correction, we find a great deal of material to confirm an assumption of historical relationship to New World practice," Herskovits wrote. "In Dahomey and among the Yoruba, flogging of an order of severity almost unknown in Europe, except as a penal device, was the rule. Children were likewise flogged—not so severely, it is true, but severely in terms of comparable modes of applying this form of discipline in white societies."

To back up his argument, Herskovits wrote that in Haiti, Guinea, Trinidad, and Jamaica, "the cries of young boys and girls being whupped for misdeeds are heard even by the casual visitor. The right of any elder to whup an erring young member of his family is vested in all Haitians," for example.[16]

Not only did Herskovits not cite historical sources for his claims, he was in fact that "casual visitor" doing his anthropological work on the Dahomey and in parts of southern Nigeria in the 1930s in colonized communities where European contact, military aggression, labor exploitation, and the influence of Christianity and missionary schools had created profound cultural changes and altered the socialization of children and parenting traditions. Herskovits's argument that beating children was integral to West Africa may have been true *after* the arrival of Europeans, but that kind of punishment, if it existed, simply wasn't written or talked about by anyone else, even among early generations of European anthropologists and missionaries. The absence of information about child punishment does not prove that Africans never hit or abused children prior to contact with whites. But oral traditions make no mention of this kind of ritualistic violence.

To get more sound answers about parenting practices back then, I turned to scholars who know better. "One can be pretty sure that aggressive punishment against children in West Africa was unthinkable," the anthropologist Murray Last told me in a phone interview. Last, a professor emeritus at University College London and a foremost authority on precolonial West African societies, has studied historical and contemporary youth violence and cultures of punishment in northern Nigeria. "To beat children was considered absurd," he said. "You might want to beat an adult for some infraction, but beating a child diminished you because an adult is older and more powerful."

Last said that according to historical records from the nineteenth century, even adult slaves in Nigeria were not mistreated with ritualistic whuppings. "If a slave consistently did something unacceptable, he was sold for export. Merely being sold was unpleasant for the slave. Children, in turn, could readily abandon their families if they were unjust in their behavior toward them." Parents exercised restraint when angry, and "justice was really very important in these communities," Last said.

Another expert, Heidi Nast, a professor of international studies at DePaul University, has written extensively about race and slavery. When I asked her about child-rearing practices in West Africa prior to the Atlantic slave trade, she agreed that there was no singular way of parenting in those cultures. "It depends on the geopolitical economy where those who were captured came from," she said. "Were they obtained from the forests where they were hunter gatherers?" Nast said that Africans from those types of societies did not physically punish and bully their children. These were societies that emphasized farming and sharing; there was no property ownership or oppressive hierarchies.

West African societies held children in a much higher regard than slave societies in the Atlantic world, which placed emphasis on black bodies as property, not human beings. In many West African societies, infant mortality was high. Because parents feared losing their children to early death, they were highly valued as sacred. Unlike in Western societies that emphasized the innate wickedness of children, Africans believed that children, especially the youngest, came from the afterlife and led profoundly spiritual lives. Adults believed children held extraordinary mystical powers that could be harnessed through ritual practice for the good of the community.

In parts of Nigeria and Cameroon and in Kedjom societies, for example, children were believed to have the power to mystically transform themselves into birds or fly invisibly through the air to meet interstitial beings. Children also had the power to play with the health of family members, and in some tribes, children were called "grandmother," "grandfather," "auntie," "uncle," or some other honorific because they were believed to be a reincarnated ancestor with strong ties to the spirit world, which granted the child a certain level of respect at birth. In Yoruban culture, boys and girls were sometimes given the names Babatunde (father has returned) and Yeyetunde (mother has returned). It was believed that coercion and hitting a child could scare off their soul. In the non-Muslim, Hausa-speaking culture in northern Nigeria, children were considered full members of the house as soon as they were weaned. The Beng people of Côte d'Ivoire believed that because children have a fragile hold on life, parents should make earthly life so comfortable and appealing for them so they would not be tempted to return to another spiritual realm.[17]

I'm not trying to romanticize childhood in West Africa or assert that it was completely free of violence. Children were indeed mistreated in ways that we in the West would regard as abusive. In some cultures, children were regarded as beasts and monsters. In Yoruban and Ibo culture, for example, twins were associated with witches and dangerous immorality. Twins held special powers that could be dangerous and so sometimes were killed to prevent them from wreaking havoc on the community. In precolonial Lagos, children were sometimes sacrificed at funerals or in times of drought to please the deity of rain.[18]

In the Gold Coast, deformed children were perceived as witches, bad omens, or God's punishment for sins of the ancestors, and so were burned alive, buried in dung heaps, or decapitated. Cutting and branding the skin, genital mutilation of boys and girls, and beatings were parts of rite-of-passage rituals. But the systematic, ritualistic whupping of children as punishment for disobedience was generally not part of West African cultures, given the spiritual beliefs about young people and their social value. And given the absence of physical brutality against slaves, it would make sense that children, who were highly valued, would not be harshly punished the way they were later on southern plantations in America and other parts of the Atlantic world.

A number of top historians of the Atlantic slave trade and slavery in Africa told me that they had not come across any evidence of the kind of harsh physical punishment of children in West Africa that black parents and children were subjected to on American slave plantations. However, the historian Paul Lovejoy pointed me to biographical accounts in which West Africans talked about being kidnapped because they disobeyed their parents. "It is possible that the threat of physical discipline may have lurked in the background," Lovejoy wrote in an e-mail. He also told me that historically, Qur'anic education of children involved whupping in some Islamic schools. "The practice involved the teacher standing above the children, mostly boys, with a short whip as they sat on the ground reciting verses in Arabic. If students mispronounced words then they got a sharp snap of the whip." Lovejoy noted that this practice is still done today in some traditional Qur'anic schools. The biography of Mahommah Gardo Baquaqua, a Muslim who was kidnapped in Africa and brought to Brazil as a slave, then escaped to New York City and wrote an autobiography, described the nature of this practice in the 1830s and 1840s.[19]

To understand the evolution of violent parenting practices among African Americans requires us to look at slavery in West Africa before Europeans turned it into a horrific race-based big business. Many slaves who were transported to America had been indentured servants in Africa, where the practice was an ancient and widespread institution not based on skin color. Africans did not enslave and sell people from their own ethnic or cultural group. This gave them the opportunity to readily sell prisoners of war and people they considered outsiders. The slavery that existed in Africa did not resemble the popular American image of gangs of black bodies on large plantations picking cotton in the hot sun under the constant threat of the whip. Slavery in Africa existed along a spectrum of dependence and servitude, and there was no strict boundary between the owned and unowned. Slaves occupied a wide range of roles and positions, and were often part of a family by adoption or marriage. They had the right to marry and to own and inherit property. Some were royal slaves while other slaves owned slaves themselves. A child of well-to-do slaves might have a better life than a poor person living in the countryside.

People sold themselves into slavery to pay off debts or to avoid starvation, to gain belonging as members of kin networks, or because it gave them the opportunity to achieve power and prominence. Their status as slaves was not lifelong, and they could envision freedom for themselves in the future. In African societies, slaves represented "human capital" and were not "property" in the way they were on American plantations. Owning slaves wasn't primarily driven by the desire to accumulate money, but was part of efforts by powerful men to acquire more wives and children and access to land, and to ensure protection from debt and abuse.

Violence did have a role.

In Africa, slaves were often, but not always, captured through kidnap and warfare. And some slaves, especially young men, were used for human sacrifice during religious or funeral rituals. Brutal whuppings, though, were not considered an effective means to get slaves to do their jobs, which ranged from domestic work to soldiering to tax collection. In the popular eighteenth-century slave narratives from African-born slaves—such as Ottobah Cugoano, who was snatched at age thirteen while gathering fruit in the woods; Venture Smith, who was kidnapped at age six and brought to Connecticut; and Olaudah Equiano, who was kidnapped at age eleven and sold to British slavers who shipped him to Barbados, then Virginia and Philadelphia—there's no evidence of physical punishment by their parents. In fact, all described having had happy childhoods before being kidnapped, with parents who gave them great affection.[20]

Historians estimate that about 12.5 million Africans were shipped to the New World before 1866, and at least two million died during the Middle Passage. About one-quarter of the slaves who crossed the Atlantic were children, defined as anyone shorter than four feet four inches. In the early phases of the slave trade, children were viewed as a bad investment and adults were preferred for the brutal forty-day trip across the Atlantic. But by the late eighteenth century, increasing numbers of children had entered the slave trade. The reasons vary. A changing, specialized market created a stronger demand in the West

Indies for labor in coffee-bean picking, for which children were better suited. Then there were families who sold their own children into slavery during times of drought and famine. The money from the sale enabled parents to purchase food, shelter, and other provisions for the rest of the family.[21]

The average age of slave captives was between fifteen and twenty at the beginning of the nineteenth century but dropped to between nine and twelve when abolition of the slave trade was imminent.[22] When the *Margarita* sailed in 1734 with ninety-three Africans, 87 percent were under age sixteen, with the youngest being ten. In 1746, the Newport, Rhode Island, merchant William Ellery wrote, "If you have good trade, purchase forty or fifty Negroes. Get most of them mere Boys and Girls, some Men, let them be Young, No very small Children." The New York City merchant John Watts wrote in 1762, "The younger the better if not quite Children, those advanced in years will never do." When the *Maria* sailed in 1790, 90 percent of the eighty Africans on board were listed as children.[23]

The fact that the majority of captives were young is significant for our understanding of the evolution of African American child-rearing practices. Bringing over mostly youth and mixing cultures meant that traditional African child-rearing practices faded the same way African languages and religious practices ultimately did. Had the slaves who crossed the Atlantic been mostly adults from the same tribes and nationalities, spoken the same languages, shared the same blueprint for child-rearing that was followed in the societies they were to be enslaved in, and been given freedom to rear their children without interference from whites, then maybe traditional African child-rearing practices could have been preserved. But since none of those conditions prevailed, to argue that whupping children was brought over from Africa is simply false.

Once on the slave ship, virtually every child was separated from his or her relatives because traders had no incentive to keep families together. Sometimes newborns were kept with their mothers, but it was not unusual for ship captains to throw the babies overboard if they changed their minds about the purchase or the if child's cries got annoying. But most young captives came without parents. Sexual exploitation of boys and girls was also common.

In this environment of kidnap, warfare, famine, death, and the increased capture of children, African adults responded by creating larger kinship networks to care for their young in the absence of parents. Over time, these networks developed new, harsher customs toward violence as a means of self-preservation and safety. (Sound familiar?)

So as the Atlantic slave trade wore on, Africans on the continent of Africa felt more compelled to advance new, more rigid coping mechanisms for the hardships of life, which included the possibility of their children being captured and sold away to an unknown world. And Africans on the continent of America felt the full weight of human cruelty as they endured life on plantations.

What united parents in Africa, North America, and other parts of the Atlantic world where millions of black people ended up, was that they all wanted to give their children the best chances of survival and they feared that they would not be able to adequately prepare their offspring for the dismal realities of their new environments.

Slave children in America played a pivotal role in the grueling daily operation of plantations run by white planters who were obsessed with profit maximization. Unlike today, when black women are demonized for producing children out of wedlock, plantation owners encouraged slave women to have lots of babies. This was especially crucial when the threat of abolition of the international slave trade threatened supplies of replacements from Africa. The new status of slave children as property owned by white people instead of their parents meant that their value had changed socially and spiritually. Being owned by racist white people also dramatically altered interactions between slave parents and children.

Once in America, Africans had to reconfigure a meaningful way to raise children under slavery because they were denied many of the same rights and responsibilities granted to free families. As in Africa, enslaved parents in America continued to emphasize respect for elders, and they formed extended networks to share collective responsibility and to care for other people's children if a parent died or was sold. So it is fair to say that American slaves maintained *some* African practices and values, but were deeply shaped by European culture, too. This created a new, unique African American culture. The two histories intersecting and blending together for four centuries is how we got to where we are.

It would be an understatement to say that slavery denied black children a quality childhood. Faced with abuse and poor living conditions, hygiene, and diet, about half of all slave children did not survive the first decade of life. The mortality rate for black children was twice that of white children until about age fourteen. This meant that slave parents had to deal constantly with a devastating number of child deaths. For those children who survived the early years of life, parents then had the task of socializing them for the cruel realities of slavery, which included brutal whuppings and torture, being loaned out as prostitutes, and the possibility of being sold away from their relatives for the rest of their lives.

"Be good an trus in de Lawd." "Be polite." "Obey your new elders and masters." These were messages slave parents had to whisper into their children's ears to prepare them for being parceled out to strangers. Owners sold kids when they needed cash to finance education for their own white children, to construct new homes, and for other minor purchases. One former slave from North Carolina recalled that his brother "was sold ter dress young Missus for her weddin'."

Under these conditions, American slavery created a new kind of black parenting whereby mothers and fathers were denied legal guardianship of their young. Slave children belonged to the plantation elite and the master's authority preempted parental authority. As one slave put it, "During slavery it seemed lak yo' chillum b'long to ev'ybody but you."

Not only did slave parents have to worry about their children surviving and completing the stages of childhood, but they also had to try to attach emotional meaning to their lives in a system that undermined family stability and parental authority. Owners punished slave children without parental consent and gave them work tasks that weren't age appropriate. Children watched their parents being whupped. "Dey didn't only beat us, but dey useta strap my mama to a bench or box an' beat her wid a wooden paddle while she was naked," one former slave recalled. Another said, "Many a day mama has stood by and watched massa beat her children 'til they bled, and she couldn't open her mouth."[24]

Since the productivity and obedience of enslaved workers was critical to the success of the plantation economy, abusive physical punishment through the sting of the lash and other forms of torture was deemed a necessary part of daily life. Masters and overseers used the whip to enforce rules, to make slaves submissive, to break rebellious spirits, and to remind the entire enslaved populations of the absolute power of white people. Children were not spared the pain of the whip, either. They could be beaten for sassing a white person, slacking off, stealing, fighting, or breaking tools. And so it was in the context of slavery that black American adults and children were introduced to ritualistic whuppings with features that still show up in child punishments today.

To be clear: not all of the physical cruelty meted out to slaves was driven by a profit motive. Plantation owners, drivers, and white women whupped and tortured slaves not only to instill deference and obedience, but also to vent their rage. Sarah Graves, a former Missouri slave, recalled that her master whupped his slaves as a pastime while another owner beat a slave because he could not "recollec ever whuppin' him."[25] Other forms of violence included the rankest sort: amputations, rapes, stabbings, shootings, brandings, and being savaged by dogs. This kind of sadistic violence was routine and often conducted in front of the entire slave community to "teach a lesson" to others.

Slaves were often stripped naked and whupped with switches and leather straps that tore open their flesh. Back then, whupping a child— whether done by depraved whites or black overseers—was a way to get that child accustomed to the reality that he or she had little power over his or her life. The mere threat of a whupping was a round-the-clock reminder to be obedient and to work without complaint. Slaves were to be seen and not heard unless called upon. It's not a coincidence that reading these kinds of narratives evokes memories from some of our own childhoods.

Enslaved parents were under tremendous pressure to make their children into docile field workers. As the historian Marie Jenkins Schwartz notes in her book *Born in Bondage*, white owners recognized the influence slave parents had over their sons and daughters and so they urged them to subdue children and turn them into dutiful and submissive servants. White owners and slave parents punished kids for different reasons. Slaveholders chastised children for their own convenience or benefit, while enslaved parents did so out of genuine concern for their welfare.

Enslaved parents were also required to teach children proper deference and demeanor in front of whites. Staring at white people, rolling eyes, sucking teeth, talking back, and questioning authority put children at risk for being whupped or sold. In her book *Stolen Childhood*, the historian Wilma King highlights an 1852 issue of the journal *Southern Planter*, which gave instructions to overseers about training slave children: "Slave children were to be taught not to run and hide from whites but to stand their ground, and speak when spoken to, in a polite manner." Polite slaves, as King notes, were expected to approach whites with bowed heads, downcast eyes, and hushed voices.[26]

Children who failed to keep up with their work tasks were whupped by whites *and* by their parents. Schwartz wrote about a five-year-old Virginia slave named Katie Blackwell who was whupped for not turning oxen in the right direction. One Alabama slave child's mother taught him to pick cotton by hitting him with a pole when he didn't follow her directions. Because the disciplinary measures employed by slaves generally pleased owners, slave parents retained most of the responsibility for disciplining their children. And they often defended their "right" to physically discipline children without intrusion by whites because they believed a whupping at their hands was better than one from a white person.[27] The right to beat a black child is a sacrosanct privilege handed down to black parents from slavery—the only privilege they got from their white masters.

The historical archives are full of awful narratives of slave adults and children being whupped and tortured. There are images of slaves strung up in distorted postures, hands tied with ropes, victims writhing in agony, bleeding, convulsing, crying, and hollering for mercy. There are gory images of skin stripped off the body from whips. Eyes are blinded, ears cropped, cheeks gashed out, jaws broken, teeth knocked out, heads cracked, pregnant women whupped so hard that they miscarried right at the whipping post. There are testimonies involving infants whupped to death by white women just for crying. And there are stories of slaves being awakened from their sleep at night and whupped for failing to complete tasks.

The Reverend Horace Moulton, a Methodist minister, wrote, "I have often heard the sound of the lash, the curses of the whipper and the cries of the poor Negro rending the air, late in the evening and long before daylight in the morning."[28] And generations later you can hear black folks tell funny stories about being snatched out of bed and whupped on the spot for forgetting to take the trash out or for not completing some other chore.

I will spare you further depictions of the graphic violence against black bodies on the plantation because we are presently living in a culture where scenes of black brutality and death play on a constant loop. But we must acknowledge that whupping black people was always about asserting power and control, whether it was done by slave masters or black parents.

After slaves were emancipated, in 1865, the rules of racial etiquette and the ritualistic whuppings continued as new kind of coercive labor system emerged that depended on black child workers. Once again, whites co-opted black parenting to make sure it performed the same kind of function in freedom as it had done during slavery. With sanctioning from the black church, of all places, black parents became extensions of the master's lash in order to instill unquestioning obedience to the rules of the Jim Crow system. Their reasoning was simple: to prepare black children to deal with the chronic stresses they would face and to keep them alive.

4

WOULD JESUS WHUP A CHILD?

Black Clergy on What Sparing the Rod Really Means

I was raised a Christian. The church services of my childhood were filled with preachers who delivered their sermons in a musical and vocal style that made people cry and catch the Holy Ghost and get a brief emotional fix to help face the next week of living while black in America.

During the hours-long services, I saw parents pinch, pop, and snatch bored and misbehaving children out of the pews, then drag them into the bathroom, where they were spanked with a hand or a comb. Sometimes the smacking and cries could be heard in the sanctuary.

I remember listening to the choir dis Buddha and Muhammad in their Gospel songs. Some of their most beautiful music ignited feelings of grief, suffering, and even a sense of shamefulness with lyrics like "Lord, make me over again." "I'm broken." "Fix me, Jesus." "Cleanse me." "Wash me white as snow." "I'm nothing without you." "I'm not worthy."

Those songs were the sound track that matched up perfectly with the whuppings every church kid I knew got at home. From the pulpit, black preachers encouraged parents to whup children for being disobedient or for getting bad grades. This religious training, however, is not the way Jesus interacted with children—with gentle hands, snuggling, kindness, a listening ear, empathy, love, justice, and by demanding that adults welcome, respect, and emulate children's nature.[1] Jesus never said, "Suffer little children to come unto me for a good butt whupping." Yet, it is constantly reinforced in church that we were all "born sinful" and that it was the parent's duty to use a "rod of correction" to guide their children out of the darkness.

There's a disconnection between what Jesus stood for and the physical punishment black Christian churches endorse. How does anyone who believes in turning the other cheek, loving enemies, forgiving trespassers, and doing unto others as you would have them do unto you also support hurting the bodies of children? Would Jesus whup a child? I found my answers in historical research and interviews with a few of the country's leading progressive black theologians.

A few years ago Zero to Three, a Washington, DC–based nonprofit organization that focuses on child development issues, surveyed African American, Latino, and white parents about the major influences on their child-rearing practices. Sixty-one percent of black respondents said that the way they were raised by their parents was most influential. But they also found that almost 50 percent of blacks were influenced more by their faith and religious leaders than by the input of pediatricians and child-care professionals or parenting information from books, magazines, websites, and television shows.

Over the years, I have read countless child abuse case files in which parents cite their pastor or "spare the rod, spoil the child"— commonly misattributed to the Bible—as justification for whupping their kids. The tenet echoes a passage from Proverbs 13:24—"He who spare the rod hates his son, but he who loves him is careful to discipline him." But it's actually taken from a seventeenth-century poem titled "Hudibras," by Samuel Butler. It's important to make the distinction between the two passages because something does, in fact, get lost in the poetical translation here. The Bible is not condoning the beating of a child. The original Hebrew word for "rod" is *shebet*, which is a shepherd's crook. In Hebrew culture, the rod was used to guide and protect sheep and to ward off wolves. It was a symbol

Major Influences on Parenting Among Key Subgroups

% saying each has a major influence on their parenting

	Whites	African Americans	Hispanics	Mothers	Fathers	First-time parents	Repeat parents
Way my parents raised me	52%	**61%**	49%	50%	**59%**	53%	53%
Faith/religous background	42%	**49%**	35%	42%	40%	35%	**44%**
Professionals' input: pediatrician, child care professionals	33%	37%	**40%**	**39%**	26%	38%	33%
Input from family and close friends	33%	34%	**36%**	36%	35%	**43%**	31%
Parenting information in books, magazines, web sites, TV shows	7%	13%	**14%**	**11%**	5%	10%	9%

Source: Hart Research Associates/Zero to Three National Center for Infants, Toddlers, and Families

of loving guidance, leadership, wisdom, and protection from outside harm. That verse suggests a more thoughtful way of disciplining children than simply hitting them.

People often use "spare the rod, spoil the child" as a way to shift the conversation away from history, science, research, devastating child abuse statistics, and other evidence of negative outcomes that result from hitting children. The phrase and the behavior attached to it is so deeply engrained that it trumps any kind of real evidence. Not to mention, there seems to be a whole lot of silence about biblical references to adult corporal punishment:

Proverbs 18:6—"A fool's lips bring strife, and a fool's mouth invites a flogging."

Proverbs 10:13—"A rod is for the back of one who lacks common sense."

Proverbs 26:3—"A whip is for a horse, a bridle for a donkey, and a rod for the back of fools."

Proverbs 20:30—"Blows that wound cleanse away evil; beatings make clean the innermost parts."

Despite these references to beating adults, we would never use them to justify hitting one another. But we don't mind trying to do it for kids.

In her book *Jesus, the Gentle Parent*, L. R. Knost argues that "spare the rod" anchors an entire parenting paradigm, which is based on Old Testament practices of rigid expectations and harsh consequences, purported to be God's way. She says that in right-wing, evangelical Christian circles, a "Biblical Chastisement Movement" bullies and intimidates parents into believing that refusing to uphold these strict parenting models will have dire consequences, from raising brats or rebels to living in opposition to "God's will." Parents are given directions on how to physically punish a child in a "godly" manner without leaving bruises and welts.

Knost cites a number of Christian fundamentalist pastors whose child training manuals perpetuate the idea that children are innately devilish, liars, and manipulators, and that their sinful nature is formed while they are in the womb. For example, in *Shepherding a Child's Heart*, Tedd Tripp, pastor of Grace Fellowship Church in Hazleton, Pennsylvania, writes, "Even a child in the womb and coming from the womb is wayward and sinful. . . . The child is a sinner. There are things within the heart of the sweetest little baby that, allowed to blossom and grow to fruition, will bring about eventual destruction."

Similarly, James Dobson, the founder of the powerful far-right-wing Christian media organization Focus on the Family, in *Dare to Discipline*, argues, "It is possible to create a fussy, demanding baby by rushing to pick him up every time he utters a whimper or sigh. Infants are fully capable of learning to manipulate their parents through a process called reinforcement, whereby any behavior that produces a pleasant result will tend to recur." This same religious leader who advocated that men shoot transwomen in public bathrooms to protect their wives and children, also adds that "a healthy baby can keep his mother hopping around his nursery twelve hours a day (or night) by simply forcing air past his sandpaper larynx. This tendency toward self-will is the essence of original sin, which has infiltrated the human family. It certainly explains why I place such stress on the proper response to willful defiance during childhood, for that rebellion can plant the seeds of personal disaster."[2]

In *The Correction and Salvation of Children*, Pastor Ronald E. Williams of Believers Baptist Church in Winona Lake, Indiana, and director of Hephzibah House, a home for "troubled" teens, similarly asks, "When should a parent start using the correction on a child that the Lord brought into the family?" His answer is clear:

> A child very quickly demonstrates his fallen, depraved nature and reveals himself to be a selfish little beast in manifold ways. As soon as the child begins to express his own self-will (and this occurs early in life) that child needs to receive correction. My wife and I have a general goal of making sure that each of our children has his will broken by the time he reaches the age of one year. To do this, a child must receive correction when he is a small infant.[3]

In their popular 1994 book *To Train Up a Child*, ministers Michael and Debi Pearl advocate hitting infants with a willow switch or a twelve-inch ruler as a punishment for getting angry, until the child gives in to the pain. Criminal complaints have been brought against some parents who have killed their children after following the Pearls' "methods," including Kevin and Elizabeth Schatz of Paradise, California, who murdered their seven-year-old black adopted daughter during a "discipline session." They beat her to death with a rubber hose that they called a "Biblical rod."[4]

Another celebrity pastor, Voddie Baucham, who is black and has called for dismantling child protective services systems, said in a recorded 2007 sermon at his Grace Family Baptist Church in Spring, Texas, that parents need to "spank often" and begin the process before children leave the crib because they come to earth willful and manipulative. Here's an excerpt from the sermon:

> "The world doesn't revolve around *you*. *Your* world revolves around *me*." That's what we need to teach our children in those first few years of their life. Because they come here and just by the nature of things, they believe that the world revolves around them. And for the first few weeks that's okay, but eventually we need to teach them that that's over, that, "The world no longer revolves around *you*. Your world, *toddler*, revolves around *me*. Around me." Folly is bound up in the heart of a child

and the *rod* of correction will drive it far from them. In other words, God says your children desperately, desperately need to be spanked.

Amen, Hallelujah, Praise the Lord and spank your kids, okay? (Laughter from audience.)

And, they desperately need to be spanked and they need to be spanked often. They do. I meet people all the time, ya' know. And they say, "Oh yeah, there have only been maybe four or five times I've ever had to spank Junior."

"Really? That's unfortunate, because unless you raised Jesus II, there were days when Junior needed to be spanked five times before breakfast."

If you only spanked your child five times, then that means almost every time they disobeyed you, you let it go.

Why do your toddlers throw fits? Because you've taught them that's the way that they can control you. When instead you just need to have an all-day session where you just wear them out and they finally decide, "You know what, things get worse when I do that."

Using religion and faith normalizes whuppings as a godly activity. Believing that God directs the practice provides legitimacy and a belief that there's a greater purpose that a switch, belt, or other version of the rod serves. "Spare the rod, spoil the child" is sold as part of one's Christian duty, when in reality it is just a way of absolving parents for inflicting violence onto children's bodies. And folks say it's "for their own good."

The irony is that while Christian teachings say violence only begets violence, a good butt whupping begets compliant and obedient children. Reflecting our investment in the belief that our children are inherently sinful, deficient, and defective, this violence becomes a method of redemption that will lead our children toward salvation and a spot in heaven.

"Spare the rod, spoil the child" leaves us believing that an obedient child is a whupped child; a respectful child is one who has felt the sting of a switch or a slap. It leaves us believing that an unruly or spoiled child, one who is a threat to family, community, and society, lives in a house where no hitting is allowed.

As Christianity is about obedience and faith, what better way to implant this idea into human beings than by starting early and

demanding submission from children through parental violence? After all, it worked to teach generations of black people how to be obedient slaves. The belief is that if children are not hit, they can't grow
up to be law-abiding citizens or good people with morals. And for
black parents raising children in a racist society, "spare the rod, spoil
the child" is a message of forcing obedience, instilling fear, guarantee-
ing adherence to authority, and beating the natural-born "badness"
out of black boys and girls. That message and the methods are racist
at the core.

"Spare the rod" is a Christian fiction that grants parents permission from clergy and others who misinterpret scriptures to justify
whupping children, just like white masters invoked scriptures to justify enslaving our ancestors.

I know this information might be hard to swallow, but we must remember that our West African ancestors did not practice Christianity
prior to the arrival of Europeans, nor did they incorporate whupping
children into their definition of healthy and responsible parenting.

The fact is, many of the Christian values we embrace, especially
when it comes to parenting, are deeply antithetical to the values of
the precolonial West African families and societies of our ancestors.
Westernized Christianity introduced new kinds of thinking about children and notions of sin into black family life, the concept of children
as "property," the notion that babies are "born evil," and that we
must hurt their bodies so they can learn, discipline their own bodies,
and achieve full personhood and then salvation in another dimension
after this life. So it's difficult to even imagine rearing children without spanking until we reject and exorcise a white-supremacist violence
veiled in Christian doctrine out of our culture.

Whupping children may have been a parenting practice that was
taught to us during slavery, but since Emancipation, black clergy have
been the most vocal supporters of this practice. Consider the following examples of the Reverend Arthur Allen, Pastor Creflo Dollar, the
ministers backing Adrian Peterson, and the preachers who praised the
"Baltimore Mom." Their actions and support of whuppings connect
directly to the history of the black church's complicit role in reinforcing violence against children.

In 2001, media reports surfaced that the Reverend Arthur Allen directed adults in his church to hold children in the air by their arms and legs while whupping them with belts and switches during services. Allen, former pastor of the nondenominational House of Prayer in Atlanta, was a self-taught minister who preached against abortion, homosexuality, birth control, and out-of-wedlock sex. Child protective services reported that more than forty children, ages two to seventeen, had been seriously beaten by their parents and by church leaders. Several children had open wounds, large bruises, and welts. One sixteen-year-old girl was beaten with belts for up to a half hour until she bled. The local news media showed heartbreaking scenes of children screaming, kicking, and biting police officers who removed them from their parents' homes.

Even after police filed criminal charges against Allen and other church members, the parents of the abused children defended their pastor's teachings on discipline. They chose foster care for their children rather than agreeing not to whup them at church services. Allen warned them that should they decide to follow the requirement from the court to change their disciplinary practices, they would be in conflict with the church and disobeying God's word.

"They'd be compromising their faith," Allen said. "Either you love the Lord thy God with all your heart and soul . . . or you don't. God doesn't accept serving two masters."[5]

Many people defended Allen and his followers, arguing that the "godless" government intervention represented discrimination against African American Christians whose practice of corporal punishment simply meant that they were doing their best to help their children rise above the economic and educational disadvantages of their backgrounds.

Georgia state representative Billy McKinney said, "This fight was not about the House of Prayer. . . . This fight was about how black people discipline their children. I know how my grandmama disciplined me. It was not out of Dr. Spock's book. White folks cannot tell us how to discipline our children."[6]

"We're going to raise our children according to the Bible," one parent insisted at the hearing to determine whether their children should be placed into foster care.

"If the white society doesn't want to whup their children, that's their business. I'm not trying to make you black, so don't try to make me white," Allen said.

Judge Sanford Jones was unfazed, noting that he regretted the parents' decision. "I hate to see these children jeopardized by what I consider to be a cult." [7]

Fast-forward a decade. In June 2012, the Reverend Creflo Dollar, a nationally recognized megapreacher and televangelist well known for his prosperity gospel preaching at World Changers Church in Atlanta, was arrested for attacking his fifteen-year-old daughter, following an argument about whether she could attend a party. According to the police report, after she walked away from Dollar and said she didn't want to talk to him anymore, he put his hands around her throat. Choking her briefly, he threw her to the ground, punched her, and hit her with a shoe.

Dollar claimed he "merely restrained" his daughter. After she hit him, he said, he wrestled her to the floor and spanked her. Nonetheless, he was arrested, charged with simple battery and cruelty to children, and released on five-thousand-dollar bond.

A few days after the arrest, he told his congregation that he didn't choke or punch his daughter, that he should never have been arrested, that the real culprit was "the devil," who was trying to discredit him, and that "all is well in the Dollar household." He likened his trials to those of the apostle Paul.[8]

A few years later, when Minnesota Vikings star Adrian Peterson beat his son, other athletes weren't his only defenders. A number of black ministers and community leaders defended the player's actions, saying that criticism of Peterson had been inconsistent, harsh, and culturally insensitive.

While Peterson pleaded no contest to misdemeanor reckless assault and faced a suspension from the NFL, he was tried and convicted in the court of white public opinion. Many white media pundits openly expressed their horror at news of both the beating and Peterson's defense of it as responsible child-rearing.

The Reverend Alfred Babington-Johnson, who heads the Stairstep Foundation, a network of churches and community outposts that works for improved access to health care in black communities, issued a statement denouncing NFL commissioner Roger Goodell's suspension of Peterson without pay for the rest of the football season. Peterson appealed the suspension, which made him eligible for reinstatement the following spring.

Babington-Johnson said that while the Stairstep Foundation does not condone child abuse of any kind,

> we are . . . clear that the black community historically has had a much different approach and attitude to the issue of physical discipline than whites. Much of the public discussion dominated by European American talking heads has not demonstrated any sense of legitimate cultural difference. Our community is not monolithic. We have different points of view, but we believe that our broader views are not being reflected.[9]

Months after Peterson made headlines, Toya Graham's pastor, the Reverend Jamal Bryant of Berean Baptist Church, said she should be "Mom of the Year" for cursing and hitting her teenage son on national television. "I wish all of the parents of Baltimore would take on her spirit and go pull your children out of the streets," he told *Inside Edition*. A year later, in May 2016, the Reverend Eric Williams, cofounder of Good Word Ministries, honored Graham at a Faith Fighters awards banquet for "using her faith to overcome life's obstacles."

So where did the black faithful get this strong belief in whupping kids in the name of the Lord? And what purpose does it serve? To answer this question we must first look to ancient European traditions, social conceptions, and religious beliefs about children.

Prior to the rise of Christianity in the fifth century AD, European children were considered easy to enslave because they were dependent beings viewed as incapable of sophisticated reasoning. Portrayed as dirty animals aspiring to become civilized humans, they were perpetual objects of violence and sacrifice at the whim of any authority. Early Christian thinkers, who took their cues on the status of children from previous Greek and Roman (Hellenistic) thought, had varying views on whether children were "born evil." One writer summarized a common medieval Christian view of children like this: "A child was not believed to be truly human simply by birthright; he was a creature in search of humanity—unpredictable, capable of animal indolence, self-ishness, and savagery."[10]

Christianity offered the hope of salvation for all people, provided they survived a set of fierce tests that followed its model for training children. Just as children were seen as being born evil and in need of harsh correction, so too were groups of non-European peoples viewed as trapped in a savage childhood state and in need of harsh treatment because they were incapable of self-rule. As the Age of Exploration and European colonization took place, black people and other non-Europeans were defined as metaphorical children as justification for their enslavement. This logic held through the Christianization of black slaves in America and even into Emancipation.

Black people in the United States, as they became Christianized in significant numbers in the early nineteenth century, could not help but be influenced by the widespread perception by white society of their savagery and immaturity.[11] So in trying to prove white society wrong and arrive at a respectability denied to us by the outside world, our people applied the Christian logic of original sin to our own child-rearing practices. But original sin was used to abuse poor white folks, too.

A parallel white, working-class version of Christianity, almost as harsh as the one black people slowly adopted during slavery, took hold powerfully among poor, stigmatized, white farmers who were violently pushed off the best land into the western trans-Appalachian frontier, and later among poor European Catholic immigrants, especially the Irish. Lower-class whites, who also suffered from centuries of marginalization at the hands of powerful elite Christians, were called "rednecks," "crackers," and "white trash."

Consider the way that the Reverend Charles Woodsman described poor whites in 1766: "They delight in their present low, lazy, sluttish, heathenish, hellish life, and seem not desirous of changing it." Like blacks and Indians, poor whites were "immoral," "lazy," and "dirty."[12]

For blacks, poor whites, and immigrants in America, Christianity has long served as a refuge from race and class oppression, but it has been a double-edged sword. Christianity provides legitimacy for the dignity of people who have been written off by society and demonized by the powerful, but at the price of what amounts to a form of self-flagellation and mutilation directed at their children to prove themselves worthy of God's grace.

Elite white Christians did not care and still care little about this self-inflicted damage as long as these benighted groups keep to themselves and don't threaten their power and wealth. The white elite has also never been susceptible to embracing a vengeful God because they can make mistakes and still thrive in society. Blacks, other groups of color, and the white poor have felt, perhaps correctly, that moral errors would doom them and their children. The scary thing is that this punitive God is something that poor and oppressed people have felt they need in order to have any shot at respectability and self-improvement. So all those who whup a child in these communities genuinely feel they are saving their young from a life of degradation on earth and the pit of hellfire and brimstone in the afterlife.

The importance of the black church as a source of empowerment, autonomy from white America, and support for black children's development is undeniable. Black churches have nurtured, guided, and consoled our people through the horrors of slavery, the nightmares of Jim Crow, and the persistent trauma in today's racial atmosphere.

The black church's evolution has been an emotional space that compensates for black peoples' lack of any real political and economic power in American society. Historically, it has played a vital role as a place where we could organize and release our emotions, stress, and energies in a constructive environment. There's no question that the church nurtured black survival under the worst conditions. But even in the black church, freedom was not truly free. Throughout our history in America, black churches have always been under surveillance, and whatever Christian theological traditions took root were always under close white scrutiny. This pressure has compromised the church's ability to function as a truly radical organizing tool and as a healthy and liberated violence-free zone to nurture black families.

To understand why so many black churches are still attached to the practice of preaching violence against children, we must examine how black Americans came to Christianity. Slave masters did not baptize and hand Bibles to our ancestors as soon as they arrived on plantations in the seventeenth century. Whites actually gave little attention to the religious practices of our ancestors for nearly a century because they considered Africans heathens, which justified their enslavement. White planters initially didn't want to convert slaves to Christianity. When some slaves won their freedom by proving that they had been baptized into the religion, and when England sent missionaries to the colonies to "save" the slaves, white planters complained.

Missionaries griped that baptism made the slaves proud and undutiful. And they certainly didn't want slaves learning how to read the Bible. The fear was that slaves would come to think that the biblical messages about freedom included them, too. Whites also feared that baptism would be a path to freedom and equality that would undermine the system of slavery and the racial hierarchy. Thus, in 1667, Virginia passed a law stating that conversion to Christianity did not change a person's status from slave to free.

Contrary to popular belief, our ancestors did not quickly embrace Christianity and its views about sin, children, and salvation. The majority of slaves continued their traditional African religious practices, and a smaller number were Muslims. When Anglican missionaries came to the colonies to spread Christianity, including to the slaves, they met resistance. Our ancestors were adamant about holding on to their African religious beliefs and to rituals and practices such as polygamy and idolatry dancing.

Our ancestors were brought to this country with clear, defined cultural, social, and religious practices informed by their African worldviews. In other words, Africans did not arrive here as Christians, except when they came from the Caribbean, where they had been "seasoned" into the religion as part of the violent two- to three-year process of obliterating the identities of new slaves, breaking their will, and severing any bonds with the past to condition them for their new lot. But those numbers were so small that those Christianized slaves didn't strongly influence the first generations of enslaved people. There's also evidence that other slaves ridiculed the small numbers of slaves who did convert to Christianity.

Transplanted into a new existence, and estranged from their traditional, religious, and cultural roots, slaves needed to configure a new spiritual cosmos for their survival. As such, slave culture became a mix of evolving attitudes and practices that originated in West Africa and then were shaped by the environmental conditions and experiences in

America. Slaves borrowed from African as well as European traditions to gradually form a new, coherent religion that explained their origins, their present oppression, and their ultimate salvation. Fearful of punishment, enslaved Africans worshiped secretly in cabins, in fields and in "brush arbors" deep in the woods so that whites could not hear them preach, shout, and sing.

By the mid-eighteenth century, white ministers were introducing more slaves to evangelical Christianity, a branch of the religion that supported slavery, and it was used as a form of social control that stressed obedience to earthly masters.

Slave preachers were expected to balance African cultural practices while promoting the gospel to accommodate plantation life. Some slave preachers encouraged slaves to accept their servitude and to expect eventual salvation from white oppression only in the next life. Those types of sermons pleased white masters because they helped to maintain control over the slave community. The slave preachers who were caught cloaking their sermons in secret messages of equality, defiance, and liberation were whupped, hanged, and even burned alive.

Slave preachers could be dangerous because they had the power to "ruin" their flock. For example, in 1831 the slave preacher Nat Turner led a rebellion in Southampton County, Virginia. Those slaves went from plantation to plantation, stole horses and guns, freed other slaves, and killed up to sixty whites in the process. Turner was captured and hanged, and nearly two hundred black people were killed during the uprising. Denmark Vesey, another slave preacher who purchased his freedom in Charleston, South Carolina, after winning the lottery, used church meetings to plan an uprising for which he, too, was executed. Fearful of future slave insurrections, whites cracked down on black churches meeting openly in many parts of the South.

By slavery's end, the practice of severe physical discipline was already deeply embedded in black culture. The black church, perhaps inadvertently, became complicit in violence against black children as a survival tactic. Between 1877, the end of Reconstruction, and 1950, approximately four thousand black people were reportedly lynched (69 percent of all victims were between ages sixteen and thirty-five, and about 4 percent were under sixteen), and white men raped black girls and women with impunity.[13] The Ku Klux Klan and Night Riders terrorized communities and burned schools and churches. Many lynching victims were sharecroppers, community leaders, and ministers who'd spoken out against the mistreatment of black people.

As the social center of segregated communities, churches helped black folks cope with the tragedy and their pain while also trying to keep up morale in the face of demoralizing circumstances. They also perpetuated a culture of fear—of God, of the white man, and between elders and children. Black churches became spaces where black folks could achieve status based on a different criteria from society, which these institutions often regarded as corrupt. In these self-contained communities, if you followed the rules, you could gain respect in the eyes of other blacks, your pastor, and of God.

Black people, like poor white folks, have long been made to feel like their low status in life is their fault, and people who feel like failures are susceptible to embracing a punitive version of Christianity under which they try to beat themselves into respectability. It's a wickedly ingenious concept and an effective way to blame and blind people who would otherwise take more radical steps to get free and destroy institutionalized systems of oppression.

During Jim Crow, black preachers still had to carefully tailor their sermons, knowing whites were always listening and would close a church and run the minister out of town in a heartbeat. The church had to help black families adapt to a regime of terror and surveillance, preaching messages that white racists would find acceptable while motivating black people to endure and survive. Whenever black churches sought to transcend this role and become open centers of activism and resistance, there was hell to pay. Our churches were brutally attacked during the civil rights movement. Churches in Alabama, Georgia, Mississippi, Virginia, and South Carolina were dynamited and fire-bombed and gutted by arson. In the mid-1960s, once the civil rights movement slowed and the laws regarding racial segregation were changed, the surveillance and intimidation of black people began to ease briefly.

Black people had some independence in the 1970s and were beginning to find their footing to work for progress. But then Ronald Reagan became president in the 1980s, bringing back aggressive race-baiting, chronic poverty, and the prison industrial complex with the War on Drugs, which have been going on ever since.

The 1980s and 1990s brought a fierce white backlash to the successes of the civil rights movement, with many of our activist giants either dead, retired, or dispirited. That racial backlash expressed itself through whites opposing school desegregation, cutting social welfare programs, and turning back the clock on civil rights protections. We also saw amped-up hostility to affirmative action programs in employment and college admissions. This is the time when many white people started seeing themselves as the new victims of racial oppression, or "reverse racism."

We saw hospitals routinely delivering substandard health services to black people; insurance companies charging black consumers higher rates than whites for car and home policies; major food retailers abandoning inner cities, which led to the sprawl of food deserts in poor urban communities; the denial of senior-level management positions to blacks; and the elimination of decent-paying factory and low-skilled industrial jobs in once booming cities like Baltimore, Detroit, Cleveland, Los Angeles, Chicago, Philadelphia, and others. These were jobs that had brought millions of poor and working-class people of all colors into the middle class during the first half of the twentieth century. When those jobs dried up, black folks were the first fired.

The retreat from civil rights led to heightened segregation and isolation of black people in blighted neighborhoods. Real estate firms and banks engaged in residential discrimination. Black working-class families who didn't have savings or good credit to purchase homes found themselves trapped in urban wastelands. Getting a loan to fix a house or start a business meant relying on "predatory lenders" who took advantage of people with little knowledge of how high-rate, short-term loans worked. The only businesses that seem to have survived in inner-city communities are barbershops, bodegas, liquor stores, beauty salons, check-cashing spots, churches, and funeral homes.

High rates of joblessness, poverty, hunger, and homelessness fostered the drug trade. With so few educational and job opportunities, it's not surprising that some young people inevitably saw selling drugs and other crimes as the only way to make a living. Increased violence from the drug trade overwhelmed communities that were already steeped in intergenerational poverty. On top of that, black communities became the target of a War on Drugs marked by indiscriminate police violence. The media fueled fear and violence by stigmatizing young black males as criminals. Federal and state governments responded with severe penalties for drug sale and possession and by building more prisons. New mandatory-minimum sentencing laws required convicted felons to serve long prison terms, and juveniles were increasingly treated as adults.

Mass incarceration has devastated black families and communities by removing emotional and economic support once provided by fathers, leading to lower rates of marriage, higher rates of black children being born outside of marriage, and increased rates of black men fathering babies with multiple women. Thousands of children have been separated from their parents and raised in foster care. And when folks do get out of prison they can't vote, apply for public housing or student loans, or get jobs.

Because of widespread unemployment, mass incarceration, and premature deaths of black men, far too many black women have been forced to raise children alone. Because we're among the lowest-paid workers in this country and highly susceptible to layoffs, some black women have had to rely on welfare and other sources of work, including drug trafficking and the sex trade. And on top of all of these social problems we witnessed the return of state-sanctioned and vigilante racial violence, fueled by the election and reelection of a black president and the apocalyptic visions of Donald Trump.

If black people had had the luxury of twenty to thirty years of breathing room after slavery, and had been able to parent without fear, then perhaps the practice of whupping might have become less widespread. But that never happened. As such, the black church continues to be a haven and survival center in many communities, but it has not made much headway in helping us destroy structural racism. Instead, we've blamed and whupped our kids for all these generational social, economic, and political problems.

A number of black clergy I interviewed say it's difficult to pin down exactly when the theological origins of "spare the rod" were fully embraced by black clergy. But they say its centrality fits within this larger religious and racial history, one that includes both black preachers who've linked whuppings to black Christian theology and those who are working to push beyond the violence, calling upon black parents to find alternative methods of child-rearing.

As I dug deeper into the research for this book, I was surprised to find allies, mainly black womanist theologians, black liberation theologians, black mystics, and of course the nonreligious, who are working to liberate black Christianity from the clutches of white theology and expression and black ministers who promote those values in their churches. These kinds of religious leaders have not been given the same level of media attention as black clergy who publicly support whupping children.

The toxic child-whupping Christianity described throughout this chapter is exactly what many of these clergy and religious scholars fled and rejected. Ultimately, they realized that it wasn't the teachings as much as the teachers that alienated and harmed them. Yes, they acknowledge that the Bible was used historically to oppress and is still used to oppress. But a more evolved and progressive Christian theology sees the teaching for what it is. So there are some black clergy trying to move out from under the oppressive hand of dogma and tradition to free the Gospel and text from the translators who seized the word and not the spirit of the message.

Some of these theologians admit that there's absolutely a culture within evangelical and fundamentalist Christianity that teaches corporal punishment, and it is stronger within marginalized communities of poor and uneducated black and white people. These churches are safe spaces—refuges, you might say—away from people and things that make the churchgoers feel oppressed. Then they get to church and beat their kids with the blessing of their pastors. It's a sad irony. But to an adult who feels that his or her political, economic, and social power has been stripped away, whupping a child provides some small semblance of power in the world. Children, in those cases, are not seen as the future and they are not repositories of our unconditional love; rather, they become another thing to be controlled and subdued.

One theologian who is addressing the intersections of race, religion, and black parenting is Lacette Cross, a Baptist minister of a multiracial LGBTQ congregation in Richmond, Virginia, who considers herself a "womanist theologian." She's doing her master's research at Union Presbyterian Seminary on black trauma and the role of religion as a coping mechanism.

The Reverend Cross believes that the patriarchal structure of the black church is part of the problem contributing to violent parenting. "Black women—often responsible for overseeing the day-to-day in the church, family, and community—fill church pews yet are rarely seen in the pulpit," she says. "Black women are shaped by the messages that come from religious leaders about being good wives and mothers, and the latter includes discipline. The interpretation of scripture can help and hinder us."

She adds: "Blacks in the early twentieth century knew that if you didn't beat your child, someone else could kill them. The belief was that 'If I instill the fear of God at home, then when you're out in the community, you won't look a white person in the eye and get killed.' You recognized your place. And you were taught to honor your mother and father, but what does it mean to honor your parents at your own expense, even though they might be beating you every week?"

These kinds of messages are so strong in black communities that even folks who don't attend church regularly, or at all, are impacted by them. The Reverend Cross argues that the way people parent is often a reflection of their image of God.

"If your image is one of fire and brimstone and a vengeful God, then it might seem natural to beat kids. But our role as parents and caretakers is to cultivate children, not beat them," she says.

The Reverend Cross recognizes that the black church has condoned physical punishment against children because of the historical role it played as a protective institution against white racist terror.

"Once we leave the church after service, we must navigate an environment that hates black bodies. At the end of the day, we have to lean on one another. I can't tell you to stop whupping your child if it keeps them from harm in the streets. The thinking is that it's better for us to take care of our own in our homes and churches than to deal with the evil, inhumane way that we are treated in the white world," she says.

The Reverend Cross said that those parents who whupped us weren't necessarily bad people; they were doing the best they could to protect us. The pain they caused was wrong, but changing behavior and culture is hard.

"We don't have enough courage, or enough boldness, or power to say, 'No, that's wrong' because we don't know what it's going to take to survive in a white-supremacist world. But we can't respond with only one solution to the systemic, multilayered issues of living black in the USA. We can't expect people to throw out a tradition they've grown up with. That's akin to throwing out Big Momma and 'nem who taught us these things." She wonders: "How do we separate the two?"

Thinking about the physical and psychological costs to children and to the larger black community, the Reverend Cross questions the ways that religion works in concert with a culture of whuppings. She believes that we need to retire the rod, but also rethink many of the messages we've learned from Christian doctrine.

"What does it mean for us to have permission to tell our own stories so that we can understand a picture of God that may not be in line with the picture of God that the church has painted. What does it mean to reconstruct our theology? What would it look like to erase everything we understand about Christianity so that we can create something new for ourselves and future generations?"

Similarly, the Reverend Leslie Callahan, a mother of a three-year-old daughter and pastor of St. Paul's Baptist Church in Philadelphia, often talks with church folks about whupping kids.

"Black church folks tend to take corporal punishment as part of our cultural inheritance," she says. "What I encounter in my conversations is a more pervasive understanding that it is the job of the parent to make their children compliant. They object to any characterization of hitting children as violence. They recognize violence as evil and acknowledge that doing violence to somebody you love is a bad thing. To call physically punishing a child violence would be to acknowledge that it's a bad thing. Parents don't always offer a real theological justification for it. They say they need to keep our kids alive. But there's a relationship between what black parents do to their kids at home and what's going on in the streets."

The Reverend Callahan describes the pervasiveness of this parental mind-set. "A lot of people say, 'I brought you in this world and I'll take you out. Children are the fruit of *my* decision. They belong to *me*.' There's a pervasiveness of that attitude. It is at the root of the village concept—the village can beat you all the way home. I never got spanked by anybody else in the neighborhood. They would call my mama and tell her what I was doing."

She highlights how capitalism, white supremacy, and Christianity are intertwined, so much so that lessons are learned even when someone isn't practicing Christianity.

"Even the folks who are not churched still harbor this cultural sense that creates the attachment towards spanking," she says. "We seem to believe that black kids are worse than everybody else. Send them to school and they are treated bad. Our kids are constantly institutionalized in the most oppressive ways. They have to wear uniforms and walk in a straight line. Zero-tolerance behavior. You have to be mean to them for everything. It's deeply embedded in white supremacy. What happens if you just love your kids?"

To convey this point, she shares the story of a single mom who brought her son to church on Bible study night so the pastor could beat him in his office. "I can hear the kid crying. I said, 'I can't stay here in this church. If you are treating your kid this way, then what are you telling him is that you can't parent him.'"

This happens a lot with boys, the Reverend Callahan says. "There's a lot of conversation in our community about the firmness black boys need. They don't get this when parented by single women, which affects the ways women think they must parent. They think they must be hard to make up for the absence of a male parent." But that's not the solution, she says. "What would be helpful to black boys would be for them to be loved more. Coddled less, but loved more. Some of the men's aggression in women's lives has to do with the anger at the women who raised them."

Despite the efforts to rationalize violent parenting with references to scripture, she does not believe that Jesus would whup a child. "No. I would talk about what the scriptures say Jesus did with children. Jesus taking a child and saying, 'Look at this child—if you welcome this child, you welcome God.' Jesus was a childless man but he centered the personhood of the child. All of us have been kids. We've all been kids, and that's a position of privilege and insight. Do you remember being a kid? Do you remember the time your parent hit you? Do you remember your outrage and the injustice of it? People have reinterpreted those experiences but you don't forget that feeling of outrage. The body holds memory. As a parent I don't want my kid hurt or injured. Spanking is not the only method of delivery of discipline. It's the easier one for parents."

Part of the issue is that despite all the revisionist religiosity and the efforts to use God to rationalize whupping children, there is no biblical or religious validation for this practice. The Reverend Callahan corrects the oft-cited "spare the rod" passage used to defend spanking.

"That isn't what the Bible said. If you're going to use the Bible as a source for this, then get it right. The notion of the rod and staff is as comforting, not provoking your children to wrath. Kids experience spanking as injustice. Rather than teaching them about consequences, you give them a sense of injustice. You can't unspank a kid. You can't restore the sense of bodily integrity. Physical discipline comes from your own ego."

There's immense power in the church and its leadership because of the value bestowed upon black ministers. Yet, changing the message from the pulpit isn't the ultimate panacea. If black preachers collectively announced that spankings should stop, and instead told parents that they should take their children's feelings seriously, whuppings wouldn't instantly become ancient history. It might, however, start a conversation that would lead to better outcomes for kids, the Reverend Callahan says.

"Black preachers say a lot of stuff that black folks don't listen to. People ignore us when they feel like it. If we decided to take a position that the health and well-being of our children require us to speak out, if we were convinced of it ourselves, then change might be possible," she says.

Similarly, Dr. Kimberly Joy Chandler, who is Catholic and whose work focuses on issues such as racism, sexism, colorism, size discrimination, and mental health, says there is no way to divorce religion from patriarchy. But there is a kind of willful blindness. "Black folks will never believe that white supremacy has influenced the way they worship and see God," she explains. "Religion is part of the intergenerational transmission of trauma from slavery. People cite Proverbs, but Deuteronomy talks about killing disrespectful kids. We have this cancerous relationship with religion because of how we adopted it during slavery."

Chandler adds that black parents often resort to beating their kids because they haven't healed from generations-old trauma. "We've reconceptualized this coping mechanism of violence and called it resilience and love. We believe that 'this is what I have to do to my child so we can survive.' Many of us don't know any better. Some of us don't want to know better because of the work it would take to go through the journey of healing," she says. "The work is so overwhelming that we go to our normal dysfunctional coping mechanism."

Chandler argues that people who whup children get some sense of satisfaction out of it because it's generally the only opportunity in their lives to assert power and dominance. But it's also "a way to navigate pain even for the moment. They really want to whup their mama and daddy and they want to whup life itself. If we really took in the overwhelming amount of pain we deal with on a daily basis, it would blow our minds. That's why we resort to these dysfunctional ways of maintaining power and control. We don't want to feel our own pain. We've got to put it on somebody else. Who is that? The most vulnerable—our children. You're acting out of this history that has not been healed. Having my child act 'right' is my social currency. 'My kids act right, it looks good on me.' They don't want to look bad in front of white people. When you don't have money, what's the next thing that gives you identity? Your children."

She goes on to explain that, "When you're beating your kid, you're beating something out of them that's intrinsically them—their assertiveness, creativity, wit, personality. People think it's strange that our boys are out here killing each other. But it's not, because they've already been deadened."

What would Jesus do? Would Jesus whup a child?

Chandler responds: "I don't have to go further than, 'Do unto others as you would have them do unto you. Love your neighbor as yourself.' The ultimate goal is that we should strive for love. 'Spare the rod' is a misinterpretation of scripture. They mean the rod of correction. You want to discipline your child with a set of guidelines and standards and showing your children how to live their best lives. If kids are doing something wrong, then it's our job as parents and adults to model and instruct what we want them to do."

To equate violence and pain with love is sadistic, she says. "That is the highest perversion of the divine. You have now shown me that my relationship with spirituality and God is dysfunctional. What else do I have if God believes it's okay to beat me?"

Kamasi Hill is a former pastor who works as a public school teacher, and as an adjunct professor teaching religious history at Garrett Evangelical Theological Seminary in Evanston, Illinois. He is divorced with no children.

Born into the black Christian nationalist tradition to a non-Christian mother and a father who was a pastor, Hill earned a PhD in religion from Northwestern University, and describes himself as having been in and out of the world of black religion. "I was a pastor for four years in the AME church, in the 'hood in Detroit and Milwaukee," he says. While he enjoyed the sense of community, the music, some of the preaching, and the affirmation he received, Hill says he was "not comfortable with the rigidity of the theology. I came from a household that was open to ideas, and my personal values clashed with the traditionally sexist and homophobic institution."

After his divorce at age thirty-seven, Hill started questioning his identity and his beliefs. "I let go of everything that wasn't a reflection of who I authentically am," he says. He returned his ordination papers. "I feel absolutely free, and I haven't turned back since." He also feels free to critique black religion. "The church has never been a progressive institution in the black community. The folks in the church are not radical," he says.

"I was a victim of abuse," he says. "I'm wearing the psychic and physical scars from my parents who meant well but they abused me. Some days there was a little slap on the head. But then my father stood on top of me and stomped me."

When he taught in an Afrocentric school in Detroit, Hill says it was legal for teachers to hit students. "But we did it low-key. Parents gave us permission." And it was mostly boys who got hit. His attitudes have since changed. "As I've evolved intellectually, spiritually, and emotionally, I have become more of an advocate for kids not to be abused."

He says that the black church has issues with the body. "We believe that the body is separate from the soul. Your body is evil, sinful. Because the body is evil, it can be brutalized, beaten, tamed. Bodily integrity doesn't even make sense to someone who is a theological conservative. The body doesn't have any value because it is a sinful thing," he says. "In black theological circles, suffering is redemptive because Jesus suffered. You get your ass beat, then it is for the good."

Echoing sentiments of others, he sees change as difficult. Even if ministers changed their tune and began to preach against spanking children, the parishioners wouldn't necessarily obey them, Hill says. "The notion of spanking and whuppings is so embedded in the cultural practices of black people, most will say, 'Amen' if the pastors say to stop, but then they'll go home and beat their kids," he says.

Obery Hendricks, a visiting scholar in religion and African American studies at Columbia University in New York City, and a senior fellow at the Opportunity Agenda, a social justice communications think tank, shares a similar view as his peers. "I've come to believe that beating young children is akin to torture," he says. "A little pat on the behind that doesn't cause pain, I wouldn't argue with that. I understand the sentiment behind whupping a child. But it doesn't fully respect the dignity of the child. I believe that children have the same right as adults to dignity."

Questioning their widespread praise, he makes clear that both Creflo Dollar and Adrian Peterson were wrong: "These are helpless children being brutalized. I was whupped. I can still remember the sting of switches because it really is torture. It's a vestige of our civilizing model of discipline we saw during slavery. You beat folk to get them in line."

Hendricks advocates Dr. Martin Luther King Jr.'s nonviolent strategy as a way of life, whether in the streets or in the home. "It's hard to reconcile violence against children. That's the model that should be followed," he says. "Not to beat children."

At the core of this is the fact that "the church is about conformity first, not freedom," he says. "The church has various means of enforcing conformity that pervade the notion of child discipline. There's a belief that there's a certain place that children should be in. And if they're not in their place then it's seen as a transgression of an article of faith. It's almost like a blasphemy. The ethos is not a diagnostic response, it's a reactionary response."

Though parents really believe they're doing the right thing for their child, they're acting out of fear when they apply corporal punishment, Hendricks says. "It's a gross misunderstanding of faith. They ignore the ethos of Jesus and what he had to say about humanity. He was about love and compassion and empathy for another person's position, which has to do with dialogue and understanding. As far as physical discipline, there's no reason to believe that Jesus said to do that. Is he supposed to be your savior and guide, or not? His teachings did not include a reactionary beating."

Hendricks further remarks, "There's a real problem when members of the clergy select part of the Old Testament when it suits them. The Bible says that sons who disrespect parents should be killed. Most ministers don't have a well-informed understanding of social forces, so they just don't think things through. They react." But the function of the church, he says, is "to model a different way of doing things."

Sharing the belief of his peers that black preachers have some power in changing our views on whuppings because of their platform, he knows there is but one potential source of change: "It could be somewhat effective if they explain well what they mean by that. They'd have to be clear, biblically, why [whupping should stop]. They would have to talk about the way that Jesus engaged people, even those who transgressed."

But that change is not likely, Hendricks says. "There's a dearth of folks willing to say things that are unpopular because it might cut into your income as a pastor," he says. "There's a lack of moral courage when it comes to standing up against social and political conventions in the pulpit."

Lawrence Rodgers is a pastor at Baltimore's Westside Church of Christ, which has a cross-generational congregation of 150 members. His church includes a parenting class and a "Mommy and Me Ministry." "People think you shouldn't reason with children," he says. "That kind of parenting approach breeds blind fear and people who rebel. We should be raising children who have an honest, critical thought process when they confront authority. We're breeding children who don't know how to deal with authority," he says.

One issue he sees is blacks studying at white seminaries and picking up bad theology. "The culture shapes the clergy. Clergy have to be careful about what they learn from white theologians about God. We have to be cognizant of the fact that their theology is what our oppression is built upon," he says. "We can't just sit in their seminaries and swallow everything. We have to look at it with a critical gaze. White theology was built on rich white men and people who thought we should be enslaved. As I study them, I have to make sure that I don't accept anything that's oppressive to me. I have to be aware of the Jesus they're teaching. I have to study another Jesus, because I can't accept anything that is oppressive to my people."

Black preachers who go to liberal schools and historically black colleges and universities might come out wanting to resist and fight the power and be liberationist preachers, "but when they encounter black Christians, a lot of their congregants don't want that spirit," Rodgers says. "So they give the people what they want. But we have a responsibility to do better. Then there's the type that says, 'I'm going to stay true to my integrity.' These kinds of people will have a very hard time. They go into established churches and get fired."

Black people have always been afraid of losing their children to racism and oppression, Rodgers says. "There's a debilitating fear—beating the child to save them from the overseer. The problem is that is cowardly. I do that because I don't want to fight the overseer myself. Cops shouldn't be beating your child anyway. You would rather beat your child than stand up to systemic racism. So they've been abdicating their own responsibility to stand up to oppression, beating kids to make them zombies to systemic oppression so that they will go along."

The Reverend Rodgers says the black minister is supposed to foster liberation from all forms of oppression, which includes violence in the home: "How do you follow that Jesus who was a revolutionary when you are slave preacher? We abuse ourselves to fit into the system. We try to shape ourselves to be accepted instead of just resisting. So we beat our kids into submission, so they won't have an opinion of oppression, so they'll rationalize it."

The message of "spare the rod, spoil the child" is very popular in black churches, he says. "They think the reason we have kids getting arrested is because their pants are sagging and Mama didn't beat them. What I teach is that the pants are sagging because the economy is sagging. They are in a depressed condition. Don't point the finger if you're not willing to help them get a job."

He teaches that "the rod" Christians are so fond of citing is best explained in Psalm 23, the prayer of the good shepherd. "'Your rod and staff comfort me.' That's not a whupping. No shepherd is going to take his rod and beat his sheep, injure and destroy them," he says. "Sheep have memory. They won't trust you. Then you'll have a hard time getting the rest of the flock to follow you. Even the sheep dog has the sense not to bite the sheep, not to harm them. I comfort the child. I use the rod to fight off wolves and predators. I'm going to use the rod to protect, not to oppress."

The complication is that "we're all trying to navigate this culture of racism and sexism and hierarchy. Some people do it by resisting, but others do it by training their children to be docile," he says.

The words of these Christian ministers, alongside our slave history and fifty years of social science research, should give us tremendous pause before we raise our hands to children. The black church itself is not the origin of the problem of disciplining children through violent practices. And I'm fully aware that black people won't abandon Christianity. The black church has gotten us through the worst of times, and it continues to have value in that role. But if black folks are going to practice this faith, we need to take a hard, honest look at its history in our lives and examine the ways that Christian doctrine has been used to oppress us and compel us to oppress our own children.

Just imagine letting go of the notion that black children are inherently "sinful," that the only way to rear them properly is to "beat the bad" out of them. If we could let go of the accumulation of guilt, sin, blame, and all the racist ideas that made us believe there's something wrong with our blackness. Imagine beginning to heal the physical, mental, and emotional scars that drive our actions and responses to our children. Imagine more understanding, more compassion, and more love. What if we made that our faith and practiced it with our children? What if we began to accept the fact that our ancestors had it right by seeing our children as deeply spiritual sacred gifts who came from the afterlife.

5

"YOU ALWAYS WERE A BLACK QUEEN, MAMA"

How Black Boys Who Are Whupped by Their Mothers Grow Up to Mistreat Other Black Women

Consider the following story: Robert Gordon, who grew up in northeast Baltimore, can still remember a whupping his mama gave him in the summer of 1978 when he was eight years old. He was taking a bath with his two older brothers. When they stepped out of the tub, their mother was waiting for them with a belt looped around her hand. The boys were still wet from the tub. Gordon, having gotten out last, watched as his mother hollered and wildly whupped his brothers into a helpless frenzy.

Gordon felt frozen in place as he watched the belt repeatedly land on different parts of his brothers' bodies—head, neck, back, legs, stomach, whatever was in the way. They jerked and grunted like electricity was coursing through their limbs.

Gordon's heart raced. He knew he was next.

When his mother finally turned to him, she was cussing and her voice was sneering as spit flew out of her mouth. She drew her arm back and brought the full swing around, with the belt landing directly on Gordon's penis and testicles, searing the tender flesh like fire.

Gordon choked on his scream. His legs buckled and his eyes rolled up in his head. And then he fell into a heap on the floor, rolled into a ball, and cupped his genitals with both hands in an effort to soothe the pain.

"Once I fell, my ass was grass," Gordon recalled, the memory bringing a flash of heat to his loins and slowing his breathing as he talked. A few moments of silence fell between us. "That was the most excruciating pain I had ever felt in my life."

His brothers laughed as he rolled around, and his mother paused for just a moment. "But then she was like, 'Okay, he's not dying,' and so the beating commenced again. I couldn't move, but she didn't stop wailing on me," he said in an unsteady voice.

Gordon paused and then let out a long sigh. "It's scary that I can still remember this. I was laying on the ground, crying and begging for her to stop, and my brothers were making light of my pain."

When the whupping ended, his mother stood there for a few moments, breathing hard with her hair askew. One of her hands was still gripping the belt while the other hand curled and uncurled into a fist. She didn't say a word. She just turned and left the room. It took Gordon several minutes to catch his breath and for his body to calm.

"I didn't get up immediately. I just laid on the floor and cried."

Nobody consoled him. His brothers continued joking and laughing.

"I guess at some point it helped me get through the pain and make light of what happened," he said. "I had welts all over my body, but we accepted that as part of the experience of getting whupped. We didn't see it as abuse because we weren't taught that it was abuse."

Gordon says he hasn't really been able to talk openly about this incident. It's only the worst example of what he experienced. His mother hit him with a bag of schoolbooks, a plastic Wiffle ball bat, and her fists. He recalls her hitting one of his brothers with a broken pool stick.

On top of the whuppings, "She did a lot of cursing. She'd say stuff like, '*Who the fuck do you think you are? You gonna stop playing with me!*' She didn't give long speeches, just a lot of 'fucks' and 'shits.'"

"I got punched in the face a lot. There were times that I got cut and she busted my lips. You didn't go to the hospital. You just dealt with it. It is what it is," he said in a resigned voice.

For a long time, Gordon says, he rationalized his mother's cruelty as love and protection. He also felt pressured by family members to accept this. But perhaps most surprisingly, he says popular messages about what black parenting looked like seemed to reinforce the notion that his mother's violent behavior was good for him.

Gordon's story is more extreme than the actions taken by most parents who whup their children today. But many, many black men experience varying degrees of this type of violence in their early childhood. And that violence, when it occurs, can cause boys to develop deeply negative, long-lasting attitudes and to project their repressed pain and anger toward women when they become adults. When a mother beats her son it damages his perception of a woman's worth and can cause him to become unsympathetic to a woman's needs.

This dynamic is infrequently discussed because it centers black men as victims of pain at the hands of their mothers, while also offering an uncomfortable reason why grown men treat women poorly. In essence, it sounds like bullshit. But decades of scientific literature have repeatedly confirmed this complex cycle of hurt.

Victims of racist oppression create their own victims. Part of being a victim of any type of violence is that it can predispose you to victimize someone weaker than you whom you love, and that, in turn, exacerbates your own victimization. If you are constantly living in fear for your children and for your own life, then it can be easy to misconstrue cruelty as love.

If we want to fully understand the sexist and racist victimization of black women in America, we must understand how racist devaluation and misogyny have sought to destroy us by orienting black mothers to be the perpetrators of physical harm against our children, in particular black boys. But the need to have difficult conversations about the abuse of black boys is bumping up against a strong taboo in the black community—criticizing mothers who whup their sons in the name of discipline and strong parenting.[1]

Gordon recalls that, for his mother, she was simply doing what black parents did. "In my mother's mind . . . you beat your kids because you love them. You do what you gotta do to keep your kids from becoming criminals," he says.

During Jim Crow, the great literary figure Ralph Ellison first described this black parenting phenomenon in a 1963 essay: "Even parental love is given a qualitative balance akin to sadism. . . . The horrible thing is that cruelty is also an expression of concern, of love."[2]

Though Gordon understands the pressures that his mother and other black women have faced, he's been unable to reject the truth that his mother's cruelty hurt him. Almost forty years later, his body still holds the pain. And unlike black athletes, rappers, politicians, movie stars, and preachers who have waxed on about their mothers' love and glorified their mothers' violence against them while repressing their true feelings, Gordon wants to tell his story authentically, even though he knows that calling out the black mother is a cultural no-no.

It took Gordon until his early thirties to realize that his mother's beatings and verbal abuse stemmed from her own issues around abandonment and emotional neglect, and frustration that his father was not in the picture. As he learned more about his mother's childhood experiences, he concluded that, "the brunt of that beating in the shower and every beating she gave me was displaced anger. She was taking her anger toward everyone else out onto me. I would get these beatings over trivial shit and I was her punching bag." In other words, his mama beat him because she couldn't confront and beat her own mother and the other men—her father and her children's father—who neglected and hurt her.

But Gordon didn't understand this as a boy. He didn't have the emotional literacy to express his hurt, betrayal, and anger at his mother, so instead he says he had to walk on eggshells for fear that she would seriously hurt him. He was always on guard, not wanting to be taken by surprise again.

Making matters worse, he didn't always know what would trigger his mother's rage, so he never felt at ease around her. His fear taught him to make himself small, and to be as obedient, deferential, and nonthreatening as possible. Looking back, he thinks that his mother flashed forward in her mind to envision a day when her three sons would be bigger and stronger than her. He thinks she created a power dynamic early on that cemented her upper hand.

"There was no discipline in her hitting me," Gordon said. "There was no love in it. It wasn't like we were bad kids. My mother would hit us in front of our friends to embarrass us. She was hitting us because she could. Because she was the authority figure and could do whatever she wanted to us."

Growing up in late-twentieth-century America, Gordon learned early that there was generally a lack of concern for his physical and emotional pain at home or in the streets because he was a black boy. All the other black kids he knew got whupped at home. For the black children in his Baltimore neighborhood, pain and trauma were commonplace.

Because he grew up not knowing what it felt like to be heard and respected, because other people tried to rationalize the abuse, because in the popular American imagination black males cannot be victims and women cannot be violent predators of children, Gordon tried to turn off his natural reactions to his pain. On top of that, black men have very few, if any, caring outlets in our communities to discuss their pain. "I spent years blaming myself for every beating, every curse and heart-stopping glare," he said.

Gordon's self-blaming response and attempts to ignore his own abuse, according to research by Howard University law professor Reginald Robinson, are not uncommon. In examining the abuse of black boys by their mothers, Robinson has concluded that black mothers who beat their sons "destroy their natural, normal response to pain" because these boys are always under attack, on guard, and unconsciously reacting to their own repressed past that is no longer present. As such, black male's first experiences with cruelty and humiliation are mostly at the hands of their parents, especially their mothers—not white America. As they grow into men, black males continue to live with the pain that their mothers planted into their bodies.

Not wanting to see the black mother as cruel, Robinson says, black boys and men for generations have accepted the internalized "lie" that slavery, Jim Crow, and racist policing practices "requires cruelty to protect black children from their own impulses. . . . The cruel black mother tragically destroys in their children what was once destroyed in them." Robinson adds that black parents then "conceal their cruelty" by citing white racism to justify the beatings and to "associate parents with safety and comfort" and love.[3]

I'm going to go out on a limb and say that black mothers who whup their sons do not truly realize the damage they are doing. And yet the racist notions of black boys as deviant and violent are ultimately reinforced by mothers who are doing their best to minimize the stressful realities of poverty, racism, sexism, and inequality.

By the time Gordon turned twenty and saw a photo of his father at the same age, his mother's harsh treatment started to make sense. The resemblance was uncanny. It also explained the nickname she gave him: Moe.

"'Your name was Ug-Moe because you were an ugly baby. Your grandmother made me stop calling you that. So I just started calling you Moe,'" Gordon says his mother told him. "She still calls me Moe to this day, even after seeing my tears upon her confession. My mother has never acknowledged my pain."

Over the years, Gordon has tried to talk with his mother, who is now sixty-six, about the beatings and her verbal abuse. But "she has never apologized," he said. The fact that she does not, or cannot, acknowledge her son's pain, and denies his truth, has caused a rift between the two.

Like many in the black community, his mother rationalized her violence against her children by calling the harsh discipline an expression of love that ultimately kept them safe and out of trouble with the law. But Gordon believes that this kind of denial and justification, and even much of the joking about being whupped, feeds the cycle of abuse in black communities and drives the truth about our traumas underground.

"She'd say, 'Look how y'all turned out. None of y'all went to jail. All of y'all went to college.' And then I would tell her, 'But you used to punch me in my face and humiliate me.' She's rationalized all this shit. It doesn't matter how I or my siblings feel about it."

It can be painful for an adult to admit that being physically hit by their parent was a form of abuse; to acknowledge that makes some people feel they are dishonoring their parents. But if a parent has beat it into their child physically, mentally, and emotionally that it is for their own good, then they start to believe and internalize physical violence as truth. And when we black folks look back on our childhoods and say that we "needed" to be hit or else we would have ended up on drugs, in prison, pregnant early, or dead, then we are essentially confirming centuries of racist ideology, which has argued that the only way to control the innately "inferior" and "uncivilized" and "criminal" and "promiscuous" black body is through painful punishment."

As a teen, Gordon admits, he had serious anger issues and got into fights as the result of the anger and frustration he'd built up toward his mother.

"I went through a period where I had a problem with black female authority—school teachers and supervisors on the job," he said. "The only way I positively dealt with black women was sexually and because of that, I became a dog."

By age thirteen Gordon was promiscuous, sleeping with seventeen- and eighteen-year-old girls, and then significantly older women once he was in college. "To have a girl smile at me, touch me *softly*—it was humanizing. It made me feel like a person. I wasn't being yelled at or hit," he said. "The main way I dealt with my anger at my mother was through my sexuality. I didn't become a misogynist or a monster, but I caused a lot of emotional damage with women that a lot of other brothers caused physically."

Gordon's behavior is not unusual for male victims of physical abuse. Researchers have shown that young boys who witness domestic violence or are physically violated by their parents are not only found to exhibit symptoms of post-traumatic stress disorder, but also to struggle with hostility and anger, substance abuse, and depression, and are at an elevated risk of committing intimate partner abuse. A study conducted by the University of Pennsylvania School of Medicine found that when boys personally experience physical abuse as a resolution to conflict in their childhood home, they may learn that perpetrating domestic violence or intimate partner violence as men is an acceptable way to resolve conflict in their adult home.[4]

As in Gordon's case, boys who are victimized as children are also more likely to have an increased number of sexual partners and engage in riskier sexual behaviors.[5]

Furthermore, according to statistics from the National Child Abuse and Neglect Data System, mothers physically abuse their children more than fathers because they spend more time with them. Mothers are also the most frequent abusers of boys, just as they are of girls.[6]

Gordon admits that he hated his mother and still doesn't know how he feels about her beyond being thankful that she gave him life.

She doesn't have a relationship with his five daughters. He has worked hard to break the cycle of abuse with his daughters, and though he has spanked them a few times, he now refuses to do so.

While this might seem like one man's sad story, Gordon represents untold numbers of black men like him who don't have the opportunity to share their experiences, or don't feel comfortable doing so. His story is indicative of how some black men feel about black women. Just look at black men's representations of black women in popular culture. No other group of men makes more money off of publicly denigrating their women. Listen to the rap lyrics of artists such as Dr. Dre, Lil Wayne, Too $hort, Snoop Dogg, and others who call black women bitches and hoes and have lyrics that spit out graphic scenarios of sexual degradation. Those artists don't publicly say that they hate their mothers. That would be blasphemous. Instead, they rap about *other* women.

Gordon's making the decision to confront his mother, speak his true feelings about her, and do the hard work of not transferring his own pain and anger onto his wife and daughters is not a common trope in black culture.

Fortunately, Gordon had positive male role models in his life, including his stepfather, coaches, and other mentors. He empathizes with struggling moms raising kids alone, especially those taking on this responsibility on top of their own histories of untreated physical and emotional trauma. But he and nearly fifty other black men I interviewed for this book agree that there needs to be an honest discussion within black communities about how black mothers are sometimes the first to, usually unintentionally, socialize theirs sons to mistreat black women.

Many of the men I surveyed and interviewed don't feel they can speak openly about their childhood experiences. But after spending weeks listening to their stories, it is clear to me that, as a community, we need to put the feelings of black children at the center for a moment so that we can deal with the feelings of our sons. It's more important to do this than we realize because we have not been dealing with the experiences of black sons, and the entire black community is paying the price.

According to Tommy J. Curry, an author and associate professor of philosophy and Africana studies at Texas A&M University, historically, scholars have tended to focus on domestic and child abuse "as an extension of the violence presumed to be associated with masculinity in this society." On top of that, "the popularization of feminism has led many to ignore the facts concerning the abuse of young boys by their parents, and in most cases their mothers, because males are thought of only as the perpetrators of violence against women, not victims of it."

Curry, who researches the sexual abuse of black males at the hands of women, and who has written the only book introducing a theory of black male abuse and trauma from internalized racism, seeks to dispel the myth that women can't commit violence against black men, or that black boys and men can't experience trauma.

"People pretend that black men are not victims of violence at the hands of women. Gender politics can't accept violence against men and boys. It puts all responsibility on black men and boys. This isn't a situation when black men are inherently evil—they have past experiences of trauma and pain. It is because of that trauma and pain that they engage with black women the way they do," he explains.

Robinson, the Howard law professor, echoes Curry as he explains why gangsta rap artists disrespect black women in their lyrics. "Few writers, feminists, and cultural commentators have actually understood why gangsta rap artists vilify women, especially blacks, with demeaning lyrics, often decrying words that wound as patriarchal oppression. Such critiques deny access to the deeper, more repressed sources for the murderous rage and corrosive hatred that such artists appear to have for black females," he writes.

The source of such rage and hatred is cruelty toward black infants and toddlers in the earliest years of their lives by black parents, especially females, Robinson says. "That cruelty gets repressed, surfacing again as nearly autobiographical lyrics because these artists unconsciously need to reveal the truth of their cruel sufferings to others, and they need others like enlightened witnesses to validate their lyric-based personal histories, without at the same time directly confronting their cruel mothers."[7]

Think about Ghostface Killah's song "Whip You with a Strap," from his 2006 album *Fishscale*. He recalls his mother's response to his temper tantrums: "Momma shake me real hard, then get the big gat / That's called the belt help me as I yelled / I'm in the room like 'huh, huh, huh' with mad welps / Despite the alcohol, I had a great old Mama / She famous for her slaps and to this day she's honored."

While cruel Mama is celebrated, innocent black women become the targets of this repressed rage, Robinson argues. He explains that these artists, who may not have been touched lovingly as children, become hypermasculine as a defense mechanism as they relive their painful childhood experiences through their music. They really want to assault the mothers who were the first to hurt and emasculate them.

It's important to emphasize that, "black men are not born hating black women. It is the trauma they suffer that teaches them the need for self-preservation," Curry says. There is no space for black men to talk about their trauma and pain, he argues. Even speaking about their abusive experiences at the hands of black women is considered misogynistic. Black men are taken to be so fundamentally misogynistic that any articulation of their pain or suffering at the hands of a black woman is simply thought to be an expression of that misogyny! So black men experience the world from a position of being made to be silent."

Curry is clear that for those of us committed to understanding early childhood abuse and its relationship to intimate partner violence in adulthood, we have to "begin admitting that sometimes the cycles of violence which so often are manifested as domestic violence against women, begin with the trauma and pain associated with the childhood violence and neglect which are far too often committed by mothers."

Given the historic disparaging of black mothers—whether Daniel Patrick Moynihan's domineering unwed mother, Ronald Reagan's "welfare queen," or "the crack mother"—it is no wonder that there is a level of defensiveness. Yet, black fathers are also demonized and critiqued. Somehow, it's okay to talk about the many ways black fathers have failed their women and abandoned their children, but calling out black mothers for whupping their children is problematic, and few people are willing to do it. But if, as experts say, men generally base the way they treat women on their relationships with their mothers, and if physical violence is associated with family dynamics from an early age, we need to consider the link between whuppings and adult domestic violence and misogynistic behaviors, whether it be physical, emotional, mental, or any combination thereof.

Simply put: if a boy growing up is hit by a parent who is supposed to love and protect him, that boy is at risk of being confused about whom to respect and about what love is supposed to feel like because the person he loves most is hurting him. The same is true of girls who are hit by their fathers. But for once, can we please center the needs of black boys all by themselves?

It is not far-fetched to assert that a boy who is hit or verbally abused by his mother might grow up not respecting her, and may very well end up beating women or engaging in other forms of violence.[8] Mass incarceration, systemic poverty, and the divestment from black communities have been antifamily, splitting apart parents and children to the point where the majority of black children are growing up in homes where many black fathers are involved in their lives, but are not living in the house.[9]

To fill that vacancy, some of their mothers—who are constantly advised that they can't effectively raise sons without men in our household—feel compelled to emulate or perform masculinity by using physical punishment as a form of "tough love" and as a deterrent for delinquent behavior. In other words, we use a negative to prevent future negatives. And some mothers bring in father figures to give their children what they think they are missing—so a stepfather, an uncle, an older brother, or even a neighbor might be brought in to whup a child. It is important to acknowledge that the violence does not need to be perpetrated directly by a woman to have the same result.

I'm not implying that black men's misogyny and violence in black communities begins and ends with black mothers, and I'm not holding black motherhood responsible for all the ills plaguing our communities. However, we are accustomed to hearing conversations about black men as absent fathers, as sexists, as violent predators, and about how some seem to avoid having relationships with black women. But we rarely seek context for how this happens.

Black men are not born innately sexist and violent. As with their brothers of other races and ethnic backgrounds, that is socialized behavior, and in the overwhelming number of cases, their mothers are the primary socializers. Knowing that all problematic behaviors can be traced to an individual's backstory made me want to explore the potential link between childhood whuppings of black boys by their mothers and their negative attitudes and treatment of black women in adulthood. Consider the following stories of black men who told me that they grew up seeing other black children around them being beaten and, like Gordon at the beginning of this chapter, thought it was the norm. Most shared that being whupped as children left them with conflicting feelings toward their mothers, doubts about whether they were truly loved, feelings of inner rage, and questions about their own sense of self-worth. Some of them admitted that their mother's beatings made them turn away from black women as intimate partners.

Brian Kevin Alsup, a twenty-two-year-old valet from Baltimore, said his mother was verbally abusive, and started beating him when he was two or three years old, using her fists, a packet of clothes hangers, a plastic T-ball bat, and other objects.

"She would use mostly her fists or whatever was around that could hurt me, but not possibly kill me. Some stuff she took out on me because I was there. She's thrown a glass bottle at me. She picked up a dining room chair and was about to hit me with it, but I screamed and she put it down," Alsup said.

His mother used verbal and physical abuse simultaneously. "She would tell me I wasn't shit. She called me the b-word. She called me motherfucker. She called me a fat pig. She called me stupid. That I was a fuckup," he said. "A lot of stuff that I spent a good part of my childhood suppressing and trying to forget. Wanting to hit her back was always going through my mind. Feeling like I hated her. Which I told her while she was on top of me beating me one day. Feeling like I just wanted to die."

Marvin Murray, a fifty-one-year-old network administrator from Lake Ridge, Virginia, was beat by his mother until he turned sixteen: "She used her hands, switches from a tree branch, belts, extension cords, and a fan belt from a car engine."

LaTroy Graham, a thirty-eight-year-old telecommunications engineer from Staten Island, New York, said his mother beat him with belts and extension cords: "One time she made me take a bath and beat with the extension cord while I was still wet."

C.M., a forty-two-year-old teacher from California who asked that his full name not be used, said he's blocked out a lot of the whuppings he got from his bad-tempered mother, who was molested by one of her own mother's boyfriends.

"Whenever I did something wrong I got whupped for it. It could have been something as small as not doing the dishes, or not finishing homework, to being defiant at school," he said. "I rarely did anything half as bad as my peers. I never shoplifted. I never joined a gang. I never tagged or did graffiti. I never had a run-in with the law. None of that."

C.M.'s mother used "anything and everything as a weapon: peanut butter jars, plates, extension cords, belts, even a machete once. Nothing was out of her scope. I will never forget the machete she had confiscated from a drunk neighbor. She hit me with it—the flat side. She didn't hit me hard, but she hit me with it at least three times. I literally thought I was going to die. I couldn't have been more than eleven years old. Later, as I got older, my mom claimed she didn't remember that day, like I was lying."

During many of his whuppings, C.M. wished his mother dead. "I remember praying to white fuckin' Jesus that Bruce Lee would come back from the dead and beat her ass. Every day I would wish for something bad to happen to my mother."

Charles Cinque Fulwood, a sixty-five-year-old writer and media consultant from Silver Spring, Maryland, was around four years old the first time his mother whupped him. He was standing on the back steps of his house with his dog. When the dog turned abruptly and knocked him off the steps, he lay on his back and cried.

"My mother came outside from the kitchen singing her spirituals and talking to herself and proceeded to whup me mercilessly for what seemed to have been an eternity," Fulwood recalled. "I distinctly remember, for the first time, asking why was she beating me when I had not done anything. 'In case you do something when I'm not around to see you!' she shouted. There was almost a little chuckle of triumph in her voice."

Fulwood's mother mostly whupped him with switches. "Sometimes she would wait until bedtime for maximum effect," he said. "Other times, she would administer the assault on the scene of whatever the real or perceived violation. But if my being bad happened at church or around company, she would say, 'Wait until I get you home.'"

Timothy McNair, a twenty-seven-year-old freelance writer from Chicago, started getting whupped by his mother when he was eight, at least two times a week, he recalled. "I remember them being very explosive and full of hate," he said. "My mother would do such things as loom over my bed with a fire iron in her hand as I slept at night in our trailer. She would wake me up and order me to go urinate or she would 'bust your damn brains out' if I wet the bed. I already had a major fear of the dark because of sexual abuse and I had urinary enuresis until I was twelve."

McNair said his mother had a penchant for instilling terror in him and embarrassing him in public. "If we were at a barbershop she would bring a switch into the facility with her because I was not to 'show my ass' by crying if the barber's clippers made me feel uncomfortable. She and the barbers would comment on me needing to not be a punk—southern black pejorative for gay. They'd laugh as she'd switch me in public and used me as a public shaming example, a lot like what parents are now doing on YouTube."

The first time twenty-eight-year-old Anthony Modesto Milian remembers being hit was at age eight. "She busted my lip open," he said. His mom died when he was thirteen and then an aunt took him in and resumed the beatings.

"My aunt would hit me almost every day. My aunt would use anything she could grab. Once she hit me with a metal pipe and another time she lacerated my head with a can of Glory mustard greens. She then kicked me out the house and made me walk to school with my head open and blood pouring down my face."

Keith McNeil, a forty-year-old reservations manager for Alcoholics Anonymous, was "popped": beaten with belts, switches, shoes, or a broom any time he gave his mother "attitude."

"She often laced her comments with profanity," McNeil said. "I usually experienced the full gamut of emotions, including fear, stress, guilt, and anger. I certainly felt that being whupped was normal, and that I 'brought it upon myself.' I felt like she hated me. She would be so intense and so angry as she whupped me that I felt that I was receiving someone else's punishment. In my mind, I remember wondering what I possibly could have done to deserve such treatment."

Rarely a day went by when McNair's mother wasn't cursing at him: "Fat fucker, sissy, punk, mama's boy, fat ass!"

Among the list of nonverbal weapons that thirty-four-year-old Roy Brooks's mother either used or threatened to beat him with were a hanger, an extension cord, and a water hose. "My mother cursed at me. She used typical curse words: 'fucker,' 'motherfucker,' 'asshole,'" he recalled.

"Many things went through my mind depending on why I was getting a beating. Sometimes I was just mentally preparing myself to take it, but sometimes I would think things like, 'I can't wait until I grow up so I can leave and never come back.' Or, 'I hate this woman.' As I got older, thoughts like 'I hate this woman' turned into 'I fucking hate this stupid bitch. She beats me and curses me out for stuff even when I'm right, and she lets these men that she dates lie to her face and get away with anything.'"

Anthony Jones, a fifty-eight-year-old electrical mechanic from Pasadena, California, was around five years old when his mother started beating him with belts, electrical cords, and switches. During the beatings, he said, two thoughts went through his mind: "I'm never gonna do that again" And, "When is this gonna stop?"

"My mother whupped me every time I did something that she thought was serious enough. She often bragged about it to family members," said thirty-eight-year-old Ramone Billingsley, a Ph.D. student and a minister from Birmingham, Alabama. His mother continued beating and threatening him up to his senior year in high school.

"If she did not hit me then she would threaten to do it in an effort to make me comply with her instructions," he said. "Her belief was 'Spare the rod, spoil the child.'"

When I asked Billingsley and the others if they had ever hit women, most of them said no. "I knew that hitting women was wrong," Billingsley said. Their mothers taught them that it was wrong to hit girls and women, even as they were abusing their sons. As a result, most of these men say they suppressed their anger for decades; others say they released their pent-up rage, but at other women in their lives—never their mothers. This is not surprising given research that suggests that abused boys often embrace behaviors and attitudes often associated with domestic violence as adults.[10]

Nickolas Gaines, a thirty-year-old from Salt Lake City, thought that being hit was a normal "black thing."

"In my circle it is, and was, completely normal and justified because you are *her* child so she could do whatever she wanted to you because it came from a place of love. It wasn't until that I got married and had my own child with my white wife [and I saw] her have such an adverse reaction to my whupping our son that I realized how deeply engrained as normative and embedded in our culture that whupping is," Gaines said.

Gaines suffered from a common rationalization by black women, who often believe that their power to whup their child is a God-given right, whereas according to interviews with low-income black mothers conducted by researchers from the University of Missouri and the University of Connecticut, "children's grandmothers, aunts, uncles, and biological fathers had to earn the privilege of disciplining through prior acts that earned mothers' trust that the individuals really cared about their children."[11] On the other hand, we can find plenty of black folks who will insist that whuppings from their black mothers made them love black women because we're "strong" and capable and demand respect.

Gaines said he didn't have any animosity toward women but "I do think having a mom who was the traditional black mom—loud, overbearing, strict, religious—made me really timid as a child. I always tried to make her happy and please her," he said. "In dating I never wanted to be with a woman who had those tendencies or personality. I wanted a strong, educated, fierce, and career-driven woman, but didn't want any of those aspects or traits that my mom had that I worked so hard to please."

McNeil lost his mom at age ten. His grandmother who raised him died a few years ago—he misses them both. Their deaths seemed to have foreclosed his ability to feel anger or bitterness toward them.

"Besides the whuppings, they were both warm and nurturing, which is why I honestly felt conflicted when I was disciplined," he said. "They made me believe that it hurt them more than it hurt me."

When Brooks reflects back on memories of his mother, the recurring theme, he said, is that she ruined his life.

"So much of my current dysfunction in personal and romantic relationships can be laid at her feet. So many of my personal failures. Not all of them, of course, because I believe that we are responsible for our own actions. But when you start off with a faulty perspective or with misinformation and you have to work to discard beliefs about yourself and people in general and relearn on a trial-and-error basis, I don't believe that I should shoulder all of the responsibility for the trajectory of my life. Honestly, in a nutshell, when I think about my mother, I wish I had never been born to her," he said.

Brooks also said that he has borne some animosity toward black women as a result of his childhood experiences. Although he is physically attracted to black women, he's losing interest in them for long-term commitments.

"I don't think that I will ever marry a black woman and I'm relatively certain that I won't date another one, at least not in the near future," he said. "I don't believe that there is anything inherently wrong with black women, nor are they deserving of being bashed as a group. I just feel that my experiences with my mother and the resulting tendency to choose women that share many of her personality traits and characteristics have turned me off from them because I just don't think I will ever find one that I'm compatible enough to be with."

"Honestly, although I loved my mother I almost grew to hate her for beating me," Billingsley said. "The beatings were so painful. I often had marks. One time my mother waited until I had taken a shower to beat me while I was still wet. It was awful. Although I knew she loved me, she had a mean side. I often felt that she was taking out her own private frustrations while beating me. From time to time mom would threaten me with, 'Ramone . . . keep on. I'm gonna whup yo' ass for old and new.'"

His resentment of his mother grew so strong that he tried to poison her by putting dishwashing liquid in her Mylanta.

C.M. unapologetically said that he hated his mother while growing up, even when she was diagnosed with multiple sclerosis during his freshman year of high school and was confined to a wheelchair.

"I was never happier," he said. "The only thought that ran through my mind was that she would never hit me again. I was thirteen. And that was when I really started to act out. I stole my mom's ATM card and stole eighty dollars from her account. I could say that part of me just wanted to have money, but the real reason was because I knew she couldn't hit me anymore, that she no longer had the strength to chase me out the house, to punch me in the face or throw a jar at my head."

For a long time, Milian said he slept with and dated only white women: "I saw all black women as a reflection of my aunt because I thought they all had the same viewpoint when it came to how to treat children. I had immense animosity for black women and black culture. Life has come full circle for me. I am now married to a black woman. I have no children and I have no intentions of treating my kids a fraction of the way I was treated as a child."

While he has never hit a girl or woman, Alsup believes that, "All of us black men were cultured and socialized to hate black women at some point. So we were all misogynists-in-training by our preteens. Some earlier. I think I really started my animosity to women after my first heartbreak. When I felt like I couldn't be loved, I just stopped loving."

Fulwood has never hit a woman but admits he has committed acts of revenge: "I did play with the hearts of many. I would gain a woman's love just to throw it away. I found pleasure in it. I had one of the indestructible Nokia phones, and it gave me a satisfaction feeling when I would dump a girl who was really into me and I would call them up, say, 'You're dumped,' hang up, and delete their number."

In college, C.M. was "extremely promiscuous," he said; "I had no respect for women." He said he never hit a woman, but he did verbally bash them. "Some of that I blame on my mom setting a bad example for black women. Some of that comes from me not having a positive male role model and part of that was just me being selfish and only looking out for my needs and wants," he said. "I never kept a girlfriend. Hell, I'm single now and I would break up with any woman who showed signs or tendencies that reminded me of my mother. I was so unforgiving. I had severe trust issues, and still do till this day. And each failed relationship I have had I attribute to not having any examples growing up of positive male or female relationships that were truly nurturing and loving."

He also said that he's afraid to have children: "I don't want to become a parent like my mother. I don't want to become violent with my kids and that fear has driven me away from having children. I am, by far, way more understanding and open-minded than my mother, but I still fear having a bad temper."

There are many contributing factors that can explain black maternal violence against boys. For one, living in a racist, patriarchal society encourages domestic violence, creating hateful divides among black men, women, and children. It then encourages us to settle our rage with physical violence against the most vulnerable among us because we can't, won't strike back at the system oppressing us all. Whupping our children is yet another well-oiled part of the violence machine that undermines us, makes us weak, and causes those we love to hate us.

Based on my interviews with black men who were whupped by their mothers, it is clear that the burdens and heart-wrenching anger caused by their fathers' abandonment, their mothers' struggles to provide for basic needs, and deficient or nonexistent systems of support were sources of the displaced physical and emotional violence they experienced in boyhood. Many of these men are products of generational father absence, which has been exacerbated by the War on Drugs and mass incarceration, economic divestment in communities of color, and state violence against black families. Some of their fathers abandoned them, are or were in prison, killed in wars, drugged out, mentally ill, or unknown. And so their mothers, living in a society that incessantly heaps insults and denigration onto black women, had to bear the weight of those absences and raise their sons to the best of their ability in a country where the threat of death at the slightest misstep was a daily reality. Black women have had to pay twice, once for their own past traumas, and then for their sons' futures.

Black maternal violence against sons is also linked to America's obsessive fear of black boys and men. That fear, which is embedded in US culture, is rooted in destructive stereotypes that harken back to Nat Turner's 1831 slave rebellion in Southampton County, Virginia, which left fifty white people murdered. That fear evolved after slavery when freed black people began to take control over their lives and build communities of their own, posing a threat to white males and the racial order. The image of black males as beaters and rapists of white women justified the lynching of thousands of black males.

The fear of black men continues to be seeded by the mainstream media, which casts black men as high school dropouts and neglectful, absent fathers, and over-reports incidents of crimes by black offenders. These negative stereotypes may impact the way black mothers raise their sons. While some mothers focus their energies on encouraging their sons to disprove racist stereotypes, others are terrified of their sons growing up. Through many generations, it is common to hear mothers, aunties, and grandmothers routinely declare that their sons—beginning in infancy and toddlerhood—are "so bad." This view sets the stage for beating boys, as if that is the only or best way to keep them in school, out of prison, or alive. As their sons grow bigger and stronger, these women may fear the possibility that their sons will exhibit violence toward them. That fear might be compounded by past abuse they experienced at the hands of other male relatives. And so in turn, these mothers may feel that they have to beat their sons into submission and complacency out of "love."

Part of the work we need to do as a community to heal the many wounds that scar us and that we pass on from one generation to the next is to allow black men the space to talk about and share their pain without challenging their manhood and dismissing their pain as woman-blaming. If we are to ever heal and progress as a people, we must look at these dynamics objectively, and not assume that black mothers and women are being attacked or shamed as we learn to understand what shapes black boys and men and their attitudes and treatment of black women.

The men I interviewed for this book told me that they've long lived in silence about the violence they experienced at their mothers' hands because any time they attempted to express their pain they were reminded, "She's your mother" or "At least she was there," as if that would make the pain and scars disappear. To really get to the root of the problem, we need to help Mama down from her pedestal and hold her, and fathers, accountable for disguising all that pain as love.

First we need to look at the fact that black mothers who whup their sons are celebrated in our culture. Whuppings are one of the few things black mothers are praised for in mainstream America. Rather than hearing and seeing men like those I interviewed, which would force us to confront their pain, we celebrate the whuppings. Rather than looking at persistent discrimination and inequality, we grab at narratives that locate success or failure in relationship to discipline, choices, values—and whuppings. Think about all the professional athletes who have praised their mamas for whupping them and the stand-up comedians who know they're guaranteed to get guffaws of recognition by sharing tales of childhood whuppings. Or think about the lyrics of popular rap songs by artists who wax nostalgically about those acts of punishment.

In his song "Dear Mama," from his 1995 album *Me Against the World*, the late Tupac Shakur reminisced about the stress he caused his poor single mother on welfare and how "running from the police, that's right / Mama catch me, put a whupping to my backside." And though she was "a crack fiend" who kicked him out into the streets, she was still "a black queen."

In the 1991 soundtrack to the film *Boyz n the Hood* there's a song called "Mama Don't Take No Mess" by the female rap artist Yo-Yo. She said that when she was growing up "we got our ass kicked" because "talkin' back is foul play." Her "down ass mama . . . had her own way of gettin' across, which was a belt of steel." She was quick to tell you "don't let your mouth get yo' ass whupped . . . Moms, didn't play the okey-doke, oke can get choked / fuck around and get yo' neck broke."

On his 2003 album *The Preacher's Son*, Wyclef Jean has a song called "Three Nights in Rio" in which he talks about getting whupped by his mom for stealing. "When I was young they called me Robin Hood / 'cause I stole from the rich and gave to the poor / Went back home, Mama whupped on my ass / Said I'll be damned if I let you live like that / Meanwhile next door neighbors drunk man / Beatin' on his wife while the kids were watchin'."

More recently, we saw the same kind of confrontation dramatized between Dr. Dre and his mother in the biopic *Straight Outta Compton*.

In one scene, Dr. Dre's mom slaps the daylights out of him for mouthing off and expressing a dissenting view, which his mother decides is an act of disrespect. In fact, the film represents this abusive act in a positive light. His mother loves him and wants the best for him. The slap is transformative and empowering. It leads Dre to leave home in pursuit of his dreams, rather than lie in his room listening to music. The message is clear: rather than pull themselves up by their bootstraps, black children need to be slapped in the name of the American Dream. Yet again we see the commonplace celebration of a black mother whupping her child into success. He becomes a billionaire and a game changer because of his mom, because she beats him to be more disciplined. In another scene, she is seen as loving and caring as he struggles with the death of his brother.

It is striking how even amid the outrage over the fact that the film glossed over Dr. Dre's history of physically abusing women, for which he later apologized, we still are okay with whupping children with impunity.[12] It is striking not only because abuse and dehumanizing violence is recast as "good parenting" but also because this is a pathway toward violence against women and other types of violence in our communities.

Famous rap artists aren't alone in their celebration of mothers who whupped them. In 1989–1990, David Dinkins campaigned for mayor of New York on a platform of whuppings. Dinkins, who would go on to become the city's first black mayor, recounted the story of how his mother and grandmother—both dollar-a-day domestics for white families—beat him for stealing. Dinkins, who was known for his dapper, gentlemanly demeanor and for being astute about not making white people feel threatened, attributed his historic success to his mother and grandmother's harsh discipline. He told a group of one hundred Latino ministers and about forty kids from East Harlem that he got caught stealing reflectors off license plates. The police took him home and his mother and grandmother, he said, were "heartbroken, crushed." When the cop left, "They took my clothes off, stood me in the bathtub, and beat me with straps. I haven't stolen a reflector since."

Professor Tommy J. Curry's belief that some black mothers play a critical role in teaching their sons to be antiwoman is not ideological or a deflection from the real violence in our communities. Rather, he argues that the abuse of black males is part of an unmentioned cycle of violence cultivated by individuals within black homes that encourages the silence of this abuse throughout our communities. This is more of a sociological reality than a theoretical one. Black males are particularly vulnerable to being distant from the lessons that corporal punishment is intended to teach. Parents often lack parental warmth when black boys are concerned. Parental warmth entails how parents articulate their care and use of whuppings as part of an overall parenting plan.[13]

According to the 2014 Child Maltreatment Report by the US Children's Bureau, child abuse has declined since 2009, but rates among black Americans remain higher than among their white counterparts. The report states that more than one-half (54.1 percent) of perpetrators were women and 44.8 percent of perpetrators were men.[14] The data also suggest that child abuse rates are higher among black Americans than among white Americans or Hispanics. According to the report, "African-American children had the highest rates of victimization at 15.3 per 1,000 children in the population of the same race or ethnicity."[15] This is much higher than the 8.8 per one thousand of Hispanics or the 8.4 per one thousand of whites.[16] This disparity does not only apply to child abuse: the fatality of children from abuse or neglect is just as concerning. "The rate of African-American child fatalities (4.36 per 100,000 African-American children) is approximately three times greater than the rates of White or Hispanic children (1.79 per 100,000 White children and 1.54 per 100,000 Hispanic children)."[17]

It is, however, important to keep in mind that "empirical research investigating ethnic differences in physical abuse is relatively scant, in part because physical abuse frequently occurs in combination with other forms of maltreatment and is thus difficult to study in isolation."[18] Consequently, the stories told in this book are rare glimpses into the experiences black men have of child physical abuse by their mothers, and contribute to our understanding of black women as specific perpetrators of child abuse toward black boys. It in no way claims they are the only perpetrators of violence against black boys, or against black children in the home. But it gives us more to think about. Black men aren't only men. They're also sons.

"Black males are punished in their own homes because many mothers have internalized the racist stereotypes that define them throughout society," Curry says. The problem is that "black boys are punished for the black men they will become, and the enforcers of this violence are not only the racist police, but those parents who are most responsible for the care of these young males, and yes, that means that the black mothers in their own homes can internalize and act on these racist tropes of black males as superpredators."

Many of the black men I interviewed said that they have reached a place of forgiveness with their mothers as they have learned more about their mothers' troubled pasts, while others remain ambivalent or keep their distance. And others continue to love black women as best they can and try to be good fathers by breaking the cycle of violence in their own homes.

C.M.'s mother passed away in 2011. Even in death he continues to hold a lot of animosity toward her. "Some of it I have accepted will be with me forever and part of it I have reconciled. Before my mom passed, I forgave her. It was hard but I did it. I don't think she ever forgave herself though," he said.

He recalled that before she died she told him that she would understand if he did not want to remain in contact with her. "She knew the damage she had done, and though she claimed not to remember every little detail, she did apologize." His mother went back to school and majored in criminal justice.

"When she got her master's and her PhD, her focus was on domestic violence, mainly from the perspective of men being victims," he says. "I think in some way, she was trying to figure herself out."

6

"TALK TO THE WOOD OR GO TO THE 'HOOD"

The Campaign to End Paddling in Southern Schools

December 2015. A few days before Christmas.

Janice Harper, a community organizer and activist against corporal punishment based in Durant, Mississippi, learned that her seventy-six-year-old father had been rushed to Greenwood Leflore Hospital. He had been sick since 2013, but now his kidneys were shutting down and his body was building up toxic fluids after he underwent emergency surgery to repair a bleeding ulcer.

Over the next few days her father's health continued to deteriorate. He was unable to eat. The inside of his mouth was dry. The skin on the bottom of his feet had turned black and he couldn't feel the doctor's pinpricks. Parts of his body were cold to the touch. He lay under a mass of white sheets as wires connected to his chest measured the beats of his weakening heart. An IV tube ran from a vein standing out in his arm to a plastic bag filled with clear fluid hanging from a metal pole. Machines beeped, pumped, and hummed as Harper beat back her conflicted emotions to put up a positive front for her father.

The writing on the wall was clear: time was running out and all Harper could do was sit next to her father's bedside and wait for him to go to God. The small, cold, indistinct hospital room humbled her. The blinds were drawn. A portable potty was folded down in a stowed position against the wall. The volume on the mounted TV stayed on low.

"My dad looked at me and said, 'I'm not coming home,'" Harper recalls.

Even as she watched her father's life slip away, she couldn't bring herself to show affection to the man she hadn't hugged or kissed in more than a decade. At age fifty-seven, she was still angry with him for hurting her body when she was a child.

"My father was a beater. Anything he could get his hands on, he would beat me and my three older brothers with. A belt. A limb off a tree. Extension cord," she says. "Up until I was thirteen years old I had to strip down to my underwear before he whupped me. But once I had developed and had my menstrual cycle my mom stepped in and said he could no longer whup me without my clothes on because I was going into young womanhood."

Harper says that her mother, who punished her by taking away privileges and making her stay in her bedroom reading books, pleaded often with her father to stop the whuppings.

"My mom would put Vaseline on our bodies after he beat us. My bedroom was next to theirs so sometimes at night when my father wasn't home I would hear her in her room crying for us. I saw that she wanted to help us but she was defenseless herself," Harper says.

Harper's father was adamant that the whuppings were going to make his children "better people in society." Her parents grew up in Mississippi during Jim Crow, when white people wielded extraordinary power over the lives of black folks in virtually all phases of life, from the cradle to the grave. Theirs was a generation of young black people coming of age in the 1930s and 1940s and enduring the terrible unfairness of limited options and terror through harassment, chasings, clubbings, illegal arrests, and sometimes lynchings for being "sassy" and "uppity," or for no reason at all. More black people were lynched in Mississippi than in any other state—533 victims between 1882 and 1946.[1] For untold numbers of black victims of race hatred, there was simply nowhere to turn for justice. Over and over again, children learned that their parents and other elders were powerless to protect them from hostile whites.

To stay alive, the Jim Crow era's black children grew up curbing their aspirations and containing their anger, all while carefully weighing their words and policing their gestures in the presence of white people. To keep their children safe as best they could, many black parents were compelled to continue the same mode of harsh physical punishment that previous generations of parents had learned from their slave masters and overseers. As the renowned black novelist and scholar Ralph Ellison put it, much of black parenting during Jim Crow was about "adjust[ing] the child to the Southern milieu . . . to protect him from those unknown forces within himself which might urge him to reach out for that social and human equality which the white South says he cannot have."[2]

Because black parents feared the possibility of not seeing their sons and daughters survive childhood, the accomplishment of reaching adulthood was not only celebrated, but elders sometimes credited "good butt whuppings" with keeping their children safe from white folks. Harper remembered her father telling her mother, "You and I got whupped when we were growing up. So why shouldn't this apply to our kids? We made it. We survived."

Whuppings might have led to survival but they also produced generations of damaged and broken people. The whuppings Harper's father dished out during her childhood not only hurt her physically and emotionally, but those painful experiences made her resent him for decades. She also cites his whuppings as the reason why she had abusive intimate relationships with men. She also admits to having been a fighter.

"My second husband was a drug addict. He would try to get my money on payday. I'd pick up a rake, a pipe, whatever was around. I even went to jail because I cut him one time. I associated all that behavior with my childhood," she says.

Her experiences, including a childhood of whuppings that continue to haunt her memories, also shaped her activism, especially after she became aware of the historic connections between slavery and Jim Crow and a persistent culture of beatings of schoolchildren in Mississippi's public schools. At the age of fifty-two, Harper became a community organizer with the Nollie Jenkins Family Center, which works with parents and children on improving public education and provides social justice leadership programs. For the past few years, youth organizers under her mentorship have been leading a "No Corporal Punishment Campaign" in Holmes County's public school system, which has 11 public schools that are 99 percent black. Through their activism, Harper and her youth organizers hope to show an important connection: the acceptance of whupping within the black family is the soil in which acceptance of abuse of black children in schools grows.

Many people outside the South are often surprised to learn that corporal punishment has not disappeared from American schools. In 1977, the Supreme Court ruled 5–4 in *Ingraham v. Wright* that the Eighth Amendment's prohibition against "cruel and unusual punishments" did not apply to corporal punishment in schools, nor did it consider paddling students a violation of the Fourteenth Amendment, which requires prior notice and an opportunity for students to be heard. The court reasoned that the original intent of the framers of the amendment was to protect people convicted of crimes from cruel, excessive, and unreasonable punishments—not students.

Justice Lewis F. Powell Jr. wrote, "The prisoner and the schoolchild stand in wholly different circumstances, separated by the harsh facts of criminal conviction and incarceration."[3] This distinction, according to the Supreme Court, was adequate justification for denying schoolchildren equal protection under the law. This ruling effectively set a double standard and sent the message that our culture has not evolved with respect to the rights and bodily integrity of children. Almost thirty years after the court's decision, in 2003, Delaware abolished the practice, then Pennsylvania in 2005, Ohio in 2009, and New Mexico in 2011. Recent efforts to ban corporal punishment in public schools have failed in Wyoming, Missouri, North Carolina, Louisiana, and Texas, while efforts to bring back the practice in California, Montana, Iowa, and Oregon were rejected.

Corporal punishment in the form of paddling students on the butt or legs with a long and thick wooden board coexists with and reinforces "zero-tolerance" and "no excuses" disciplinary policies in large, high-poverty urban school districts outside the South. These stringent tactics have resulted in black students being disproportionately suspended, expelled, and arrested for the most minor of offenses, such as chewing gum, failing to finish homework, tardiness, talking back, rolling their eyes, cursing, or violating the dress code. Studies have shown that the removal of students from the classroom through suspensions and expulsions far too often sets them up for poor outcomes ranging from failing grades, to dropping out of school, to becoming incarcerated.[4]

When it comes to physical punishment of students, they are required to bend forward and place their hands on a desk or wall. The staff person administering the hits is supposed to be the same gender as the student being paddled but that isn't always the case. Sometimes the school's handbook specifies how many times a student can be struck or on what part of the body. Some principals wrap paddles with tape so the blows hurt more.

The paddles are sometimes up to thirty inches long, half an inch thick, and from two to three inches wide. In 2014, the *Nation* reported that teachers in Holmes County, Mississippi, tell students to "talk to the wood or go to the hood," slang for choosing between being punished with a paddle or serving an out-of-school suspension. Students even bestow the paddles with names like "Mr. Feel Good" and "Big Daddy."[5] Some districts require punishment to be administered out of view of any other students, but this doesn't always happen. In March 2015, a video that circulated on social media showed a Florida teen being held down by a group of male classmates while her teacher paddled her.[6]

Activists have reported that paddles are sometimes drilled with holes to cut wind resistance and deal a more stinging blow. In Madison, Florida, elementary and middle school students are hit with Plexiglas paddles about eighteen inches long, seven inches wide, and a quarter-inch thick. At Holmes County High School in Bonifay, Florida, students make paddles in woodshop class from ash wood planks according to teachers' instructions.

Despite the fact that corporal punishment is theoretically illegal in the US military, in prisons, and in mental institutions, paddling continues to flourish in public schools in nineteen states, mostly in the South. While more than a hundred nations have banned the practice of corporal punishment because it violates international law, which recognizes paddling as a form of violence against children, the United States continues to allow teachers, principals, and coaches to paddle more than two hundred thousand children each year.

Forrest Wickman explains in a piece on the history of the paddle published in *Slate* that its use has roots stretching back to the eighteenth century, when European sailors beat seafarers for slacking off or sleeping during work. The paddle was brought to America as a way to punish slaves without scarring their bodies because they were considered valuable "property." James Glass Bertram wrote in his 1869 *A History of the Rod,* "In order not to mark the backs of the slaves, and thus deteriorate their value, in Virginia they substituted the pliant strap and the scientific paddle." The historian Darius Rejali explains in *Torture and Democracy* that "a scarred slave was a troublesome one, and no one wanted to purchase trouble."[7]

While it is less clear exactly when or why the paddle became the go-to instrument for physical punishment in schools, legal experts say that corporal punishment gained traction in the aftermath of the launch of the War on Drugs and several horrific school shootings in the 1990s, 90 percent of which were committed by white upper-middle-class perpetrators.

The availability of sophisticated weaponry, mixed with growing anxieties about lawlessness and juvenile delinquency, fueled the rise of metal detectors, police officers on school grounds, and a punitive approach to teaching in urban, mostly black and Latino schools, and gave further legitimacy to the practice of paddling in majority-black rural districts in the South. Instead of instituting more severe school discipline policies for students at the white upper-middle-class schools where mass shootings were actually happening, black and brown children in poorer schools faced harsher consequences.

Over the past two decades, school paddling has come under increased scrutiny in the United States as several thousand kids have suffered bruising, broken bones and blood vessels, nerve damage, and other physical and psychological injuries as a result of "school discipline."[8] Aside from the damaging physiological and psychological impact of paddling, opponents have also noted the inconsistency between the outrage over students bullying each other in schools and the fact that educators still have the legal right to bully and injure students with paddles.

Faced with increased criticism, several states are reluctantly taking measures to ban the practice, mainly out of fear of lawsuits. In the nineteen states where paddling is legal in public schools, the law gives educators the right to hit students as long as they are in compliance with the local board of education's policies. There's also an "immunity clause" that protects school staff from being held criminally responsible when a child is injured. In Mississippi, for example, the law states that "no teacher, assistant teacher, principal or assistant principal shall be held liable in a suit for civil damages alleged to have been suffered by a student as a result of the administration of corporal punishment."[9] This is a far different world than the one for parents, especially those of color, who may whup a child, leaving bruises or welts, only to be arrested and charged with felony child abuse and then lose their child to the foster care industry. That's because there is no "immunity clause" for black America.

"When I began to advocate for families and researched that children were being paddled in schools, this concerned me. No real work had been put forward," Janice Harper notes.

Harper spends much of her time at Nollie Jenkins Family Center working with youth organizers on educating black parents, students, and the broader community about the effects of corporal punishment. Their focus isn't simply about presenting the science and teaching the history of corporal punishment but also about giving voice to victims of corporal punishment: the youth who are bearing the brunt of the pain. Talking to their peers about this issue and encouraging them to keep "violence journals" documenting any verbal or physical altercations they witness at home, school, or within their neighborhoods, youth organizers and Harper are moving the conversation forward by circulating petitions and demanding the abolition of the paddling of students.

"I know firsthand what it feels like to be a victim of corporal punishment and I agree that it should be abolished. It only made me angry with the person who inflicted the pain upon me, my teacher, and it particularly angered me with my mother, who let this happen as if there was nothing wrong with it," Randarious Cooper, a youth organizer with Nollie Jenkins, wrote in a statement.

In June 2014, several youth organizers bravely took their fight to the Holmes County School Board, which is all black. Curshevia Robinson, a fifth grader at the time, testified about being paddled by a computer science teacher who she said "didn't like me." She also spoke about witnessing other students returning to classrooms crying and limping after being beaten and the damage that being paddled caused her.

"I felt embarrassed. Ashamed. Belittled. Worthless. Disliked. I felt like I didn't want to go to school," Curshevia said as she spoke confidently into the microphone at first. The teacher, she said, had grabbed her by her school uniform, bent her over her desk, and paddled her in front of the class.

"While she was paddling me, she called me all kinds of names like 'ugly' and 'dumb.' She told me I was worthless and I wasn't going to be anything when I grew up." That beating, she said, "Took away my confidence and self-esteem."

Curshevia was too upset to finish her testimony. But her story is an example of how self-hatred, untreated trauma, and internalized oppression compel some black educators to beat the creativity and freedom from the spirit of a black child to force them to conform to the limited expectations surrounding them. And when our children cry out for us to see them as whole people, to feel their pain and to spare the rod, their pleading falls on deaf ears. Despite witnessing her tears, hearing testimonies from several students, and hearing pleas from parents in the audience, the Holmes County School Board held firm, refusing to change its disciplinary policies.

In addition to Durant, Mississippi, where Harper is based, the Nollie Jenkins Family Center serves several other majority-black towns: Tchula, Cruger, West, and Goodman. Many black residents in these historically self-contained communities throughout Holmes County, which is sixty miles north of Jackson, on the edge of the Mississippi Delta, live on lands that were once slave plantations. Following Emancipation, those plantations became tenant farms that kept black people on subsistence income and in an unyielding state of terror. During the civil rights era, these communities figured prominently as staging grounds and organizing bases for voter registration campaigns.

Today, Holmes is the poorest county in America's poorest and fattest state. Forty-two percent of the county's residents are obese, and the average life expectancy is seventy-three years for women and sixty-five for men—a full decade shorter than the US average.[10] Mississippi ranks number one in the nation for teen pregnancy, sexually transmitted diseases, illiteracy, and high school dropout rates. A practice that dates back to integration of school through "forced busing" in the 1970s, most white parents in Holmes County either home-school their kids or send them to private Christian academies while black students attend substandard public schools.

Holmes's highly segregated towns are governed almost entirely by black elected officials. But the mass exodus of black folks seeking a better life in the North during the 1950s and 1960s, along with white flight after the fall of legalized segregation, drained these towns of money, resources, and opportunities. There are poor whites but many others live in beautiful manicured homes while struggling black folks live in trailers and homes a step above shacks. Economic hardship, social strife, and racial inequality have remained constant bedfellows. Boarded up storefronts and empty homes sit in disrepair. The unemployment rate consistently hovers near 20 percent and more than 50 percent of children live below the poverty line.

There are few thriving businesses in these towns, which means a small tax base without much revenue to spend on improving schools. In a few towns, such as Tchula, liquor stores make up the majority of the businesses. The scarcity of jobs and lack of opportunities for kids has yielded little, if any, sense of purpose for young people, who hang around in public spaces with little to do. Kids as young as three suffer from obesity and high blood pressure, ten-year-olds have been diagnosed with diabetes, and school buses are overcrowded because only two students can fit in seats made for three.[11] Some of this is due to longstanding culinary practices. But much of it is the price of rampant environmental injustice and toxins in foods, which also affect children's brain development and behavior.

Eddie Carthan, a black former mayor who was once heralded as the prospective savior of Holmes County, has acknowledged that in many ways black communities in the Delta are locked in a past of racism and economic bondage. But he has also argued that black folks have been complicit in their own failure to progress. In a 2015 interview with the *Atlantic*, he said,

> Three or four generations of people raised on welfare—everybody knows the problem. . . . Single-family homes, drug-infested neighborhoods, the youth always on social media, exposed to everything. Earrings, nose rings, lip rings, baggy pants. I'd expect they'd show some appreciation, but a lot of them don't know their history. That's a challenge. It's very difficult for the teachers to even teach school. They're rebellious. They have the freedom, the resources. They don't have the restraints we had in the '60s.[12]

Carthan's view is commonly held among the older generation of black leaders, clergy, and parents living in Holmes County (as well as much of white America)—that black children these days are naturally wild and aggressive, less respectful and more troublesome than their elders were when they were coming up. They believe that to maintain order in the home, the classroom, and the community, obedience needs to be inscribed onto children's bodies through humiliation and pain. By his logic, you'd think that black children are born "bad" and that the adults in their lives and their environments aren't the primary things shaping them.

These attitudes, which rely on entrenched racial stereotypes about black people's behavior and lack of a moral compass, all while erasing the root causes of the real issues, ultimately feeds widespread support for whupping children in homes and paddling students in Mississippi's public schools. In the 2012–13 school year, school staffers paddled students 351 times, up from sixty-eight the year before, according to a report by the *Nation*.[13] Some larger school districts in the state reported paddling their students more than a thousand times.

All paddling is not created equal. The number of black students and white students enrolled in Mississippi public schools was nearly equal that year (255,625 black and 237,910 white, according to the National Center for Education Statistics) but the number of black students receiving corporal punishment was nearly three times that of white students, according to a report by the US Department of Education's Office of Civil Rights.[14]

Reflecting these entrenched racial beliefs as well as history, it should not be surprising that some of the most vocal defenders of school paddling are black people. Defenders of the practice in Holmes County have argued that paddling is an effective disciplinary tool that is mandated by the Bible. They claim that paddling teaches poor black children that they must obey rules because failure to respect authority has potential devastating and deadly consequences. Supporters of paddling also argue that black children live in a different social reality from their white counterparts, necessitating different educational approaches determined by black communities.

Anthony Anderson, a minister and member of the Holmes County Board of Education, told the *Nation* that students who learn the importance of "rules and regulations" through the paddle will be less likely to get into trouble—or act out violently—as adults. And besides, "There was no other alternative given in the Bible," he said.

Yushekia Creswell, a parent of a child at the Spann Elementary School in Jackson, who was interviewed for *The Board of Education*, a documentary about corporal punishment, said, "I grew up with paddling in the school system and I think it was really helpful."

In that same film, Josephine Kelly, principal at Cardozo Middle School in Jackson, reflected on the effectiveness of paddling in that school before it was banned. "It would only take one and it would get around that somebody got paddled and nobody did anything for the rest of the day because they knew, okay, you're go'n' get paddled for real."

Nzinga Gibbs, a teacher at Cardozo, echoed the sentiment that students see paddling as a deterrent from acting out: "They avoid a lot of getting into trouble because they don't want the embarrassment of getting paddled."

Dornise Milton, who also teaches at Cardozo, blamed the deterioration of home life for the rise in school discipline problems: "Nowadays, a lot of them have to raise themselves. A lot of them pretty much have to do everything on their own and so they fear no one. Some of them, they don't even fear death. They definitely don't fear authority."

The logic behind these comments is that without a strict family structure, schools need to step in and fill this disciplinary void. Without parents instilling discipline with the switch or belt, teachers and principals must wield the paddle for the good of the community. This is the kind of response we witnessed in October 2015 when an out-of-control school resource officer at Spring Valley High School in South Carolina attacked a foster child in a classroom. The officer, Ben "Officer Slam" Fields, yanked the sixteen-year-old black female student out of her desk by her neck and then threw her across the classroom before arresting another female student for coming to her defense. It made national news.

The black male teacher stood by, motionless and silent, as the other students looked on in terror. Their reactions, along with the fact that the victim did not scream or try to defend herself during the attack, indicate how commonplace violence likely is in those students' lives. Despite the student's suffering a broken arm, bruised ribs, and other injuries and having millions of people watch her beating on constant loop, some of the harshest reactions came from black people. Folks took to social media to argue that this child must have done something to anger this hulking white man. It was especially disturbing to listen to grown people debate the respectability politics of a black child. When the teen returned, she was faced with a hostile environment and eventually began to avoid going to school.[15]

As Tracey Michae'l Lewis-Giggetts wrote of the incident in *DAME* magazine, too many black people "have stopped defending our children. Because of the very real weights we carry, we have stopped fighting for them. We hesitate to step in on their behalf. We have left them psychologically, emotionally, and spiritually alone, to fend for themselves. Then we have the audacity to complain about them being disrespectful."[16]

Beyond rationalizing destructive practices, such arguments in favor of corporal punishment turn the spotlight back on black youth, letting white supremacy off the hook. Too often, we turn conversations about structural inequality back on ourselves, particularly our youth. Never mind that militarized police target our children, while the rise of law enforcement in our schools, the proliferation of zero-tolerance and no-excuses policies, and the misuse of suspensions and expulsions are systematically pushing our children out of schools and into prisons, with some black educators facilitating the flow of black children through the school-to-prison pipeline with harsh discipline practices.

Not to mention, the mass school closings and consolidation of schools in different districts are poisoning the learning environments in low-income communities. It's clear that Jim Crow's educational legacy of starving majority-black schools so they don't adequately prepare our youth for full participation in a democratic society lives on. During Jim Crow, white supremacists supported policies of coercion and force over black lives, which included providing educational experiences that inculcated social deference and rudimentary skills in reading, writing, and math that would prepare black children for a lifetime of menial labor.

In January 2015 the Southern Education Foundation released findings showing that for the first time in fifty years the majority of US public school students in prekindergarten through twelfth grade were living in poverty.[17] Whether they attend public or private schools, poor students are being given an education that consists of little more than test prep, sometimes starting as early as kindergarten and pre-K.

Why? Some education advocates say it partly stems from a fear, akin to panic, on the part of parents, teachers, and school officials that children will be stuck in poverty permanently and become candidates for the underground economy and prison if they don't perform well on tests. But some of it is also due to state and national policies, which mandate closings of schools whose students perform poorly on tests or call for state takeovers of entire districts where schools fall into that category. Such policies inspire what amounts to an atmosphere of perpetual panic. Principals and teachers in virtually every high-poverty school fear that their school could be closed and that their staff will lose their jobs if their test scores aren't raised.

Despite structural problems, far too many people across the racial spectrum have come to believe that black children's behavior is the true enemy of peace and black progress. It's much easier to call a black child "bad" than it is to do the hard work of getting to the root of that child's behavioral issues. It's much easier to whup a black child than it is to admit that we can't, won't, or don't know how to destroy the system that produces the problems in our communities and encourages violence against our children, and then criminalizes us for it.

The fact is, the terrifying damage imposed by slavery and Jim Crow to black children is now being repeated in Mississippi's all-black districts, where paddling has been institutionalized and continues to be supported by black parents who sign opt-in forms granting teachers and administrators permission to assault their children's bodies for minor offenses. We must look at the ways that we perpetuate this culture of rationalized violence through paddling in school systems. The education of black children in these districts, which are already systematically disadvantaged, erodes their self-esteem, sense of bodily integrity, and dignity, and forces them to internalize societal values about age, power, gender, race, and class. Children complain that the teachers are insensitive and callous in their treatment of students. Like parents who whup, schools are complicit in the process of shaping children to accept violence as normal and to demand respect through aggression.

In addition to Mississippi, the other states that allow corporal punishment in public schools include Alabama, Arizona, Arkansas, Colorado, Florida, Georgia, Idaho, Indiana, Kansas, Kentucky, Louisiana, Missouri, North Carolina, Oklahoma, South Carolina, Tennessee, Texas, and Wyoming. Private and charter schools in every state except Iowa and New Jersey also allow corporal punishment. It's not surprising that most of the top ten paddling states were also the top ten lynching states in the early twentieth century.

An analysis of US federal data from 2009 and 2010 revealed that one child was hit or paddled in public school every thirty seconds. A *Washington Post* report found that nearly 60 percent of the students being hit in school live in Texas, Mississippi, Georgia, or Alabama— states that "happen to have among the largest African American populations. Blacks constitute about 16 percent of public school students in the United States but 35 percent of those who receive corporal punishment. That leaves a situation at majority-black districts in the Deep South where physical punishment is a relative routine part of the public school experience."[18]

According to data from the US Department of Education, throughout the South, more than four thousand students receive corporal punishment in school every year. In some districts, parents have to sign a consent form allowing their children to be hit in school, but in many, they do not. Districts in Florida, Alabama, and Mississippi have reported that up to as many as 80 percent of parents have opted in to the beatings.[19] In districts that have banned the practice despite its still being legal in the state, teachers, principals, and superintendents have reported that when parents are called about a misbehaving child they often respond by saying, "Just whup 'em," and send the child back to class.

Nationally, black students and students with disabilities are disproportionately subjected to corporal punishment. Although students with disabilities constitute 13.7 percent of all public school students, they make up 18.8 percent of those who receive corporal punishment, often for behaviors arising from their disabilities, such as autism or Tourette's syndrome. Teachers are not properly trained to teach these students, whose behavioral problems stem from the fact that they are neurologically limited.

In a statement from the American Civil Liberties Union (ACLU), one Mississippi high school student described the administration of corporal punishment in her school this way: "Every time you walk down the hall you see a black kid getting whooped. I would say out of the whole school there's only about three white kids who have gotten paddled." She also noted that darker-skinned black children are likely to be punished more severely because "it takes more to let their skin be bruised" and lighter-skinned students should be hit less because "it'll leave marks."[20]

While support for these practices is widespread, a grassroots movement to get corporal punishment out of schools has been gathering steam over the past decade. Anti-spanking organizations such as For Kids' Sake, Parents and Teachers Against Violence, The Hitting Stops Here, and No Spank have been demanding that children should no longer be excluded from the legal protection against assault and battery that applies to adults. These groups hope to pressure states, schools systems, and, eventually, the US Congress to ban corporal punishment. Their efforts, to say the least, have been glacial. The ACLU, Human Rights Watch, the Southern Poverty Law Center, the Dignity in Schools Campaign, and others have produced investigations and

Paddling and Lynching in the United States

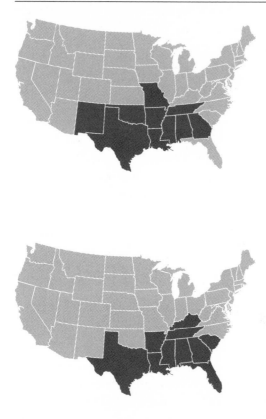

Top ten paddling states

1. Mississippi
2. Arkansas
3. Alabama
4. Tennessee
5. Oklahoma
6. Louisiana
7. Texas
8. Georgia
9. Missouri
10. New Mexico

Source: U.S. Department of Education, Office for Civil Rights, 2000 Elementary and Secondary School Civil Rights Compliance Report

Top ten lynching states

1. Mississippi
2. Georgia
3. Texas
4. Louisiana
5. Alabama
6. Florida
7. Arkansas
8. Tennessee
9. South Carolina
10. Kentucky

Source: The Charles Chesnutt Digital Archive

reports, and along with other local grassroots organizations have also been pushing for legislation to ban corporal punishment and for resources that would give funds to educational agencies so they can develop and implement Positive Behavioral Interventions and Supports in schools. Many schools are beginning to implement Positive Behavioral Interventions and Supports, which have produced greater academic achievement, significantly fewer disciplinary referrals, increased instruction time, and staff perception of a safer learning environment.

Yet, the fight continues to be an uphill battle. These modern-day freedom fighters have been unsuccessful in the courts. In 2010 a federal lawsuit was filed on behalf of a Tate County, Mississippi, high school student requesting a ban on paddling in the state, claiming the punishment was unfairly applied based on gender and race. The lawsuit was filed on behalf of William Cody Childress, a sixteen-year-old student at Independence High School, who claimed he was struck twice "with excessive force" for looking at a camera in class in September 2009. The student said the paddling was so severe that it hurt him to sit or use the restroom for days. A federal appeals court declined the student's request to pursue his lawsuit.[21]

A few years later, in March 2014, a federal appeals court rejected the lawsuit of a Mississippi eighth grader, Trey Clayton, whose paddling by a school administrator caused him to faint and then fall face-first to the concrete floor, splitting his chin, breaking his jaw, and shattering his teeth, court papers said. According to the lawsuit, the paddling left bruises and welts on Clayton's buttocks. Clayton and his mother sued the administration, Jerome Martin, and the school district under the Eighth Amendment and the Fourteenth Amendment's due-process clause. A three-judge panel of the US Court of Appeals for the Fifth Circuit in New Orleans ruled unanimously that it was bound by the US Supreme Court's 1977 decision in *Ingraham v. Wright*, which upheld the constitutionality of corporal punishment in schools.[22] Movements seeking bans on corporal punishment in schools have faced similar intransigence within the political structure. Two congressional bills, H.R. 3027 and H.R. 5005, were introduced in 2011 and 2014, respectively, by Representative Carolyn McCarthy (D-NY) and H.R. 2268 in 2015 by Representative Alcee Hastings (D-FL), but did not make it out of committee.

Outside of Mississippi, many black leaders and communities staunchly support and defend corporal punishment as a necessary part of rearing and educating their children. The *Nation* interviewed Troy Henry, a black board member of St. Augustine High School in New Orleans, who said, "We feel as if we know what is best for our kids." In 2011 Henry fought against an effort to abolish corporal punishment at the all-male and historically black Catholic school because "the margin for error is much smaller in black communities, especially for black boys."[23] Messages like this tell the world that something is wrong with our children and they can succeed only with constant intimidation.

Even in cities outside the South, increasing numbers of black children who are being educated at experimental charter schools such as KIPP in twenty states and the District of Columbia, and the eleven thousand kids attending the thirty-four Success Academies in New York face discipline but without the paddle. In the 2012–2013 school year, there were an estimated six-thousand-plus charter schools serving about 2.3 million students in the United States, and that number has kept growing.

Many charter schools operate under the philosophy that high dropout rates of poor black children and the large academic achievement gaps between those children and their white counterparts can be reduced only if schools demand more, hold students to higher expectations, and stick to rigorous uniform teaching methods that supposedly prepare students for success on high-stakes tests. Starting in kindergarten, students in these charter schools are taught submission, obedience, and self-control as core values through routine humiliation. Children are yelled at, made to face the wall, denied the right to use the bathroom, and punished for minor infractions such as not walking properly through the halls, talking too loudly, and asking too many questions, or for poor performance on standardized tests.

Many black folks continue to support these educational regimes with "no-excuses" and "zero-tolerance" practices, which are found almost exclusively in schools where students of color are the majority. We do this while ignoring how harsh physical punishment and other punitive psychological treatments deprive our children of the self-confidence and resilience needed for them to bring about change both in their personal lives and in the hurting communities they live in. For too many black children, schools are not a refuge from the whuppings they receive at home or the violence they witness in their neighborhoods, but rather are yet another zone of intimidation.

So how did this happen?

Throughout the nation, there has been massive divestment from public schools, promoted by leaders of both political parties and corporate America in the name of cutting costs and lowering taxes. This divestment, coupled with a marked increase in standardized tests, has led to overcrowded classrooms, elimination of the arts, and growing disciplinary problems as public schools fail to provide culturally relevant curriculum and activities to engage and inspire students. Into the breach, promoted by the same forces that defund public schools, have come charter schools, which promise rigor, safety, equity, and better educational outcomes to desperate parents seeking alternatives to crumbling schools that the powerbrokers starved of resources in the first place. But what many charter schools offer instead are draconian discipline and relentless test preparation.

And herein lies a great irony . . .

The elites promoting charter schools, from which they profit in numerous ways—from generous tax credits and breaks to the exorbitant fees paid to management companies running these schools—cater to the conviction of many black parents that their children can succeed only in the harshest and most intimidating of environments.[24] Charter schools have been very effective at marketing themselves to black parents by claiming that harsh disciplinary measures and constant test prep will put their children on a path to college rather than prison, the streets, or a life of permanent poverty. Given the fears that black parents have of losing their children to the streets and crime and the cultural belief that harsh discipline is the only way to save them, the charters' sales pitch has fallen on receptive ears, even though the evidence is not there to support their claims of more successful outcomes.

Charter schools have survived and expanded their market because they have shrewdly assessed the deep-seated fears of black parents and their preference for strict discipline, and developed a profitable marketing strategy based on those fears. It is like selling violent movies or music, but in this case they are selling a violent education. The CEOs and principals justify the tough disciplinary methods and governing ideology by claiming that it is what parents want and what black children need, regardless of the race of the teacher. Charter schools proudly market themselves to parents as institutions where no behavior problems will be tolerated and children will learn in an orderly environment. While the paddling in all-black districts in the South is likely being done mostly by black educators steeped in the culture and communities of their students, the educational violence that black children are being subjected to in charter schools is being carried out by sophisticated and highly educated people who would never treat their own children this way. Charter schools would never market this model of harsh discipline and pedagogy to white middle-class parents.

The psychological intimidation practiced by charter schools, just like the paddling practiced by schools in the rural South, could not be sustained without support from black parents. And black children all over the country are being maimed and psychologically impaired as a result. If black parents didn't buy into this idea that our children need strict forms of discipline at home and in schools, these modern-day Jim Crow brokers couldn't sell that kind of education to us for profit. But because we constantly tell the world that our children behave worse than previous generations and need more whuppings, people are cleaning up on the idea that our kids need a special brand of zero-tolerance discipline to be successful. Charter schools provide this environment, all the while enriching their promoters while producing results no better than those of public schools.[25]

There is so much money invested in charter schools, largely because of a 39 percent federal tax credit, that many interests in both political parties, along with the major players in today's postindustrial economy—bankers, hedge fund managers, and real estate developers—are committed to defunding public schools in support of expanding charters, and in the process they have shamelessly pressured governors and mayors in states such as New York, Washington, New Jersey, Illinois, Louisiana, Mississippi, and elsewhere. So many jobs have been created by this misery industry built off black parental fears and punishment practices, be they in foster care, criminal justice, or charter schools.

Janice Harper clearly sees the many connections among history, structural racism, and black parenting practices. That's why her organization and local students have been fighting back since 2012. They've been collecting signatures, lobbying school board members, and spreading the word through social media. They face an uphill battle because a majority of the school board, which is predominantly black, supports the paddle, and she hasn't been able to get local pastors on board.

Both black and white teachers and administrators are paddling children, but no one has compiled statistics to see whether white administrators are doing it more than black administrators. Some advocates speculate that given the segregation of public school systems, most black children are being paddled by blacks who might feel but not recognize their own racial bias against black students. It's worth mentioning, too, that the idea of a black male principal paddling a white female student probably wouldn't go over too well. For example, in November 1987 in Pell City, Alabama, a white mother was sentenced to six months in jail for assaulting a black assistant principal with a twenty-two-inch paddle, opening a bloody gash on her forehead, after the assistant principal paddled her child, who had been paddled earlier that day by a white teacher.[26]

"There are plenty of black administrators and teachers hitting," says Dan Losen, the director of the Center for Civil Rights Remedies, part of the Civil Rights Project at UCLA. "Black teachers have bias against students. They might not be consciously aware of it. With so many negative stereotypes bombarding us, to think that you can—because you happen to be black—be completely immune to them is false. Those stereotypes affect your thinking, perceptions, and judgments. You have to acknowledge something before you start solving the problem."

Many activists have acknowledged the racial disparities in school-based paddling. Dennis Parker, director of the ACLU's Racial Justice Program, found that students of color, especially black girls, are far more likely to be paddled than their white peers.

"So many of the problems in discipline disparities are the result of this idea of what is perceived to be threatening," Parker says. "People respond to black children differently and are more likely to read behaviors as being disrespectful and insubordinate. Teachers are more likely to punish black children because they are not aware of their own biases and how those biases affect the ways they interact with students."

These biases impact which students get paddled and why. Parker found that white kids were paddled for clear violations such as drug use, property damage, and bringing weapons to school, while black students were more likely to be punished for talking back and other forms of insubordination. "Things that involve someone's perception of your behavior," Losen says. "When we looked at individual reports we found incidents where black kids were punished for questioning what a teacher told them. This kind of behavior is seen as a challenge that is not divorced from race."

Most of the teachers and principals in Holmes County's black schools are black and some of the teachers, Harper says, keep paddles in their desk drawers. And most parents sign the opt-in form granting permission to hit their child. In some cases, parents are called to the school to administer punishment in front of everyone.

"We live in a Bible Belt state and so we hear all the time . . . children should be beat, seen, and not heard," Harper says. In the Bible Belt, fundamentalist Christianity is a deeply rooted part of child-rearing practices. These pathological narratives of violence are displayed on highly visible religious billboards along interstate highways throughout the South, with such statements as "Use the rod on your children and save their life."

Harper says her organization is starting to talk with local black ministers to raise awareness about the dangers and destructive influences of corporal punishment in schools. "We're trying to get people to think differently. We're telling pastors, 'You have a lot of young children coming inside your church and you're teaching and condoning beating. How can we address this behavior in a positive way?'"

So far she hasn't gotten much support from black ministers. While "some teachers agree with us and support our work . . . they don't support us in a meaningful way because they are afraid of losing their jobs. This is a lonely fight," Harper says. She also notes that even the influx of mostly young, white teachers from Teach for America hasn't helped to solve the problem. Harper and others say TFA teachers don't know the history and culture of black children in Holmes County, and those who defend corporal punishment in the schools gripe about TFA teachers' criticisms of the practice and their refusal to participate. The paddling of students may horrify TFA teachers, but they are still comfortable with intimidating black children through scripted learning.

While fighting corporal punishment often feels like an uphill battle, Harper is committed to working for change. "We're trying to eliminate this practice across the Delta, but a lot of black parents really do feel our kids need this and so many kids have gotten used to it. They just brace themselves to take the beating and then they just go about their day," she says.

By high school, some students have shown resistance to principals who have tried to paddle them, resulting in their being suspended, expelled, arrested, or sent to alternative schools. Many students either stay silent about being paddled because of fear or because they feel there are no adults in their life who want to make it stop.

A half-century after *Brown v. Board of Education*, activists, lawyers, parents, children, and organizations including the Southern Poverty Law Center, the National Women's Law Center, the Dignity in Schools Campaign, Parents Against Spanking, the Center for Effective Discipline, and the NAACP Legal Defense and Educational Fund, to name a few, have brought much needed attention to the issue of disproportionate suspensions and expulsions and other techniques to push black children out of schools. But in spite of the fact that the civil rights community and grassroots activists have been leading the call to end corporal punishment, they're facing strong resistance from black communities.

Most defenders of corporal punishment base their support not on data and science, which shows negative outcomes for children, but on how they themselves were raised. Dan Losen says that paddling kids is not educationally sound or justifiable. Through his own research and work with the Southern Poverty Law Center, he has found that even in districts where paddling is practiced, many schools opt out. In some cases, the entire district has opted out.

"All the research says it is harmful. Just because the culture or community gives it permission, or the courts say leave it to discretion of the districts, doesn't mean that the practice still isn't good for kids," Losen says. "We have seen girls hit by male principals and disabled kids hit. Why are we as a society so upset when we see men hitting women, but we allow this in schools? We are putting paddles in the hands of people who are supposed to report child abuse, and the same schools that are hitting are also suspending and kicking students out at disproportionately high rates. Schools have become harsh, uncaring, unforgiving, and punitive environments."

Losen's findings are backed up by other research that has found that aside from the infliction of pain and physical injury that often result from paddling, these violent disciplinary methods negatively impact student academic performance. A report by Human Rights Watch found that in states where corporal punishment is used, schools perform worse on national academic assessments. The ACLU found that none of the paddling states scored in the top 20 percent of eighth-grade performance on the National Assessment of Educational Progress. In fact, 60 percent of the paddling states scored below average or worse in eighth-grade performance. Two-thirds of states that do not allow paddling in schools had graduation rates above the national average in 2004, while 57 percent of corporal punishment states had graduation rates below the national average that year.[27]

The Society for Adolescent Medicine has found that victims of corporal punishment often have deteriorating peer relationships, difficulty with concentration, lowered school achievement, antisocial behavior, intense dislike of authority, a tendency for school avoidance and dropout, and other evidence of negative, high-risk adolescent behavior.

A 2008 report from the ACLU and Human Rights Watch asserts that corporal punishment not only does not stop students from acting out, but also is harmful to their educations and futures. "Studies show that beatings can damage the trust between educator and student, corrode the educational environment and leave the student unable to learn effectively, making it more likely he or she will leave school," the report states. "African-American students are punished at disproportionately high rates, creating a hostile environment in which minority students struggle to succeed."[28]

The practice of corporal punishment is not preparing kids for a future of happiness, much less empowerment and success, but rather pushing them out of schools and preparing them for a brutal life of incarceration. Ironically, according to the ACLU, in many states, children receive greater protections against the use of corporal punishment in juvenile detention facilities than they do in their schools. As noted by the American Psychological Association, the use of paddling does not improve behavior, but can instead increase the likelihood that students will fall behind academically, have future behavior problems, drop out of school, and become involved in the juvenile or criminal justice systems. Corporal punishment doesn't protect our children but instead contributes to increased chances of their being swept away by the prison industrial system.

Over the past twenty years, researchers have made great strides in our understanding of brain development and trauma. Various traumatic childhood experiences such as homelessness, abuse, food insecurity, and neighborhood violence are forms of toxic stress that can negatively impact learning, behavior, and health across the lifespan. A 2011 study by the Vermont Department of Heath found that children with three or more "adverse family experiences" were less likely to engage in school, and more likely to shut down or act out because the part of the brain that provides inhibitory control is affected. Families of such students were more likely to be contacted by the school about their children's behavioral problems. As such, paddling and other punitive forms of discipline retraumatize already traumatized students. Dennis Parker's research concluded that the practice not only negatively affects children, but also contributes to the first stage of what's known as the school-to-prison pipeline.

Amir Whitaker, a staff attorney with the Southern Poverty Law Center who has studied educational psychology, says that paddling pushes students out of schools and into prisons because the practice creates a climate in which they don't feel welcomed.

When he was a student at the mostly black Plainfield High School in Plainfield, New Jersey, in the 1990s, his school brought in a new principal, the famous bat-wielding Joe Clark depicted in the film *Lean On Me*. Neoconservatives loved Clark because when he was principal at Paterson's Eastside High he used physical intimidation and verbal abuse to get "lazy" and "boisterous" black children in line. Metal detectors and sophisticated security systems, Whitaker says, changed the climate.

"It took an hour and a half each day to go through the metal detectors. Teachers screamed at us. The security system made school feel like a prison. I would go home instead of subjecting myself to this," Whitaker recalls.

Because of his poor attendance, and the fact that he was labeled a "bad kid," he was placed in alternative schools. Both his parents were in and out of jail and he moved around a lot. "I felt alienated at school," he says. "The school gave up on me. My experiences in school led me to see how school environment heavily influences student outcomes."

In 2007, Whitaker taught for a year in South Africa as part of a fellowship program, and it was the first time he witnessed children being hit in the classroom. When the teacher lost control of the class because a couple of kids were acting up, he pulled out a ruler, lined up the entire class, and gave each student three licks on the hand.

"I noticed it didn't work with the students and it devastated the learning environment. Some of them thought it was funny that the whole class was getting whupped. But it changed the tone of the classroom and the demeanor of some of the students who stopped participating in class," he says.

Whitaker didn't know that corporal punishment was still legal in almost half of American schools until he started researching educational law in Florida in 2011. "I was shocked when I discovered it was a tool kit for discipline," he says. "Basically, we have legalized assault and battery."

Whitaker points out the irony of today's antibullying measures in public education. "Corporal punishment is bullying that involves a larger, older person using their size and strength on a child as an advantage. There's been all kinds of antibullying legislation because of suicides of schoolkids. We don't allow our children to hit and bully each other but we give license to teachers and administrators."

Whitaker believes that within black communities there's little resistance to paddling in schools because it is frequently practiced at home and is seen as an integral part of black culture, arising from an unjust history. "We've had centuries of whuppings during slavery, public lynchings, night ridings, and we've learned that that's how you control and put fear in children. Today's paddling is a consequence of hundreds of years of oppression and harmful racist policies."

He says the Southern Poverty Law Center is trying to combat the practice in places such as Alabama and Mississippi, "but the parent says, 'No, if my child acts up, whup his ass.'"

The story of Janice Harper's personal pain and her work with young people in Holmes County illustrates how the wounds of childhood whuppings can have a lifelong influence on parent-child relationships.

Ultimately, she made peace with the father who hurt her body, and she turned years of unspoken rage into passionate activism in hopes of saving other children from the suffering that marked her flesh and spirit. On her final visit with her father just before he passed away, his hazy eyes looks into hers and he took her hand and apologized for "things that have happened."

"It felt like it all went away and had never happened. I felt like my father's little girl for the first time in my life," she says. Her story symbolizes the hope for the kind of conversion experience we should inspire between black parents and children in communities across this country.

7

"I'LL BUST YOU IN THE HEAD TILL THE WHITE MEAT SHOWS!"

Why Black Comedians Joke About Whuppings

Humor masks some painful truths about growing up black in America. While often lamenting the realities of racism, the persistence of white privilege, and the daily battles of existing while black, much of black comedy explores the more personal challenges facing our communities, particularly when it comes to child-rearing. Black comedy also captures how black people cope with the pain inflicted onto us by white America and the pain we inflict on ourselves.

If we *really listen* to the jokes black comedians have told us about the struggles of parenting, what emerges is a dystopian hellscape where parents resent their children even before they draw their first breath, where children are routinely threatened by their parents in an attempt to get them to "act right" in a white world waiting to crush them. Without most of us realizing it, black comedy provides yet another cultural reminder to black children that because the world is a dangerous and racist place, parents must hurt them to get them ready for it.

Many stand-up acts are little more than black men confessing their childhood traumas and brutalization of their own children.

Kevin Hart jokes about punching his nine-month-old daughter in the throat for wanting juice.

Bernie Mac declares, *"I will fuck a kid up!"*

Bruce Bruce advises parents to set the tone for their child's day: "As soon as your kid wakes up, beat 'em because they've done *something* wrong."

Reflecting back on his childhood in his 2015 film *Chris Tucker Live*, the comedian said, "My father beat us like slaves." And then he described how he and his brother were ordered to go into the basement, strip naked, and spread over a couch while their father whupped them with a strap.

The underlying message from these comedians is that, for black children, their very existence is a source of constant irritation to their parents. Requests for food, attention, toys, and information—all normal child behaviors—are met with scorn and violence. Before our children have their innocence destroyed by their first direct experiences with racism, each developmental milestone is met with black parents diminishing them through shame, ridicule, physical force, and even the threat of being taken out of this world by the people who brought them into it.

There is even violence in the nurturing of our children when they are physically injured or sick. Richard Pryor said that after his grandmother whupped him with a switch, she treated his wounds with a cotton ball and peroxide, and then promised to whup him again if he acted up. His audience responded in laughter.

Black comedians also jest about how "soft" today's children are because they cannot withstand poverty, illness, injuries, or painful beatings from adults. The overarching message is that black children should expect no empathy or kindness in the world, even from their closest relatives.

And yet we laugh at these messages. We find humor in the pain. And we use this entertainment in an effort to persuade ourselves that we turned out just fine. But what's most disturbing about our laughter is that it demonstrates our inability to recognize that there's something fundamentally wrong with beating a child until "the white meat shows," as Bernie Mac famously threatened his nieces and nephews. The audience's laughter tells us that the whuppings we received have made us numb to our own pain and immune to the continued violence we witness. We have either suppressed our negative childhood experiences or obliterated them from our minds so that we cannot empathize with our children's pain and vulnerability.

Consider the Peabody Award–winning *The Bernie Mac Show*, an upper-middle-class-black-family sitcom that aired on Fox from 2001 to 2006. Mac plays a loving but gruff and exasperated uncle, whose childless, picture-perfect life with his wife is interrupted when they agree to take custody of his drug-addicted sister's three children.

The premise of the sitcom was based on Mac's own life, and he incorporated it into a legendary routine in the very popular stand-up comedy film *The Original Kings of Comedy*.

"I got three fuckin' new kids in my life," he gripes to the mostly black audience, which roars with laughter. As he ticks off their ages— two, four, and six—the audience collectively groans.

With a mother who became more and more neglectful as she fell deeper into her addiction, life had been bad for his two nieces and nephew. They were going to end up in foster care if Mac didn't step in. It wasn't surprising that they had their own emotional baggage when they arrived at their uncle's home. Mac describes them as if they are pathological street urchins. The two-year-old, he says, is the bossy, cunning one—a little "heifer" and the ringleader who "works for the devil." Mac makes fun of the four-year-old's wide-eyed expression, speech delay, and constant rocking—developmental disabilities caused by her mother smoking crack while pregnant.

"She don't talk. She don't say *shit*. All she do is just look at you," he says while widening his eyes as the audience cackles. He says he told the child that if a fire breaks out in the house she "better have a whistle or something. . . . I ain't got time to be lookin' for no deaf, mute muthafucka!"

Mac then calls the effeminate six-year-old boy a "faggot . . . the first one in the family," whose sexuality "hurt my heart." When the boy cries or wets himself, Mac tells him to "act like a man!" When Mac tells the two-year-old, who has snuck into the kitchen to get milk and cookies, that she can't have any, he says the child looked at him as if she wanted a piece of him, so he squared up in a boxing stance for a fight. The message here is that black children should not ask for food or want for anything, that they should make themselves invisible, and that they are never too young for an adult beating.

Throughout the stand-up act, Mac cusses at the kids and repeatedly calls them "sumamabitch," "motherfucker," and "punk-ass." He admits to the laughing audience that he constantly fought back the urge to call the children other names like, "you ugly son-of-a-bitch" and "you stupid muthafucka you." Other punch lines also evoke wild laughter from the audience: "Fuck that timeout shit! These kids bad. . . . When a kid gets one years old, I believe you have a right to hit them in the throat or stomach."

It is difficult for me to laugh at that line, given what I know about child abuse statistics. Children under age one are the most vulnerable victims of abuse, accounting for around 40 percent of all fatalities from abuse and neglect in this country. The majority of children who die from physical abuse are under age two, and studies show that black parents have reported spanking and yelling at children as young as four months, with the frequency increasing as the child gets older.[1]

In that same stand-up act, Mac jokes about opening a day-care center where parents can send their "bad-ass kids" to receive three months of free service. There would be no need for secret cameras because he promises to be transparent about his disciplinary practices. He says that if a mother picked up her child who had a knot on his head, and she asked, "What happened to my son?" he would answer, "I took a hammer and slapped the fuck out of him."

Mac's language would be cleaned up for his television show, though the violence still resonates. In the opening scene of the pilot episode, Mac looks at the camera and says, "I'm gonna kill one of them kids. Don't get me wrong, I love them. . . . I know what you're going to say. 'Bernie Mac cruel. Bernie Mac beats his kids.' I don't care. That's your *opinion*."

Mac's classic threat to the children is "I'll bust you in the head till the white meat shows." That line is akin to another oft-repeated threat from black parents: "I'll slap the black off you." His child-rearing tactics eventually get him in trouble when one of the children calls social services. Throughout the show, he defends his disciplinary practices by explaining that he is trying to instill respect in the children.

As one TV reviewer wrote in 2001, *The Bernie Mac Show* is a "brutal view of how a dysfunctional family might be made to function again. From Bernie Mac's perspective, that means employing strict rules, verbal abuse and corporal punishment to teach the values of personal responsibility and self-respect. What raises so much of the pain is seeing Bernie Mac attempt to instill these values in children whose young lives have already been damaged, perhaps beyond healing."[2]

This idea that traumatized children who had rough beginnings can be fixed with a "good butt whupping" also appears in Tyler Perry's 2002 play *Madea's Family Reunion*, which was later adapted into a 2006 movie. The no-nonsense Madea, who is played by the cross-dressing Perry, fosters an angry and rebellious runaway whom she whups with a belt even though corporal punishment of foster children is generally prohibited by state agencies.

One of the classic themes in all black parental comedy is to compare "these kids today" with the previous generation. Popular comedian D. L. Hughley, whose adult son has Asperger's syndrome, quips that "kids these days got diseases I ain't never even fuckin' heard of. 'I'm bipolar.' That means I have two different personalities.' We could have never told our mothers any shit like that . . . 'Mom, I'm bipolar.' . . . 'Well both you muthafuckas go in there and clean that goddamn room!'"

For Hughley, good parenting meant a teething child got a face-numbing dose of whiskey on the gums. Mothers chewed and sucked the juice out of pork chops to feed their babies. And a child left alone in a hot car should never set foot outside the car for cooler air, lest they get a whupping for being defiant. Like Mac, Hughley paints a picture of babies who come into the world cursing, and of mentally ill toddlers whose presence is neither desirable nor worthy of celebration. Children are a source of constant need, warranting adult violence from domineering and uncaring black parents.

Meanwhile, in his 1994 comedy film *You So Crazy*, Martin Lawrence jokes about resenting newborns from the moment they emerge from the womb because they are a threat and source of competition to their fathers. As Martin reflects on the birth of his child, he describes the child as "that little mutherfucka." When the newborn's head pushes through the vagina, he turns to the doctor and complains that the child is "tearing up the pussy! Look at that hole. I can't follow that."

Weeks later, as the new mom's body is healing from the birth process, Martin lurks around for weeks wondering when he will be able to have sex with her again. He jokes about testing his wife's tolerance for penetration by thrusting his fingers and hand inside her vagina. As his wife is breastfeeding, Martin expresses jealousy because the baby is using "his titties." In another moment, he laments how his efforts to suck on the "free titty" prompted the newborn to rolls his eyes in disgust. His wife's "titties" were the babies' for now, a fact that infuriates him, just as Bernie Mac's nieces and nephews interrupt his ability to walk around the house naked and engage in "fuckin' hard" with his wife.

But this is no laughing matter given the preponderance of women of color who cannot breastfeed their newborns without facing jealousy, domestic violence, and trauma. Female victims of sexual and physical abuse are less likely to breastfeed their children, and for women of color, this is especially harmful. That's because "we are not only navigating generational trauma but also face barriers to maternal health education. African-American women and Latinas experience higher rates of intimate partner violence and abuse, up to 35 percent more than white women, making the intimacy of breastfeeding and nurturing an infant much more difficult," wrote Sevonna Brown and Esperanza Dodge.[3]

For a black child, the very act of birth, of coming into life, and trying to grow is an annoying interruption to male pleasure. Kevin Hart, who also called his infant daughter "stupid" and "an asshole," plays on this theme in one of his routines. Hart jokes about how having car seats throws off his "game" with the ladies who aren't his wife. "Don't focus on the negative," he tells the women who inquire about the car seats.

Another recurring theme in black parental comedy is the denial of feelings to children, especially those who have just been whupped. In one of his routines, Arnez J. turns his microphone into an extension cord and dangles it at a white woman in the audience. Reminding her that she doesn't know anything about being whupped with an extension cord, Hot Wheels tracks, or Christmas tree lights, he jokes, "Welcome to our world, white people!"

He recalls being hit so hard that his mother knocked the sound out of him. After the whupping, he was sent to his room to calm down, only to be brought back to receive an explanation. Still whimpering and trying to adjust back to normal, he struggles to speak fast enough about what caused the parental wrath. His silence compels intervention as his parent beats him again. The moral of the story is made clear as J. announces, "Ain't nothin' wrong with beatin' your kids. Most of us were beat and we turned out fine." The audience applauds.

In his 1983 stand-up comedy film, *Bill Cosby: Himself*, "America's Dad" performs in front of a live audience at the Hamilton Place Theatre in Canada. While offering his views on family—namely, marriage and the trials and tribulations of parenting—he describes the nightly bedtime ritual in his home. After dinner, he and his wife give instructions to their five young children. They are the same instructions each night: "Go upstairs . . . take off all your clothes . . . get into the shower . . . please turn on the water . . . Please use soap . . . rinse yourselves off . . . dry yourselves off . . . put on clean pajamas . . . get into the bed and go to sleep!" Each instruction Cosby recalls is met with raucous laughter from the audience.

He continues the setup: "Now if these brain-damaged children would do that, there would be no beatings." He looks at the audience knowingly. "But there's going to be a beating tonight."

Cosby describes warning his children to do what they're told, lest they pay the price. "And the children kiss me and they pat me on my head and they smile and look at me as if to say, 'Dear man, thank you for your kindness and your wonderful attitude about this whole situation. But you don't understand . . . we cannot sleep through the night unless we've had a good beating.'"

When the children inevitably begin acting up and hitting one another, Mrs. Cosby steps in because she's had enough.

"My wife turns around, grabs a yardstick. She holds it like a samurai warrior. She then makes an announcement that the beatings will now begin. . . . My job is, I am the goalie. The children come at me and I kick 'em back into play."

The beating ends. The stick has been broken onto the children's bodies. They're back doing what they're supposed to be doing, only now they're crying, too.

Mrs. Cosby, meanwhile, returns to the kitchen to calm down, only she can't stop grumbling her frustrations aloud to herself: "Gonna tell me you're *not* gonna do something when I tell you to do something? I mean, you *move* when I say *move*. Think I carried you in *my body* for nine months so you can roll your eyes at me?! I'll roll that little head of yours down on the floor. . . . I'll beat you until you can't grow anymore!"

Black parents' threats to beat their children until they can't grow anymore subconsciously echoes the larger societal attitudes about black children's inevitable passage into adulthood. Such a message says, "I'm so terrified and feel so inadequate about parenting you through puberty and so I want to attack the part of you that's growing up."

In one of his routines, Mike Epps continually riffs on how black mothers deal with their sassy teenage daughters entering puberty. "You know those black mothers love jumpin' on their daughters. They got that little rival thing." He makes it plain: if a daughter gets smart with her mother, the mother should smack her and threaten to knock her head between the washer and dryer. "Black mothers love to do that first jump-off," Epps says.

After the beating, Epps says the mother then calls a friend to shame the daughter—"I had to knock Shaneika's muthafuckin' . . . I tried to kick that bitch all behind the damn washer and dryer!" He notes how the mother further shames her daughter by discussing her sexual development with others. "I guess 'cause she got titties she think she runnin' somethin' 'round here. I had to let her know, 'Buy your own tampons! Until you can buy your own tampons, don't say a muthafuckin' thang to me.'"

This is yet another example of how children, in this case a daughter who has entered puberty, are perceived as threats to parents. And they must be beaten down for "getting too big for their britches." What Epps depicts is a scene where a teenager is denied privacy, denied the sanctity of experiencing a healthy progression into womanhood, and shamed for it with a beating and gossip, and for her inability to purchase her own tampons.

In comparing black and white parenting styles, Epps also says that black parents will beat their kids anywhere—"church, the parking lot, court." Describing a disrespectful white male teenager who cusses at his mother, threatens to kill both parents, and spends his free time in the garage making bombs with no investigation from the parents, he depicts white parents as too permissive. And that has deadly consequences.

"White people, your kids will kill you!" Epps proclaims, adding that white parents don't beat their children and give them too much unsupervised time alone in their homes. The more responsible black mother has "instincts like she's in Vietnam." She will ask questions when her child is spending too much quiet time alone in their room. According to this logic, permissiveness and the lack of beatings leads to white pathology, whether it is backtalk or mass shootings. But whuppings in the black community lead to respect and civility.

Black parents criticize white parents for being "permissive" and latch onto a sense of moral superiority because they would never let their children behave "like those little white children." The truth is that what spells freedom for white parents and their children is not having a history of racial dehumanization and violence. It is immunity from widespread studies, media images, and stereotypes that demonize black parents and blame them for social ills inside and outside of the black community. It is the ability to live in a society where as a white parent you don't have to teach your child what to do with their hands when confronted by a cop or how to live in constant racial terror. Black parents work overtime to rein in their children early on, because there is nothing outside the family unit that can protect them from the countless threats and blows of racism.

Watch the different ways that small black children and small white children move through public spaces. The black children are seen by everyone as a nuisance, as unruly, and threatening, and so their parents work to clamp down on their behavior, grooming them to be small, silent, and as close to invisible as possible to avoid attracting trouble. White children are imbued with racial swagger from day one—the sense not only that they belong and have a right to an expansive presence in any environment, but that they are deserving and important and in charge.

It's easy to see why black comedians are so outspoken about our child-rearing practices. Comedy and, more recently, social media are really the only vehicles that black people have to critique racism and white privilege, and within that, white parenting and child-rearing. After all, white people are constantly demonizing black parenting as the source of violence and other problems in our communities. So we return the favor by insisting that we must beat our children to keep them from growing up to be bombers and mass shooters like white kids, even though there is no evidence that black kids are at risk of committing such crimes.

We really need to stop citing the rise in school shootings as an argument for why our children need to be whupped more; it simply does not compute. Harvard University researchers found that the rate of mass shootings, which are committed mostly by adults, has increased threefold since 2011, occurring on average every sixty-four days, compared with an average of every two hundred days from 1982 to 2011. The more than 350 mass shootings in the United States in 2005 were perpetrated almost exclusively by white men. A good number of the 174 school shootings that have taken place in America since 2013 were committed by adults and white male teens.[4] How does that correlate to black kids needing to be whupped when they aren't the ones committing the bulk of these crimes? We're over here agreeing that our kids need more-punitive discipline and whuppings by saying these school shootings are happening because black children aren't being physically punished enough. This isn't just comparing apples to oranges; it is comparing apples to a car.

"They have no evidence. It's all speculation," says Alvin Poussaint, a black psychiatrist at Harvard University. "What they're trying to say is 'We like to beat our kids and it's good for them. White people don't beat their kids, and it's not good for them.' It's not good thinking. They don't know what happened to those mass shooters when they were kids or what were they like as youngsters. Sometimes they experienced psychological abuse, which can be as bad as physical abuse. When a kid is told they can't do anything right, they get very damaged and feel rage at the abuser and at the world."

Dr. Poussaint sees the comparison to white people's permissive parenting as yet another rationalization used by black parents to legitimize their own violence against their children. "They don't have any proof that beating their kid tones down misbehaviors or the violence in the black community. In fact, it is probably the opposite," he says. "By beating their kids, they are more likely to turn out violent, because spanking and beating is legitimizing violence. It tells children that hitting is an appropriate way you interact with people and express your frustration."

Yet, comedians continue to send the message that whuppings will save us.

But why do we laugh at the act of verbally abusing and inflicting violence upon children? What function does the humor serve for the joke teller, and for the audience doubled over in laughter? How did we get to the point where so many people invert violence, pain, and trauma as love and responsible black parenting?

The great Harlem Renaissance poet and activist Langston Hughes wrote in his 1965 introductory note to *The Negro Book of Humor* that "humor is what you wish in your secret heart were not true, but it is, and you must laugh. Humor is your own unconscious therapy." It's no wonder that so many black male comedians spend so much time in their stand-up acts joking about 'ass whuppings,' especially if the topic is guaranteed to draw hearty laughter and applause. Many black people laugh at these descriptions of violence against children because that is the only way we can absolve our parents and caretakers of their violence against us and keep from having to grapple with the contradiction that the people who loved us and were supposed to keep us safe also hurt our bodies.

Hughes's insightful words speak directly to the ways in which black comedians have provided "therapy" in a very bizarre way, for themselves and their audiences. The comedic stage is in some ways a public therapy because it provides a space for the expression of joy, love, pain, and trauma. This is especially true for black Americans and other marginalized communities whose experiences with violence are often rendered invisible or insignificant.

Comedy becomes a means to be heard. For men, and in this case black men, comedy serves as a means to discuss feelings, to be vulnerable, and to expose some of their pain to a world that is already injurious to black bodies. Joking about whupping kids isn't just a therapeutic way to work through pain. It's actually a temporary balm and a form of humor that becomes complicit with the perpetuation of violence in our communities. As one psychologist put it, "Humor can be used as a mask that shields both the wearer and those around him, from the pain underneath."[5] Because the violence against black children is expressed in the context of comedic entertainment, we are given permission to enjoy it.

Dr. Poussaint explains that people who joke about whuppings are trying "to ease some of the pain or deny the implications of it by turning it into comedy. They are saying that it's legitimate to beat black children because they are lesser beings. And they are playing to white people by saying that their violence toward blacks is okay because blacks do it to themselves. White people listen to them and laugh. By infusing a fun aspect to it, the jokes deny the damage. With the parents I've talked with over the years I very seldom heard them talk about doing any damage to their children."

During the Adrian Peterson controversy, the pop-culture writer and LGBT activist Katie Barnes wrote about how comedians help perpetuate cycles of violence in black communities. "Black comedians are artifacts of black culture, and help craft how that culture is reproduced. Through laughing (and sometimes cringing) at their jokes, we internalize messages about what the 'Black experience' is," Barnes wrote. She further reflects on the implications of Bill Cosby, Sinbad, Chris Rock, Kevin Hart, and other black comedians celebrating the abuse of black children. Barnes argues that these comedians are not actually advocating for violence against children, but their words still send implicit messages of what is culturally acceptable and appropriate.

Barnes adds: "It is also worth noting that this form of discipline is not relegated to 'man's work'; Cosby and Sinbad both discuss female participation. For Cosby, it was his wife that actually performed the beatings while Sinbad spoke of his mother giving him a whupping for his attitude, her arm extending eight blocks to drag him back to the house."

Whether black comedians are unconsciously perpetuating violence or not is irrelevant. In finding humor in the violence against black children, these comedians normalize the message that responsible black parenting means wielding the switch or belt. Their jokes about the verbal and physical violence also stabilize the idea that black children are inherently "bad" and need to be attacked. We might as well say, "Yes, white America! We agree. Our kids are bad as hell. They need to be shamed, verbally abused, and beaten. See how we laugh about it." It's no wonder that the most graphic descriptions of violence result in the most boisterous laughter.

Ray Winbush, a research professor and director of the Institute for Urban Research at Morgan State University and a psychologist who has published a number of books on racism and black culture, including *The Warrior Method: A Parents' Guide to Rearing Healthy Black Boys*, says that black folks, and America writ large, are comfortable seeing black bodies get beaten.

"We want to see the beatings and when we do, we laugh," Winbush says. Since the end of slavery, black America has never had a chance to have conversations about how we were brutality punished by our white oppressors. After enslavement, approximately four million black people were released and left to fend for themselves. "We literally had nothing but the clothes on our backs," Winbush said. "The trauma of enslavement should have been directly addressed by professional counseling, which was just emerging in American psychology as a profession."

"With each laugh, we are complicit in perpetuating violence as a point of comedy, allowing it to further burrow its acceptance underneath our skin and within our consciousness," Barnes wrote in her commentary piece. While black folks aren't the only community that uses humor to laugh at their own personal and collective pain, the costs and consequences, such as the school-to-prison pipeline, persistent inequality, gun violence, and the trauma of our history, are unique.

Throughout history, humor has helped many groups of oppressed people survive their suffering without losing their minds. We joke when the pain overwhelms us and because we feel helpless, knowing that we can't control or diffuse the racist structural realities that surround us. All oppressed groups use self-deprecating humor. Think about Jewish comedians who joke about their "overbearing mothers." During World War II, Jews in concentration camps joked about the Nazis and their own dire situation.[6] Think also about concentration camp comedies such as Jerry Lewis's *The Day the Clown Cried*, a film that was never released except for a short excerpt recently circulated online, and Roberto Benigni's *La Vita è Bella* (*Life Is Beautiful*). Scholars who've analyzed Nazi and Holocaust comedy have argued that the humor was used in jokes and films to prevent overwhelming sadness from consuming audiences. The comic relief was a coping mechanism that allowed victims to adapt to their miserable conditions and find refuge from constant fear and violence. Yet, this humor became commonplace once the violence was over, while whuppings are still plaguing our communities. The humor continues to fill a void left by a history of white-supremacist violence.

Nothing was given to our ancestors to help them psychologically deal with rape, incest, beatings, maiming, the murders of relatives, and the selling of relatives to unknown parts—all of which had been a routine part of black lives for generations. The severed bonds between husbands and wives, parents and children, and siblings were already deeply traumatic, but many were retraumatized when reunions did not happen, when they learned that loved ones were either dead or still alive and remarried. None of these historical traumas was addressed professionally; instead, only the barest custodial needs of the newly freed blacks were addressed.

"We had the Freedman's Bureau, but no counselors waiting for us. So suicide, drunkenness, and abandonment were common immediately after Emancipation, and most of it was directly due to not having a place to talk about what had happened to us," Winbush said. "The church was the biggest outlet, and perhaps this is why the number one place where black folks go to seek counseling remains the clergy. We did not get the therapy and protection we needed; black people built folklore and entertainment around our trauma. Black parents started using words like 'I will beat you within an inch of your life. I'll hang you. I will slap the black off you.'"

Winbush also notes that "comedic violence" used by black entertainers often followed a defeat of white supremacy. For example, immediately before and after the Civil War, the country witnessed the rise of minstrelsy and its associated violence among white folks and ultimately black folks in stage acts. The comedic violence gained popularity among black vaudevillians at the turn of the twentieth century, and then that form of entertainment emerged again after this country's defeat in the Vietnam War.

"It's as if white America literally takes out its frustrations on us and we try to psychologically absorb and reflect it by directing that violence toward ourselves in our comedy, as if when white folks see this, they'll lessen their violence and defeatism toward us," Winbush says. "We are master channelers of white violence toward us. We convert their violence toward us into gallows humor."

Vaudeville entertainment and comedy emerged during the worst period of racial unrest in America—post-Reconstruction—characterized by lynchings, the destruction of Rosewood, the Red Summer of 1919, when hundreds of black people were killed in race riots in more than thirty cities, and the Scottsboro Boys' rape trial. Vaudeville was hugely popular because it was considered more family friendly than the variety show entertainment that had come before, and it grew into a national network of hundreds of theaters. Before television and movies, it was the main form of mass entertainment, combining short plays, music, acrobats, magicians, animal acts, dancers, and comedy. One generation removed from slavery, black comedians used slapstick humor to process the trauma of slavery and survive their experiences with Jim Crow America.

It is ironic that after World War I, the popularity of vaudeville occurred alongside horrific racial violence, Winbush says. "Black vaudevillians channeled this Sturm und Drang (storm and stress) into their acts with slapstick violence directed at their own people in a symbolic yet futile attempt to show that we were willing to be the psychological whupping boys and girls for American white people."

Humor serves many purposes in surviving and processing oppression and trauma. It creates a sense of solidarity in those who are laughing at the people who beat them—in this case, black parents and grandparents. In the heat of the humorous moment, the person telling the joke can turn their childhood pain into something that feels better. This can help them to hurt less, and cover up their pain. But no matter how loud, long, or raucous the laughter, that pain never goes away. And when both the comic and the audience have a shared experience of that pain, it becomes a collective form of release and bonding.

Humor gives us a break from the painful realities of abuse. But it also allows us to deny child abuse as a problem in our communities.

Scientists say laughter can lift our moods by releasing endorphins and helping the brain to relax and feel good in the face of pain. Winbush says laughter is a useful therapeutic tool for survival that helps to banish anxiety and replace fear: "If you're not into drinking and taking drugs, if you want to physically medicate, then you can laugh about the pain."

On the surface, the ability to laugh at one's pain can be considered courageous, and comedic gifts can be used as a shield. And the fact that people are prone to pursuing pleasure and avoiding pain helps to explain why we often laugh at those things that threaten us or cause us to suffer. Difficult topics can become easier to talk about in the context of humor. While it can feel paralyzing to deal with one's pain, humor and laughter are great (if temporary) stress reducers. They can even help people grieve and find comfort when they need it most. Laughter can increase some people's tolerance for pain, and over time, painful events that once made people very upset can be viewed as funnier once they feel more detached from the situation.

Jeff Baylock is a twenty-seven-year-old Chicago-based comedian who performs in local bars, restaurants, and at colleges. He's been on the hit TV show *Empire*. He jokes about the whuppings he received from his single mother.

"My mother is legally blind. She used to hit me in my face with pinpoint accuracy," he says. "I was always like, 'Damn, you're blind, but how can you still hit me in the face?' She would say, 'I can smell your head movement.'"

Sharing these jokes has left Baylock feeling depressed once he's off-stage. "Comedy puts you in a happy place. I joke about my mother's whuppings, but there have been times when I got back home and cried."

When asked why he and other comedians joke about whuppings, he explains the technique behind creating material. "You want to be as original as possible. It's best to crack jokes about yourself. When you focus on your own life—they can steal from general topics, but not steal from your life," he says.

"The deal is you take the pain that you have gone through and you make it funny. I used to get bad grades. My mom would say, 'Go get that switch.' You take your pain and make it funny. A lot of people like hearing drama and what happened to you. Sometimes you can spin it and exaggerate it. It's funny to them."

But why joke about being beaten? "The audience is expecting jokes," he says. "They are prepared to laugh, not to say, 'Aw poor kid, you got beat.' They're not trying to be depressed. You rarely hear jokes that are positive, especially with black comedy." Baylock says he has stopped performing comedy for mostly black crowds. "I like doing comedy for white people. I could mess around with them better, and get paid more. I can do less of the crass, violent stuff for white crowds than for blacks."

And he is not alone.

Chloé Hilliard, thirty-five, is a full-time, Brooklyn-based comedian who performs about 95 percent of her shows for white, hipster-type audiences. She says that most comedy stems from making light of something painful as a coping mechanism. "Like rape jokes," she says. "We try not to normalize it but make these atrocities more palatable for the audience."

While a small part of her story, Hilliard refuses to integrate whupping jokes into her routine. "I was disciplined as a child but not beaten like my parents were. I didn't get the switch. There was no wailing and dragging me through the house. My parents made a conscious decision not to beat me like a wild animal. We were taught how to rationalize our behavior and understand where we messed up," she says.

But "when it comes to comedy, people want to talk about the pain in a funny way," she says. "I talk about being overweight."

She explains why she and some black comedians don't lean on the whupping jokes with white audiences. "White audiences don't have a basic understanding of beatings. White people don't have that experience. Black people understand the culture of being oppressed, being whupped, not having a voice. We *have* to know how to behave. Know our place. White people's sympathy ruins the joke." Yet, she sees danger even sharing these stories with black audiences.

When black comedians share their tales of childhood pain with black audiences, "the comedy validates the whupping," Hilliard says.

"Parents can say, 'I'm right for what I'm already doing.' It's so deep into our DNA to whup a child."

She does see a generational shift, though, saying, "Comics in my age group don't joke about it as much."

Comedy can also be a source of recognizing; it can spotlight truths and force us to confront our trauma. Unlike the other famous comedians I've discussed, Richard Pryor, who in his 1979 *Live in Concert* film vividly described being whupped by his grandmother, offered insight to a child's memory of the pain. "My grandmother is the lady who disciplined me, beat my ass. . . . She would say, 'Richard, go get something so I can beat yo' ass with it.'"

He described being ordered to get a switch off a tree and snatching the leaves off of it before getting whupped with it. "I see them trees today, I will kill one of them muthafuckers." He pretended to stop a car, get out, and try to twist and yank the tree out of the ground so that it will never grow up to beat anybody. "You won't be beating nobody's ass. . . . That's some hell of a psychology—to make you go get a switch to beat your own ass with it." Pryor then chronicled the long, scary walk back into the house, cutting the wind with the switch as he yanked it back and forth in his hand. He listened to its distinctive whistlelike sound. He hoped for snow or that his grandmother would have a heart attack so she couldn't whup him—and then proceeded to dance around on the stage as if he was getting whupped.

While Pryor's routine is a source of humor for many, it also forces us to confront our fear, trauma, and pain resulting from whuppings. Though he told the story in a funny way, he didn't celebrate the whuppings or defend the practice. Instead, he confessed how he wanted to grow up and destroy trees so they won't bear switches that could be plucked off and used as weapons on other children. He wanted to break the cycle of violence. He didn't speak from the patriarchal, abusive position of inflicting pain on a smaller person. He actually infantilized himself to show us the unfairness and fear from a child's perspective. The sights and sounds—his crying and whining and screaming and begging—and his reenactment are so visceral.

While it's uncommon, Pryor is not the only comedian to use the stage to disrupt the whupping narrative. Former child comedian, Lil' JJ, now twenty-five, offered a subversive routine at Harlem's Apollo

Theater in which he carried forth Pryor's truth-telling about being whupped as a child. Like Pryor, he brings the audience to a space in their minds where they can recall what it *really* felt like to experience the fear of being hit.

As he takes the stage, Lil' JJ, fourteen at the time, tells the audience, "I want to talk to y'all grown folks." He proceeds to mock the adults for saying that they're always talking about how "kids today" are so bad and how much they lie.

"Y'all be lyin', too," he says, ticking off examples like the Easter Bunny, Tooth Fairy, Santa, and the Boogie Man.

"Y'all be lyin' when y'all whuppin' us."

While pretending to be a parent spanking a child, he laments the ultimate lie parents tell: that they are whupping the child because they love them. "You not whupping us 'cuz you love us. You whupping me 'cuz you mad." As he pauses to punctuate every word with the simulation of a hit, the audience has little choice but to confront his words and the ways that violence penetrates his body with pain.

What's brilliant about Lil' JJ's routine is that he speaks from a child's perspective, all while pointing out that parents who whup their kids do so not from a space of love or virtue. He's able to show that kids are just like adults and they behave the way adults teach them. His message is that children and adults are the same. But when a parent whups a child for committing the very infractions that adults have failed to master, they are actually beating out of their child the negative parts of themselves that they are ashamed of.

8

"DON'T BE A FAST GIRL"

How Hitting Your Daughter
Can Trigger Early Puberty

One common goal of black parents is to pace the budding sexuality of their young children as they grow into adolescence. This is especially true for girls, as a young woman's chastity is somehow a reflection of her family's values. In a lot of families, there are firm rules around what's permitted. No makeup until a certain age. No dating until a certain age. No short skirts or tight shirts. Don't be fast. Stay out of trouble. And whatever you do, don't bring home any babies.

These rules are pretty universal across ethnic and class groups. But some may argue that for black parents the strictness is even greater because the consequences are clear. Girls who've broken these rules make for easy, cautionary tales about lost opportunities, bad choices, not listening to parents, and the importance of keeping one's knees closed. Not to mention, a fast black girl seems to confirm stereotypes of wanton black female sexuality.

Beyond steady exhortations not to do it, sex is generally not a topic of polite conversation in our homes, our churches, or the larger black community. It touches on too many taboos and toxic racial and gender stereotypes. On top of that, generational traumas—rape and forced breeding during slavery, gynecological abuse and forced sterilization by white medical practitioners, misogyny, sexual objectification in popular culture—have deeply impacted how black girls are reared by their parents and other elders.

Black parents see a correlation between sexuality and more hardship. That's not something they would ever choose for their child.

Religion also plays a significant role here. Parents who are steeped in religion respond negatively to any hint of sexual activity. That stifles important conversations about it even more.

Then bubbling just beneath the religion and the male-dominated structure of our society, where protecting a girl's virginity is crucial, are the respectability politics that encourages parents to keep young black bodies under control. And so we whup girls to try to maintain that control and to maintain in them a semblance of innocence. By keeping our kids "young," we somehow feel we are protecting them from the stereotypes and criminalization that get directed at black bodies.

In our culture, many people believe that raising up good children requires policing their bodies through force. But decades of scientific research on the biochemical consequences of spanking a child indicate there is reason to believe that hitting a child can accelerate puberty and sexual maturation in girls.[1]

For fifty years, scientists have studied how the impact of children's experiences—including how they are parented—can rewire their developing brain's physical structure or social and emotional function. We've learned that drinking and smoking during pregnancy is harmful. Breastfeeding is good for an infant's psychological development. We've also learned that good nutrition is key to children's cognitive development. And now pediatricians and other biomedical researchers have added spanking to the list of practices that need serious consideration because of the potential harms to children's developing brains.

The pain and stress that come with receiving a hit can alter what's called the hypothalamic-pituitary-adrenal (HPA) axis, which is a series of nerves and hormonal channels that is a major part of the neuroendocrine system, which controls reactions to stress and regulates body processes such as digestion, the immune system, mood, emotions, and sexuality. Exposure to only mild stress in early childhood can enhance HPA functioning and help young people develop lifelong resilience to stress, but repeated stress can cause the HPA axis to become hyperreactive.[2] So when parents hit their child to correct misbehavior, what they can't see is the immediate biochemical response their pain has caused their child's body and how over time it can cause emotional and physiological damage. It's akin to a kid being fed a constant diet of junk food and then eventually developing obesity or diabetes.

The 1990s saw the beginning of extensive research by psychology professors from the University of Rochester on how physical discipline, unpredictable environments, and chronic stress impact brain growth. Constant hollering, belittling, threatening, and hitting your child sets off biochemical responses to stress that can change the physiology of their brain and lay the groundwork for a low IQ, a quick temper, aggressive and delinquent behavior, depression, suicide, drug and alcohol abuse, an inability to regulate impulses, dysfunctional relationships, and perhaps most surprisingly, early intrusive sexual thoughts and activities. A 2012 study published in the *Journal of Behavioral Medicine* revealed that beating and insulting children can put them at risk for adult cancer, cardiac disease, and asthma.[3]

In other words, the body keeps score.

Scientists at Harvard Medical School have compared neuro images of brains of maltreated (emotional, physical, sexual, through neglect) and nonmaltreated children, and even followed groups of females from infancy through adulthood to gain insights on the impact early-childhood stress had on their emotional and physiological well-being.[4] The maltreatments include poverty, community violence, parental abuse and neglect, or harsh discipline. The research has focused on the stress hormone cortisol, which is released when children find themselves in frightening, anxiety-producing situations, such as being threatened or hit by a parent. Cortisol gets released by the pituitary gland and sets off fight-or-flight responses to feeling threatened.

Children who are being whupped don't have the option to fight or flee. They must submit to the experience without grabbing, blocking, or defending their bodies. This triggers the release of cortisol, which allows children to manage the immediate pain and stress. Having elevated levels of cortisol for a short period of time is not harmful, but if this fear response is experienced repeatedly, it can damage a young brain and lead to diseased neural networks. Researchers have found that preschoolers and grade school children whose pulse, respiratory rate, and cortisol levels fluctuate most in response to environmental challenges displayed aggressive behaviors and entered puberty earliest when they had grown up in stressful home environments.[5]

Researchers also say that repeated elevations of cortisol can result in children becoming desensitized to fear, making it easier for them to experience danger and pain and normalize abnormal behavior. Think about how many adults who were hit as children can't remember the trauma and fear they actually felt at the time but say that being hit was a good for them because they've only held onto the rationalizations used to justify the violence against them.

"The cortisol response is great and useful when it is fired episodically. The problem is that when kids are exposed to chronic violence, adversity, threats, fear, and hitting, too much cortisol becomes poisonous and undermines the psychological functionality of the brain and physical health." says Jay Belsky, an expert in the field of child development and family studies and a professor of human development at the University of California, Davis.

Belsky adds: "If the release of cortisol becomes chronic, then the system loses its capacity to mount a stress response. Hitting kids is not only painful, it is frightening. Parents induce fear by hitting. They say, 'I want them to be afraid of me.' But the fearfulness extends beyond the immediate situation of being hit. It produces anxiety, worry, and hypervigilance. When a child is walking around feeling fearful, threatened, and uncertain, their stress system is being provoked. What parents don't understand is that they may be undermining their child's ability to cope in the future. That is a problem for dealing with real situations."

Belsky highlights how toxic stress is harmful for a child's health because it becomes "biologically embedded" under the skin and increases inflammation. This accelerates aging and shortens the lifespan because it makes them prone to illness, obesity, high blood pressure, diabetes, heart disease, and cancer.

"Beating children, scaring them, exposing them to chronic adversity, and the fear it produces, from the body's perspective, has biological affects that are very similar to experiencing the subtle and not-so-subtle slights of racial discrimination. Your body doesn't know the difference," Belsky says.

In other words, children's bodies experience a parent's hitting in much the same way that a black adult experienced incidents of white racism. A chain reaction is set off: Breathing speeds up. The heart races. Muscles tighten. And then people fight, take flight, or try to protect themselves as they endure the hitting.

Dr. Martin Teicher, a neuroscientist at McLean Hospital and Harvard Medical School has been researching the effects of child maltreatment for more than thirty years. His research has shown how sexual and verbal abuse, witnessing domestic violence, and experiencing corporal punishment can negatively impact the development of a child's brain. During his residency training in psychiatry, he examined brain scans of a few patients suffering from borderline personality disorder, suicide attempts, and symptoms suggesting temporal lobe epilepsy. Many of these patients had noticeable shrinkage of the hippocampus—the part of the brain that forms memories, organizes and stores information, and is responsible for emotional management, logic and reasoning skills, self-control, and communication. He noted that all of these patients had one thing in common: a history of childhood maltreatment.

He decided to look deeper. For the past decade, Dr. Teicher and his team at Harvard Medical School have scanned the brains of hundreds of subjects who experienced regular corporal punishment and those that had no exposure to corporal punishment. In 2008, he and his team completed a five-year neuroimaging study of the impact of corporal punishment on the brain. He scanned the brains of forty-six mainly middle-class, well-educated subjects, half of whom had been corporally punished and half who had not.[6]

"All the subjects that we looked at were hit at least once a month, through several years of childhood," Teicher said in a telephone interview. Gray-matter volume in portions of the prefrontal cortex was reduced by 19 percent in the subjects who were corporally punished compared with those who were not hit. "The prefrontal cortex is the last maturing part of the brain and it is associated with impulse control, executive function, the ability to make right decisions, judgment, learning, being productive in life, being able to correct and modify behavior, being able to infer what others are thinking and feeling. This is what we rely on for higher cognitive function. Harsh corporal punishment appears to compromise this," he said.

Teicher's study is significant because many people say there's a "thin line" between spanking and abuse. Crossing that line is often defined by visible injuries: the sight of a bruised child, broken bones or blood streaming from a child's body, and charred skin. If medical intervention or child protective services are needed, it fits the definition of abuse. While none of the participants in Teicher's study fits this category, their brains still told a story of trauma and injury that will last a lifetime.

The defense of corporal punishment, the dismissal of the science, and the vigor and violence evidenced in their argumentation is not surprising. People defend what happened to them "because if I say it was a bad thing that hurt me, set me back and challenges me as an adult, that will truly be upsetting and will cause me to reframe how I view my parents, my childhood, my religion. It will call into question a number of things I don't want to question," said Teicher. "But the science tells us that corporal punishment is a failed experiment for producing a beneficial protective effect against antisocial behaviors or incarceration."[7]

Leslie Seltzer, an anthropologist at the University of Wisconsin's Child Emotion Lab, and her colleagues have been studying how stressful parent-child contact can overload a child's body with stress hormones.

Including girls of different racial backgrounds—who were victims of severe abuse, not spanking—her study looked at the experiences of her girls within the Madison community. In lab experiments in which she placed adolescent girls in a stressful situation and then took samples of their saliva and urine, Seltzer surprisingly found that girls with histories of harsh physical discipline didn't experience the cortisol rush that we would expect. Instead, these girls showed very high levels of oxytocin, known as the "comfort" or "cuddle" or "love" hormone that causes people to feel emotionally bonded to each other, and acts as the body's built-in counter to stress.

Seltzer and her colleagues discovered that when placed under a stressful situation, girls with a history of harsh physical discipline had their oxytocin levels nearly triple from their baseline, which was already three times higher than the baseline levels of girls that had no history of harsh physical discipline. Oxytocin is a powerful hormone that gets released into the bloodstream when we experience warm feelings such as love, trust, security, attachment, comfort, and protection. Our levels of oxytocin surge when we hug, kiss, have sex, give birth, and breastfeed. A surge in a hormone associated with sexual pleasure is not the sort of thing you expect to happen to a girl when she is threatened or hit by a parent or guardian.

"To be clear, I am not suggesting that hitting children releases oxytocin," Dr. Seltzer explained to me. "I am suggesting that children who are abused show an oxytocin response to a separate stressor applied in the lab. This is in stark contrast to girls who are not abused, who release cortisol in response to stress. . . . We would predict that girls exposed to repeated stress in the form of parental abuse should be motivated to establish other relationships. We know that oxytocin motivates social approach of novel individuals and is involved in the regulation of sexual behavior."

What this means is, when you threaten or hit your daughter, the part of her brain that controls emotions, memories, and arousal gets activated into a state of hypervigilance and readiness to respond to danger. The amygdala in her brain gets the message that danger is coming and so it generates an emotional response that releases oxytocin. Over time, as her brain develops and she receives whuppings, this ripple of hormonal changes can permanently rewire her brain. Furthermore, her nervous system will run on a continuous high, as she constantly anticipates more threats.

That is what happens physiologically when a girl grows up with whupping as her caretaker's approach to discipline.

The consequences are stunning.

Having higher levels of oxytocin can trigger early puberty and may remove inhibitions around decisions to engage in risky sexual activities. The stress of being threatened and hit has actually damaged her brain. Researchers have found that these girls have higher levels of intrusive sexual thoughts, consume more pornography, and masturbate more frequently. They may also struggle to compartmentalize their sexual preoccupations, control their impulses, and refrain from the very temptations that their parents want them to avoid.

Let's be clear: none of these activities are "bad things" in and of themselves. But by the time parents respond to a girl's perceived promiscuity, they don't realize that they may have been sowing the seeds for this behavior in infancy or adolescence by hitting, yelling at, and threatening her. If parents are whupping their daughters to reinforce family values around remaining chaste, then they need to understand how they're working against themselves. Put plainly, repeatedly subjecting a girl to threats and hitting puts her more at risk for engaging in unsafe sexual behavior, teen pregnancy, and a tendency to choose aggressive, violent partners later in life.

"For much of human history, abused girls who experienced early puberty and engaged in earlier sexual behavior had more children than those whose pubertal timing was delayed. That's irrespective of race," Seltzer says. "Growing up in a difficult, highly unpredictable environment should favor early reproduction. It's an evolutionary argument. Perhaps it's better to reproduce now, rather than wait for a tomorrow that might never come, if the environment is that risky."

Seltzer is expressing an idea that Belsky was the first to advance, highlighting the evolutionary basis of the reproductive response to exposure to adversity early in life. Indeed, as he points out, "There's evidence that family conflict of a variety of kinds, including hitting, speeds up girls' physical maturation. They enter puberty earlier. Girls who enter puberty earlier get involved in sex earlier. If you're creating a stressful fearful environment in your home, that's sending a signal to the kid's body that their future is precarious," he says. "It says to the child, 'I may not endure to get to reproductive age. Therefore I should hurry and mature to increase the likelihood that I will be able to reproduce before I die.' Living things have one fundamental goal, which is to pass on genes, to be reproduced. When that is threatened in a female child, she matures sooner. Plants do it. Animals do it. So do humans."[8]

This drive to reproduce early does not happen consciously in a child's brain. "Nature hasn't left that biological process to your conscious. The body senses the risk that 'I've got to hurry up and develop because what's most important is reproduction,'" Belsky says. As such, when a parent whups his or her daughter, "It may be the case that you're the producers of their very behavior that you disdain. You have caused the very thing, or contributed to the very thing that provokes your hostility. That hostility continues to send the message to the child that 'You don't care about me. Your actions are telling my body this.'"

But the ramifications don't end there.

Psychologically, hitting your daughter impairs her sense of trust and self-confidence, and it sends confusing messages about boundaries and her right to bodily integrity. The pain tells her that she is not in control of what happens to her physical self.

Making matters worse, the general public is seeing this humiliation play out more and more through the rise of a phenomenon known as "digi-punishment."

Adults whupping children used to be considered a private matter. *"What goes on in this house stays in this house,"* our elders warned. But technology has changed all that. Now parents are able to put their business into the Internet streets thanks to social media. Despite their intentions to teach their children a lesson and to make a statement about what responsible black parenting looks like, now these public whuppings are forcing a much-needed discussion about that so-called "thin line" between discipline and abuse because people are able to see firsthand how physical some parents' discipline gets.

With the popularity of websites like Facebook and Twitter, free video sharing websites like YouTube and LiveLeak, and video blogs like Worldstar Hip Hop, the Internet has become a cesspool of viral videos showcasing all kinds of graphic violence: brutal knockout punches and beatdowns, stabbings and shootings, rape and suicide, public sex acts, "cyber banging" and "drill music" glorifying gang murder, torture, and carnage.

We're also seeing a steady stream of photos and homemade videos of adults shaming and beating children and trading their self-esteem, privacy, dignity, and trust for "clicks," "likes," "shares," "emojis," and praise from their peers and strangers.

Ironically, a few parents who gained cyber fame from whupping their kids on camera with belts, extension cords, and other weapons, claiming that they were disciplining their child to save them from the penal system, ended up being arrested for child abuse. While most black parents don't hit their kids with a camera rolling, the parents in a growing trend of viral videos represent an important facet of the black community: those who believe that physically punishing a child is necessary to build character, to control behavior, to keep them out of trouble, and, by extension, to prevent the erosion of the entire social order. Parents continue to post these child-shaming videos in hopes of achieving fame and "inspiring" others to mimic their parenting practices. The message these parents and those who cheer them on are sending is that to address the chronic issues in the black community, we must whup, humiliate, and denigrate our children for their transgressions.

Kevin Geary, a writer and founder of the parenting website RevolutionaryParent, notes in a piece titled "The Viral Popularity of Child Abuse" that none of the parents in these videos wants to be publicly shamed or assaulted themselves. But to teach their children a lesson through fear and intimidation, they are game to record and upload.

"Parents are thirsty for approval from their peers and nothing is hotter right now than showing Facebook and Instagram and Pinterest how much you're dedicated to Team Adult by all the creative ways you make Team Child suffer," Geary writes. "'Everyone look! My kids were arguing so I forcibly isolated them together in a tee shirt with condescending phrases written on it."

Geary adds:

> We hit them (to teach them not to hit), we rage at them (to teach them to communicate in a nicer way), we coerce them with punishments and rewards (can you teach authenticity through inauthenticity?), we discard their intrinsic desires while force-feeding them our brand of "education" and "life experience," we teach them that their emotions are undesirable (while we rage and shame and play the victim card and bitch about everything under the sun), we love them conditionally (while claiming it's for their own good). . . . And most of all, we see nothing wrong with *us*. It's always the child that's broken and needs fixing. No matter how obviously hypocritical we are as parents, the child *deserved* it.[9]

If you visit YouTube and enter keywords such as "whupping" or "ass whupping" (and it's various spellings, like "whooping") into the search engine, you'll see video titles such as "Kid Tries to Pray His Way Out of a Whooping," "16 Year Old Son Gets a Whooping,"

"Butt Whooping Try Not to Laugh or Grin Challenge," "How to Get Out of a Whooping," and "How to Beat Your Kids Tutorial."

While parents whup their kids on video for a host of misbehaviors—acting out in school, being disrespectful, stealing, lying, bullying, sexting, and getting bad report cards—one of the more disturbing genres of these viral videos is when parents whup their daughters for exhibiting their budding sexuality. All of these videos include countless comments that mostly blame and insult the girls, calling them "little whores" and "bitches." While a few viewers express outrage and the potential harm the beatings and posting of the videos can do to the girls, hundreds more express absolutely no empathy.

Consider some of the most popular ones below.

"Dad Goes Nuts When He Sees Dirty Text Messages from a Boy on His Daughter's Cell Phone." (WorldStar Hip Hop, May 2011—more than 7 million views)

In a shaky video, a father is being filmed destroying his teenage daughter's cell phone with a metal baseball bat. After smashing the screen with the tip of the bat, he hits it down the street a few times. He then backs her down in a threatening manner, with the broken phone in one hand and the bat in the other hand, screaming, "I oughtta whup yo' freakin' ass! You got boys talking to you crazy. You lucky I don't go up on your freakin' ass in the middle of the street!"

There was lots of sympathy for the father in the comments, as if he had no other choice: "We need more parents like him." "I just did my daughter same way. They want to be grown before their time and my daughter 14." "Every man hates it when his daughter is having sex . . . he lost his mind . . . I feel ya homie . . . home run." These were common sentiments.

"Mother Puts Her Daughter on Blast for Talking to Dudes on Facebook!" (YouTube, May 2013—more than 1.2 million views)

In this video, we don't see the face of the angry mother as she cusses and screams at her fourteen-year-old daughter for sending salacious messages to "niggas" on Facebook who sent her "nasty-ass pictures of they dicks anshit." The mother changes the password to her daughter's account, and yells, "For the record, she's 14 motherfuckin' years old and nobody ain't g'on do shit with her! She ain't fuckin'!" The mother then threatens to beat her daughter and post it on Facebook.

Most commenters supported the mother's tactics. "This needs to happen to all the selfie whores," one wrote.

A few commenters who took issue with the mother's verbal abuse were assumed to be white. A viewer ranted in response:

> You white people saying that this is child abuse are soo fucking stupid. I am soo fed up with you people. We know that your parents never talked to you like this because they let you do whatever right? Right. It's not our fault white people don't care bout their children. Everyone is raised differently. If that's how she talks to her daughter then so be it. I'm tired of only seeing these comments in videos like this seriously y'all need to go get busy with your cousins and sisters and stop coming at black people sideways. We let you slide with shit this year waay too much. You all sound FUCKING dumb. Idk why we haven't killed all you baking soda humans yet. Don't say shit to me.

"Father Punishes Daughters After Finding out They Put a Twerk Video on Facebook." (LiveLeak, May 2013—more than 10.7 million views)

It was initially reported that Greg Horn, a thirty-five-year-old father from Dayton, Ohio, had whupped his two daughters, ages twelve and fourteen, with an extension cord after they filmed a twerk video that they posted on Facebook. After the video went viral, it was later reported that he beat them as punishment for sneaking out of the house.

"Whup that trick. Whup that hoe," a commenter wrote in response to Horn's video.

"We need more black fathers to step up and do this," another commenter wrote.

The girls suffered welts and open wounds on their legs and thighs. The girls' mother alerted the police and Horn was subsequently arrested and charged with child abuse.

"Not On Xmas: Mother Fights Her Daughter for Having Sex in the House!" (WorldStar Hip Hop, December 2013—more than 3.1 million views)

In this grainy video a mother confronts her daughter about having sex in her house, repeatedly slapping the teen in the face while the girl is texting on her phone. The mother then viciously punches, kicks, and drags her daughter from the bed to the floor by her hair.

"Get up, bitch! . . . Get tough, bitch! Don't play with me, hoe!"

The teen takes the beating and immediately picks up her cell phone and starts texting again like the attack never happened.

"Mother Punches Her Daughter Dead in the Face for Having Sex in the House! (Sad Situation)" (WorldStar Hip Hop, March 2014—more than 2.8 million views)

A mother who suspects her teenage daughter of having sex in her house approaches the girl with her fists clenched.

"You fucked him in my house?" she asks.

As soon as her daughter says no, the mom clocks her in the face, knocking her backward against the wall. "Bitch, you lyin'!" she yells, continuing to punch the girl through the doorway.

"Mama Don't Play: Mother Whups Her Daughter for Being a Thot!" (WorldStar Hip Hop, December 2014—more than 2.1 million views)

In this December 2014 video featuring a mama who "don't play," her teen daughter cries as she anticipates the pain of an extension cord snapping against her bare legs. The mother yells, "I refuse to grow a THOT!" (THOT, an acronym for "that hoe over there," is a new term for "slut.") The daughter, who is wearing white panties and a T-shirt, is spread across a bed with her head buried in a pile of clothes. She tries in vain to protect herself from the hits.

"Quit being a fuckin' THOT! You not a hoodrat. Bitch, I refuse to grow a fuckin' hoodrat in my house. Didn't nobody show you to be what the fuck you not!"

Out of breath after a nearly a minute of nonstop hitting and yelling, the mother takes a break. "I'll be back. That's part one." She then tells the person filming to recharge her phone.

"Beat that THOT-wannabee's ass," one viewer wrote in response to the video.

Aside from the pain of the vicious beating, the mother has exposed her daughter's body for millions of viewers, including to potential sexual predators who get aroused by such scenes, and put her at risk for being recognized by members of her own community. She doesn't want her daughter to be a THOT, but she whups her half-naked body like one. And since this video has had such wide reach, what will this teen think of her own self-worth when she looks back on the video and reads the hurtful comments of strangers who agree with her mother's sentiment that she is dirty and despicable?

"Dad Whups Daughter for Dressing Like Beyoncé" (WorldStar Hip Hop, March 2015—more than 13.4 million views)

After she went missing for three days, this teenager's welcome home is a brutal whupping from her father. Wearing a tight black dress, she is beaten in the middle of the street with a strap and then humiliated in the virtual streets, as her father grabs her by the hair and calls her "bitch" and "hoe."

Encouraging the beating, a woman yells, "You thirteen, hoe. You wanna be a woman? Put it on Facebook. . . . You know you ain't grown, bitch."

What better way to groom your daughter to become pimp-bait than by teaching her that men who claim to "love" her can also beat the shit out of her because she did something to displease him? This video also raises other important questions: Why was she missing? Might she have run away from an abusive parent, one who is now only sending a message that she should have stayed away?

A few months later, a similar video emerged on the website EarHustle 411 showing a father striking his daughter with a belt ninety-one times while a woman recorded the whupping, which was eerily similar to a brutal beating scene in *12 Years a Slave*, a movie depicting the horrific experiences of an enslaved African American prior to the Civil War.

One commenter defended the father who whupped the teen daughter who had been missing for three days: "He just trying to whup the trick and hoe spirit out of her. That young lady might change her ways and grow up to be something productive."

"Good. That's what these bitch-ass kids need these days," another viewer commented on the same video.

The fathers in these videos are trying to exert control over their daughter's bodies, especially their sexuality. They are also trying to dissuade their daughters from letting others exert control over their bodies. Moreover, they are clearly mad that their daughters are exerting control over their own bodies and sexuality. These fathers are already teaching their daughters about the way society at large demonizes black girls and women for their sexuality.

These popular videos raise some important questions about parent-daughter relationships, especially with mothers, since most of the videos I've seen feature this combination. Whereas other videos focus on fathers using shaming and violence to protect sons from the police and violence, these videos see black freedom as coming through controlling black female sexuality. The intensity of the beatings and misogynist name-calling by the parents, especially by the mothers, seems to increase as their daughters enter their teen years. The assaults on daughters are often done in the name of "protection" and keeping daughters from unwise or premature attention or relationships with boys and men.

Most of these viral videos have sparked debates over the question, *Is this discipline or abuse?* But such a question, unless posed by misogynists or racists, would not be asked of a video involving a man hitting a woman, or the police beating a black person. The fact is, we live in a society where hitting another adult is deemed an "assault" and hitting an animal is called "cruelty." We raged when we saw a viral video of a white Texas cop slamming a black teenage girl to the ground at a pool party in 2015, and again when we saw a school resource officer yank a black teen out of her desk and toss her across a classroom, also in 2015. But where is the outcry against black parents brutalizing their children in these viral videos?

We are so used to centering the actions of the parent wielding the belt, the switch, or the cord, and *not* centering the experience of the child bearing the brunt of the pain. Not only couldn't adults get away with hitting one another, including their intimate partners, the way we seem to let them hit children, but you cannot even treat *animals* this way. Animal abuse stories cause huge amounts of outrage, but hitting a child is often shrugged off as "tough love." Think about the controversy over the NFL's Michael Vick's abuse of dogs, or the dentist who killed Cecil the lion. Are kids less important than animals?

Unlike domestic abuse involving adults, people seem to be incapable of *immediately* recognizing the violence for what it is when an adult is hitting a child. And so they go through a process of having to deduce whether what they are watching is abuse. And the folks who ask the discipline-or-abuse question are often trying to match up the violent actions of the parents with their "intent." If a parent's intent is "loving" protection, then that often excuses the violence against the child. But at the end of the day, intentions are irrelevant. "Abuse" and "discipline" both involve physical violence coming from two distinct places, one loving and the other malicious and neglectful. But from the child's perspective, the hurt and the pain are indistinguishable.

While black parents of today have to deal with social media and a culture saturated with sex, previous generations of parents had to adjust their child-rearing practices in response to white America's sexual objectification of their children in other forms of popular imagery.

Black females have been eroticized since the first European explorers traveled to Africa in the sixteenth century and concocted artistic depictions comparing black and European women's bodies to support their racist colonial schemes. To them, our bodies, namely our breasts and butts, and behaviors were strange, animalistic, and hypersexual and freakish. Later, white American slaveholders used those negative depictions to normalize violence and rape against black women and girls.

As Marie Jenkins Schwartz notes in her book *Born in Bondage*, "Racial stereotypes of the day encouraged sexual abuse of slave youths parted from their parents by allowing white exploiters to blame the black victims for their predicament. Many white male southerners considered black women inherently promiscuous because of their supposedly insatiable sexual urges," and they claimed that young slave girls commonly solicited "the caresses of men of their own race" and also "sons of their masters, overseers or any other white men in the neighborhood" while white women denied the reality of their men's abuses.[10]

The plantation economy relied on black women to produce future generations of the slave population through their wombs. And because enslaved women's unborn children increased future earnings, slaveholding families ensured that our ancestors were "multiplying women" who bore plenty of children. Adult women who didn't regularly produce children were threatened with being sold to another plantation.

Owners even resorted to monitoring women's menstrual cycles through the distribution and storage of rags used to absorb the monthly flow. Schwartz found that white "masters, mistresses, and overseers came to know whose period was late, scanty, suppressed, painful, irregular, or characterized by excessive bleeding."[11]

Given the specter of incessant bodily violation, invasion of privacy, violence, and racial terror, it isn't surprising that there was a great deal of silence about sex because slave children were vulnerable to sexual exploitation. While mothers tried to prepare their daughters for the possibility of sexual exploitation as they approached puberty, "they hoped to prolong childhood for their daughters," Schwartz writes. "Girls who knew a lot about human sexuality hardly qualified as children in the minds of their white owners, a fact that caused some parents to wait too long to address the issue. As a result, girls might reach the age of maturity with no clear understanding of the human reproductive cycle. A few even went to their marriage beds without knowing what to expect."

Talking about sex was considered taboo and slave parents took measures to keep children from learning too much by telling them "fanciful stories about storks and other imaginary means of human reproduction" and even whupping an inquisitive child with a switch. Despite the secretiveness within slave communities, Schwartz argues that young people still sought to create intimate relationships with one another during their mid- to late teens.

"For them, as for other youths, the attentions of a special boy or girl brought joy and excitement. Because their lives were otherwise more notable for neglect, impoverishment, hard labor, and distress, everyone wanted someone to cherish. In addition, youths who were working as adults and subject to slavery's worst features considered themselves entitled to the privileges of adulthood, including love and its sexual expression." Sex, love, and marriage offered young slaves physical release and an emotional haven.[12]

After Emancipation, white men continued to promote the sexualization of black women and girls, both for their own pleasure and because black children were still a primary exploitable plantation labor force. Black females continued to be white men's preferred partners for unpunished sexual exploitation. Sexual conquest of black women and girls remained a central white male fantasy well into the twentieth century. The historical record is full of testimonies of black females being routinely abused by employers, cops, bus drivers, and other authority figures, who retained power over black women's bodies by limiting and policing white women's and black men's sexual and marital choices.

Throughout the Jim Crow era, white men used physical violence as a means of coercion, control, and harassment, with the ritualistic rape of black women prominent. Ferdie Walker, who was born in 1928 and grew up in Fort Worth, Texas, recalled being harassed by white police officers and bus drivers at age eleven on her way home from church. "They'd drive up under there and then they'd expose themselves while I was standing there, and it just really scared me to death. . . . This was broad, open daylight with the sun shining. . . . That was really bad and it was bad for *all black girls*, you know."[13]

It is no wonder that when Rosa Parks was arrested on December 1, 1955, and released to her family that night, the very first thing her mother asked was, "Did they rape you?" Because she knew. All black women knew.

In her book, *At the Dark End of the Street*, Danielle L. McGuire tells the story of Gertrude Perkins, a twenty-year-old black woman who was accused of public drunkenness in 1949. The cops stopped her while she was walking home. They took her to a railroad embankment and repeatedly raped her at gunpoint, forcing her to have "all types of sex relations."

In 1946, Viola White refused a bus driver's order to move out of her seat. The police were called. An officer beat and arrested her. She filed a lawsuit. The officer retaliated by seizing her sixteen-year-old daughter, driving her to a cemetery, and raping her. As the officer thrust himself inside her, she stared at his car and focused on memorizing his tag number. Still, the officer was never charged. He was allowed to slip quietly out of town.

Claudette Colvin was called a "black whore" and then yanked from her seat and kicked down the aisle of a bus in March 1955. Officers joked about her breasts and bra size.

This was, and is, the reality that black women face in America. As McGuire writes, "Away from the public glare and in the backseat of a White man's car, anything could happen." They could take a black woman wherever they wanted and do whatever they pleased with her without fear of punishment. "It was the worst possible situation for a young black woman—something generations of mothers had warned their daughters to avoid at all cost." As the civil rights activist Fannie Lou Hamer reminded us, "A Black woman's body was never hers alone." Nor was—or is—a black girl's or woman's body ever protected, nor is she able to feel safe from the threat of harm.[14]

Young black children also remained objects of fear and sexual fantasy. They were victims of unpunished lynching and rape, and they also figured prominently in the public circulation of pedophilic pornography controlled by white artists and printing companies.

Black children's scantily clad or nude bodies figured prominently in white people's erotic fantasies that were illustrated in colorful picture postcards. Black children were turned into commodities, profitable objects of a libidinal Jim Crow economy. Consumer goods were part of a psychological ecosystem of pleasure derived from the spectacle of black pedophilic projection and humiliation. For the artists, the mainly white consumers, and private exchangers of postcards, the climax was not necessarily experienced genitally, but through the affirmation of a false sense of superiority that their consumption aroused.

The production of this racist child pornography began after Reconstruction and lasted until the 1950s, when black women's groups and the NAACP pressured publishers to stop their production. The desire to control, ridicule, and sexually violate black children through consumer goods served as a source of sadistic pleasure for white audiences. White artists drew images of unescorted and unprotected black children with engorged lips resembling vaginas, exposing their private areas, seducing viewers, simulating oral sex on fruit, namely watermelon cut in the shape of vaginas, masturbating, selling sex, getting pregnant during adolescence, engaging in sex with trees and animals and engaging in scat (feces) play.

These postcards were drawn by white artists, produced and mass-marketed by white publishers in the North and South, and purchased by white consumers who collected, archived, laughed at, and enjoyed them. During their heyday, these cards sold for around a penny. But today they are auctioned for just a few dollars to upward of a hundred dollars, such as a 1910 image by female artist Frances Brundage (1854–1937), who illustrated a black girl child with her dress strap exposing her bare shoulder and her lips wrapped around a banana.

The yellow peels resemble a pair of pants dropped, exposing an erect white penis that is inserted into this black girl child's red lips, which are engorged like a vagina. Her eyes signify struggle as her left hand extends outward to hold her balance or to hold onto the viewer, who could imagine his own penis in this child's mouth.

Images like these postcards denied black children innocence, normalizing their sexuality as savage and pathological. The black child's body was consistently represented as nude, as available to be gazed at, and as a source of sexual pleasure. These pornographic postcards made clear that black childhood is brief, or nonexistent, that black children cannot be distinguished from adults because they can't control their sexual urges. The acceleration of black children's maturity into perceived adulthood has long been a core historical feature of antiblack racism, which continues today through the fixation with the black child's size, criminality, and sexual behavior.

While surrounded by such perverse racist imagery, it is understandable that black parents throughout history have struggled to keep their children innocent, to shield them from negative messages that the white world sends about their sexuality. Black parents and community leaders created their own counter images, from portraits of clean, well-dressed children to Tom Thumb weddings and best-baby contests, that sought to humanize their children. They also dreaded the possibility of their children conforming to white people's racist stereotypes and thus worked to produce counter-images in black news publications, books, and comic strips and regulate behaviors that would possibility confirm white America's stereotypes of us.

Today, degrading stereotypes of black girls and women remain a staple of our culture. As in earlier times, the persistence of these pernicious stereotypes compels action: beatings. That is, if white America thinks that black females are jezebels and whores, whuppings become a way to punish and control black girls for potentially reinforcing those stereotypes. This is very similar to parents who beat their sons for acting like "thugs" to deflect racist stereotypes about black male criminality. Ironically, the beatings actually implant and affirm the very behavior they are designed to discourage.

While many of the parents and their online fans are trying to beat the emerging sexual agency out of black girls to keep them innocent and from harm, they might be surprised to learn that that hitting, and other types of intimidation, which often begins as young as age two, according to a number of surveys, just might contribute to early puberty and those young girls becoming sexually active at an earlier age, and engaging in coerced, risky, or masochistic sex.[15]

There's also a relationship between corporal punishment and sexual abuse. "The hitting tells the child that 'my body is not my own. I'm not in charge of my body and other people get to do with it what they want to do. What's the boundary between hitting and sexual abuse? Adults think those are two different things, but a young child doesn't always know the difference," Harvard psychiatrist Alvin Poussaint said in an interview.

He added, "Parents don't understand the connections between structural racism, the legacies of slavery, and their own behavior. They may not see the connections. They see it in a personal and emotional way. These are my kids. I need to beat them. The biggest manifestation is rape. Some of these men beating their daughters is sexual. They get vicarious gratification from beating their daughters in the streets or in their panties. It's about power and control over their daughters. It's about sexual relief. When you look at the physical violence, listen to the language . . . This is a way of doing something sexual with your children."

This may be difficult to understand because that's a big accusation to hear. But Poussaint explains that sexual release is not always about achieving something physical—like arousal or an orgasm. It can be achieved through power and control over another person's body through violence. Children who are hit don't always regard their bodies as being their own personal property. Physically hitting children trains them to accept the idea that adults have absolute authority over their bodies, including the right to inflict pain. And being hit on the buttocks, or while nude, teaches them that even their sexual areas are subject to the will of adults. The child who submits to a spanking one day might be at risk for not being able to say no to a molester on another day. People who sexually molest or exploit children have a sixth sense for picking out victims among children who have been taught to be submissive and to believe that adults have absolute authority over their bodies.

While violent and painful, being hit on the buttocks can stimulate immature sexual feelings in some children. They have no control over those feelings, nor do they understand what is happening to them. The awful consequence is that some of these children form a connection among pain, humiliation, and sexual arousal that endures for the rest of their lives. A common refrain is "I got my ass whupped and I didn't ever feel aroused." But more than a dozen researchers have contributed to the weight of evidence.

Sigmund Freud first wrote about this phenomenon in his 1905 *Three Essays on the Theory of Sexuality*: "It has been well known to all educationalists that the painful stimulation of the skin of the buttocks is one of the erotic roots of the passive instrument of cruelty (masochism)." And in 1919 he argued, in "A Child Is Being Beaten," that "sexual perversion" in adulthood is rooted in corporal punishment during childhood.[16]

In his 1924 book *Love in Children and Its Aberrations*, Oskar Pfister, a Swiss psychoanalyst, noted,

> I have had constantly to do with neurotics in whom sadistic feelings were first aroused by corporal punishment; after the sadistic impulse thus awakened has been repressed and forms the starting points of very malignant aberrations about which it would be very disingenuous to aver that they would have developed without the free use of the rod. . . . The number of those who are harmed through beating, especially upon the buttocks, is undoubtedly very great.[17]

"Spanking on the buttocks can produce definitely erotic sensations, including sexual orgasm, in some children. Some of these children have been known to cause themselves to be spanked, by misconducting themselves on purpose or pretending distress while receiving the desired punishment," John F. Oliven wrote decades ago in *Sexual Hygiene and Pathology*.[18]

Shere Hite, a sex researcher and sociopsychologist, wrote in 1995, "When a child is hit on the buttocks . . . [t]his kind of violent touch can be sexualized in the child's mind not only because of a real flow of blood into the genitalia, but also because of a longing for intimacy with the parent: if painful physical touch is the only fulfillment of that longing, then this can 'feel good.'"[19]

Haim Ginott, a child psychologist who wrote the best-selling classic *Between Parent and Child*, argued that frequent spankings can have a negative impact on sexual development. "Because of the proximity of the sex organs, a child may get sexually aroused when spanked. Or he may so enjoy the making up that follows the punishment that he will seeking suffering as a necessary prelude to love."[20]

Adding to the chorus on the risks of hitting, Seltzer clarifies, "Spanking doesn't have a positive effect in deterring undesirable behavior. Instead, it causes anger and is associated with a host of undesirable outcomes: depression, anxiety, externalizing aggression, self-injury, and incarceration. It's difficult to dismiss the weight of evidence that physical punishment is harmful and does not produce better behavior."

She says it asks people to "admit to themselves and others that a behavior they've already engaged in has caused harm to someone they love. Frankly, I don't know if all forms of physical punishment are permanently harmful to all children. It's certainly possible that some such punishment, especially if rare and not severe, won't do much in the long term. If it is possible that physical punishment, however culturally condoned, may be causing early puberty and sexual behavior in girls . . . is it worth the risk for your daughter?"

The irony is that so many parents whup their kids thinking it will keep them from being "bad" and prevent these very behaviors. All children need lessons about appropriate behavior, but discipline that rewires children's physical and mental hard drives damages their ability to function in healthy ways. And parents who are concerned about their daughters' healthy mental, emotional, and sexual development might want to consider the scientific evidence that spanking is not the best way to "train up" a girl to develop healthy, happy relationships at an appropriate age and stage of life.

Like black parents' determination to disprove white stereotypes about black male "thugs" and protect their sons from police, the judge, and a life of crime, the determination to beat the sexuality and the potential reinforcement of disreputable stereotypes out of their daughters has long-term consequences, and causes emotional, physical, and bodily scars. It contributes to a culture that denies violence against black girls and women, which equates physical and sexual abuse with love, and otherwise renders our bodies and sexuality as objects of shame and pathology deserving of discipline and punishment.

9

THE PARENT-TO-PRISON PIPELINE

How Wisconsin's First Black District Attorney Connected Hitting Children to Criminal Justice Outcomes

On the evening of June 20, 2016, East Baton Rouge, Louisiana, parish deputies arrested thirty-year-old Schaquana Spears on two counts of cruelty to juveniles. Her ten-, twelve-, and thirteen-year-old sons had stolen a hoverboard, several pieces of electronic equipment, and clothing from a neighbor's house. So she grabbed an electrical cord and whupped each of the boys until their bodies were covered in cuts, bruises, and blood.

After her oldest son told child services about the whupping, Spears was arrested, and she also lost her job. As reports of her story went viral on social media, people praised her actions and expressed outrage that she was being punished for being a responsible parent. In a tearful interview, Spears expressed genuine shock at what was happening.

"I couldn't believe it. I just kept crying," she told the *Washington Post*, and told another media outlet, "Was I wrong? I don't think I was. If I wouldn't have done anything, people would be asking 'Where is the mother?' 'Where are the parents?' I decided to be a parent, and I'm the bad guy?"[1]

In an interview with a local TV station, Spears explained, "I thought I was showing them this is not what you do. You do not steal people's stuff, what they work hard for. I know how that feels. I've had my house broken into. Everything I do is for my kids. I didn't want them to commit another crime."

In another interview, she said, "I'd rather discipline my kids than for them to be beaten in the street, caught in someone's home murdered, or in someone's prison and me having to visit."

Others offered similar justification, as she emerged as a hero in the court of public opinion. Even the neighbor whom her children robbed offered public support for Spears.

"If it was me," said the neighbor, "I'm gonna beat you before I let the cops kill you. I'm gonna do what I have to do. I'm not gonna let [my children] steal and kill and do all of that. I'm not gonna let them fall victim to the streets."[2]

Spears's despair and dedication to her kids were clear in each interview. Yet she made no mention of her children's pain and injuries, or of the uncertain future they potentially faced in foster care.

"I can't live without my kids," she pleaded. Her articulate and painful statement, however, was all about *her*. The public sympathy was equally about her: that *she* might go to jail; that *she* might lose her kids; that *she* had lost her job; that *she* was being unfairly punished. Such empathy and concern did not carry over to her injured children.

As the furious debate over Spears's actions and her arrest continued, East Baton Rouge Parish district attorney Hillar C. Moore III announced that no charges would be filed against her. I participated in a local radio interview with Moore just days before his announcement. Moore, who is white, testified about his own childhood experiences, saying that he, too, was whupped with switches, a wet rag, and even a pot when he got out of line. He credited his successes, including becoming a district attorney, to the discipline he received as a child and said he turned out fine.

The Louisiana Department of Children and Family Services saw things differently. While announcing that the thirteen-year-old child would be placed in the custody of child protective services, it offered a short rejoinder on the difference between discipline and abuse. While reiterating its support for "reasonable, constructive discipline" as "a healthy part of parenting," it said behavior like Spears's crosses a line "into abuse when it leaves a child cut, burned, bloody or bruised."

And with that, Spears became yet another tragic story of a black mother who clearly wanted the best for her children, even as they made a terrible mistake. Her decision to reach into her parenting tool-box for an extension cord put them all between a rock and the hard place within a system that is dedicated to protecting children but also feeds those same children into the juvenile and adult prison pipelines.

There are no obvious or easy solutions to these difficult situations. The feeling of vulnerability and powerlessness of black parents like Spears only makes matters worse. Many black parents genuinely be-lieve that hitting their kids is perhaps the best or only way to keep them out of prison. Sadly, they find out that their weapon of protec-tion leads all too many black parents into jail and pushes kids into foster care, which is a fast track to prison because foster children have a very high risk of being incarcerated later on.

Over the past decade, we've been hearing a lot about America's "school-to-prison pipeline." Scholars, activists, child advocates, civil rights organizations, and legal experts have looked at a confluence of forces, including the increasing criminalization of adolescent behav-ior and the stringent "zero-tolerance" and "no-excuses" philosophies that have dominated national school policy since the 1980s, and have disproportionately pushed black and Latino children out of schools and into the criminal justice system.

There's been much debate about the root causes of the school-to-prison pipeline, but few have discussed the role parents play in help-ing to facilitate the flow of children of color through this pipeline. As we examine the widespread acceptance of whuppings, and the criminalization of black parents for using the practice, alongside the failures of a rigged foster care system and a thirsty prison industry, we see a reality where the state is moving black children from their homes in the name of "protection" only to push them onto a path destined for incarceration.

Ultimately, black children are the victims caught between a rock and a hard place. They are first victimized by parents who hurt their bodies to keep them alive and out of prisons, or because they are frustrated or lack parenting skills. And then they are hurt by the violent intervention of state agents whose policies set them up for more potential abuse in the foster care system with educational failure, harmful psychiatric diagnoses, poverty, and incarceration instead of support and resources for healing. Despite promises of "protection," black parents and the child welfare system seems to unconsciously partner in disabling and criminalizing future generations of young black people.

There are some black people who have leadership positions in the child welfare system, medical community, and even the criminal justice system who are thinking about the connections among parenting, educational outcomes, and black people's interactions with the criminal justice system. I want to share the story of one man who is trying to make a real difference, and the obstacles he's encountering along the way.

Ismael Ozanne, a lifelong resident of Dane County, is the first black district attorney to hold office in Wisconsin's history. He's seen the criminal justice system from front to back and he has been trying to change the culture of child disciplinary practices in what has been deemed the worst state in America to raise a black family. Black folks in Dane County, where Ozanne works, and other communities throughout Wisconsin have lived under tremendous stress and faced unyielding injustices and racial inequalities for decades.

Ozanne is the first district attorney in the country to connect the dots between how parenting practices impact criminal justice incomes. In recent years there have been hundreds, if not thousands, of initiatives nationwide focused on addressing implicit bias and racial disparities in policing, police brutality, mass incarceration, child abuse, and the foster care and juvenile justice systems. His efforts are pioneering and unique. But first it's essential to understand the environment in which he is operating.

In 2014, the Annie E. Casey Foundation, in "Race for Results: Building a Path to Opportunity for All Children," examined the connections between the well-being of American children and educational access, socioeconomic status, and home life. The report ranked Wisconsin the lowest of all states, with a score of 238 (the average was 345) on its ability to prepare black children for educational and financial success.

On the other hand, it was ranked tenth nationally in its preparation of white children.

Madison, the state's capital and a college town of forty thousand students, has long prided itself on being a liberal utopia governed by progressives. Its residents proudly speak of its quality public education, good jobs, access to health care, human services programs, a relatively high standard of living and, in general, a progressive outlook on social, economic, and political questions.

Over the years, Madison has been top-ranked for quality of life and the eighth-happiest and -healthiest city in the country by Bloomberg. Despite its glowing media image, Madison is also a city of immense racial inequality and hypersegregation. The black-white racial disparities are equal to or higher than the national average when it comes to unemployment. The city's criminal justice system is marred by racial disparities. Wisconsin leads the nation in black male incarceration. It spends more money on prisons than education for the poor.

Dane County, located in southern Wisconsin midway between the Mississippi River and Lake Michigan, was an important railroad and manufacturing center in the early twentieth century. While it's now one of Wisconsin's wealthiest counties, it also has one of the highest rates of income disparity in the nation, largely along racial lines. In the 1970s, Dane County began to attract many African Americans from low-income areas of cities such as Chicago. Most settled into neighborhood pockets of subsidized living ravaged by poverty, limited opportunities, crime, and drugs.

Today, half of all black households in the county live in neighborhoods with no churches, full-service grocery stores, restaurants, civic clubs, job placement organizations, retail outlets, or family support services. Most black children there are being raised in neighborhoods that are not healthy, safe, or connected to opportunities that will give them the best chances of becoming productive citizens.

As far back as the 1980s—with the start of the era of Reaganomics and the War on Drugs—black children have grown up in chronic poverty, with toxic stresses impacting their health, brain development, and social and emotional well-being. Here is a snapshot of the disparities highlighted for the year in that Casey Foundation report:

- The unemployment rate in Dane County was 25.2 percent for blacks (compared to 18 percent nationally) and 18 percent for whites (compared to 8 percent nationally). There were twenty-five applicants for every job opening. In the post-recession economy, people with a prison record had to compete with thousands of college students working in local jobs to support their education, the unemployed and underemployed skilled workers for a limited number of jobs.
- The median black household income was $21,000 compared to $64,000 for whites.
- Nearly half of black students—48 percent—were not proficient at reading by the third grade, compared to 11 percent of whites.
- Blacks were over six times more likely to be poor than whites. The child poverty rate was 74 percent for black children— the highest in the nation—compared to 5.5 percent for white children. The Casey report stated that, "this 13 to 1 disparity ratio may constitute one of the widest black/white child poverty gaps that the Census Surveys reported for any jurisdiction in the nation."
- Some 14 percent of black babies were born at low birth weight—twice that of white babies. The black infant mortality rate was 17 per 1,000—more than four times that of whites, at 4 per 1,000 live births.
- Black students were 15 times more likely to be suspended than white students.
- Only 50 percent of African American youth in the Madison Public School[s] graduated while 85 percent of white students completed their high school education on time.
- Black youth, who are less than 9 percent of the young people in the county, made up almost 80 percent of all the local children sentenced to juvenile prison.
- The arrest rate for black children was 469 per 1,000, versus 77 per 1,000 for whites. One in eight black male residents were incarcerated, which is double the national average.
- More than half of black men in their 30s and 40s have been incarcerated in state correctional facilities.

These numbers have remained dismal since the release of that 2014 report. It is against this backdrop that Ismael Ozanne is fighting to help disrupt the parent-to-prison pipeline by helping black people see how corporal punishment increases their children's risk for negative educational outcomes and for interaction with the police.

Ozanne, a Democrat, ran for Wisconsin attorney general in 2014. Raised by his black mother and white father, his parents taught him about the struggle for racial justice. His father taught at Tuskegee University. His mother grew up dirt-poor in segregated Alabama and was active in the civil rights movement, becoming the youngest member of the Student Nonviolent Coordinating Committee. She participated in Freedom Summer, registering people in Mississippi to vote. In his autobiography, Stokely Carmichael called Ozanne's mother "a gutsy little sister."

While his mother was whupped as a child (she was sent outside to pick her own switches), Ozanne can remember being spanked only once. Though family members criticized his mother for not spanking, Ozanne says, "She treated me like a human being with an opinion and thoughts. She expected her kids to be expressing their thoughts and feelings. She said she was raising leaders."

After graduating from the University of Wisconsin Law School in 1998, Ozanne began working for the Dane County District Attorney's Office as the assistant district attorney. Not a traditional "law and order" prosecutor, Ozanne tried to see beyond the crimes people were accused of committing. He considered the environmental factors that drove a person to break the law. He focused on their actions rather than seeing them as unredeemable criminals.

Over the years, Ozanne found that most inmates had reading and education levels below the sixth grade. Their childhoods had been filled with abuse and neglect, and many had experience with child protective services. There were widespread mental health and addiction issues among the inmates he encountered. This opened his eyes to the connections among early childhood experiences, low educational achievement, and incarceration. He also learned about the role of historical trauma in black life, and researched how parenting impacted brain development in children who had been abused and neglected.

In a May 2014 interview with the University of Wisconsin's *Badger Herald*, Ozanne said, "If we reduce abuse and neglect, we can keep those kids out of the foster care system, we can keep those kids out of the delinquency system, and we can keep them from walking into the adult system, which will have the impact we're looking to have on the criminal justice system."

When he took office in 2010, the Dane County criminal justice system was being aggressively scrutinized for warehousing more people than any other county in the state. It faced scathing reports about racial disparities in its own system and other measures of life. Members of the black community couldn't decide whether they'd support Ozanne because he was heading a bureaucratic institution that had long abused them. Shortly after taking office he tried the case involving a white child who had been abused and confined to a basement for six years. After that case, his office saw a sudden spike in cases—mostly from persons of color.

"This caused us to ask, 'What's going on?'" Ozanne says.

Having taken office with a commitment to addressing issues that impacted children, Ozanne turned the attention of his office to the issue of child abuse. "How do I address racial disparities, equity, and equality in this community? How do we deal with the community perception that the system is no longer fair? What are the implications for the criminal justice system and community safety?"

An alternative approach was needed.

Ozanne encouraged his staff to undergo cultural competency training and workshops on implicit bias. They reflected on racial disparities locally and nationally, and within themselves, hoping to understand the cultural context of corporal punishment beyond the stereotypes. Parents of color are responsible for more than half of the child abuse case that come into his office, even though they represent less than 15 percent of Dane County's overall population. He found that between June 2011 and June 2012, police referred 174 cases of child abuse to his office—54 percent involved minority offenders.

His office also began to research the impact of corporal punishment on families nationally, and found that the vast majority of the physical abuse and fatalities of children were rooted in parents' use of spanking. Parents who were angry and frustrated were most likely to go too far. Parents who regularly hit as a form of discipline were at higher risk of severely abusing or even killing their child when they were tired or frustrated.

Ozanne recognized that the issue was not bad parents. Many were not aware of the real impact of hitting their child. Looking at referrals to the system, he notes that, "You are also seeing people who love their children, who want to see their children succeed, trying to do the best they can. We read all these studies coming out about brain development, the impact of corporal punishment on brain development and child behavior. Many of these people were coming into the criminal system for the first time. We feel that if we can change their behavior we have protected that child and every other child in that home."

To better understand the roots of corporal punishment, he and Amy Brown, director of the Victim Witness Unit, studied the science behind the practice. Their findings led to the creation of the Deferred Prosecution Unit's Child Abuse Initiative to address racial disparities and corporal punishment. The goal: to bring the issue of corporal punishment and racial disparities to black communities, and educate parents in a professional and community context that included partners in the faith community.

Brown explains that such a program could result in fewer children becoming injured and killed. If their office could find alternatives for well-meaning parents to discipline without violence and avoid criminal records, then families could be saved and taxpayers could also save money. "It would be better to offer educational services and support for parents rather than permanent felony convictions," Brown says.

Ozanne adds: "Here I am, the DA charged with the enforcement of the Constitution of the United States and the State of Wisconsin, upholding law and order in our community along with all the studies coming out about racial disparities and the impact of the system in general. As a prosecutor the answer is not that we can't be holding people who abuse children accountable. People say we're prosecuting too many people. Well, say that to a victim. We need to think about how to keep people out of the system, how to keep kids out of that slow walk into the adults system, and protect kids from abuse."

He remained concerned about the effects of corporal punishment on children's developing brains. The child abuse cases he saw typically involved parents who started hitting their children when they were about two years old, when a child's brain is rapidly growing and developing.

"That's when it is developing all of its skills and problem solving and reasoning and logic to actually succeed further in life," Ozanne says. "If you start to use physical discipline in that window, you start to rewire the brain. You start the brain not thinking about problem solving, not thinking about reasoning and logic or figuring out how something works. You start that brain thinking about how I can avoid pain. How can I avoid this uncomfortable feeling? How can I not be afraid? And if that is what you are doing and you have a bunch of other children who are not dealing with that, in a sense what you are saying is, 'I am going to make sure that every child has a head start on my child. I am going to rewire my child's brain. And instead of my child getting to where they need to be, prepared for school because they have already figured out how to reason and logic and to use their voice, now my child is worried about what they need to avoid doing.'"

Despite Ozanne's intentions, not every parent has been receptive to his message. He confronts resistance from some in the black community who feel that the government is preventing them from using a parenting tool that will help keep their children from running wild and getting into trouble at school and in the streets. Ozanne knows how deeply parents believe that if they don't hit their children when they're young, then the system will do it later.

He has publicly acknowledged that blacks in Dane County have suffered from racial bias in the criminal justice system. This has produced toxic results of continuous fear and mistrust that has impacted the child welfare system's ability to provide meaningful protection to victims of abuse and to help the offending parents. Racial bias deters people of color from reporting abuse to a system that they see as unfair to their own kind, and it provides offenders with a psychological "out" to blame the system for their wrongdoing and avoid taking responsibility for their behavior, Ozanne argues.

According to Ozanne, research shows that "physical discipline really causes more disobedience in children, causes more aggression in children, causes the risk of involvement in risky behavior such as drug use or unprotected sex or whatever you want to look at. They can cause a higher risk of mental health issues."

One thing is clear: experiencing physical punishment increases children's aggression levels. Some young people who experienced physical punishment as teens were more likely to physically assault their partners as adults, according to a 1996 study by Murray Straus of more than 4,400 adults.[3] While functioning as a reflexive response to pain, children are also learning from their parents' behavior that violence is an appropriate method of getting what you want.

Another study, published by the journal *Child Abuse and Neglect* in 2010, found that parents who had experienced corporal punishment as children were more likely to approve of using corporal punishment on their own children. Similarly, children whose parents approved of and used corporal punishment were more likely to approve of spanking and to think that hitting was a good strategy for resolving conflicts with their peers and siblings.[4] In fact, many studies point to increased aggression, antisocial behavior problems, future domestic violence, future child abuse, and criminal behavior as direct consequences associated with experiencing corporal punishment. Children who experience child abuse and neglect are 59 percent more likely to be arrested as a juvenile, 28 percent more likely to be arrested as an adult, and 30 percent more likely to commit a violent crime, according to data from the US Department of Health and Human Services.[5]

Knowing the science and the scholarly landscape, Ozanne was determined to try to reduce the number of criminal convictions for parents arrested for child abuse. He set up his deferred prosecution program so that child abuse offenders who meet certain conditions can sign a contract and attend up to eighteen months of intensive parenting classes to learn better disciplinary techniques, rather than go to jail. While he has a special concern for black parents and children, the program is open to all races, aimed specifically at parents who

- Committed the abuse in the context of excessive discipline
- Have a recent history of alcohol or drug abuse, and who are willing to undergo treatment through drug court
- Have admitted guilt, shown remorse for their behavior, and are working cooperatively with law enforcement and the Department of Human Services

- Have no past criminal record
- Use corporal punishment as a culturally acceptable form of discipline

The program not only allows defendants to avoid prison but can lead to charges being reduced or dropped altogether if the parents successfully complete the program and stay out of trouble in the year after the initial charge. Parents who engage in the most serious cases of abuse and neglect are not eligible for the program and are prosecuted to the fullest extent of the law. And deferred prosecution cases are not expunged from the system. Court officials and the public can still find information online and at the courthouse regarding the original criminal complaint and its resolution even if a defendant successfully completes a deferred agreement.

When Ozanne's program was launched in 2014, twenty people were enrolled—nine white, ten black, and one Asian. Ozanne told local media that it wouldn't help anyone to lock the parents up without giving them the tools they needed to improve. His objective was not just to punish them for their crimes, but to change their approach to parenting. Fostering an adjustment in their behavior would help protect the child in the future, while keeping the parents out of the system.

Despite his passion for justice and his commitment to addressing the huge racial disparities in Dane County, Ozanne faces several stiff challenges. Some critics accuse him of going soft on child abuse. Many black parents and community leaders question his credibility and expertise on the topic of spanking black children given that his mother is white and didn't spank him. Others are understandably apprehensive of the district attorney's initiative since they have been so disproportionately hurt by the criminal justice system in the past.

People have also accused Ozanne of trying to take power away from parents.

He recalls, "I've had people say, 'You need to get off this beating children stuff—you're taking power and parenting tools away from parents.' So many parents say, 'I'm doing this so the police don't have to.'"

Ozanne recognizes all the skepticism and is working to address some of these suspicions through reforming the entire system. He has established new "community courts" in an area of the county where black males ages seventeen to twenty-five were disproportionately impacted by arrests. The program steers them toward accepting responsibility for their crime and repairing harm to victims instead of charging them with crimes. His critics see his efforts as race-based justice programs in order to achieve a modicum of arrest parity. Milwaukee County sheriff David A. Clarke Jr. called Ozanne's approach "pure lunacy," saying it throws dangerous youths back into the community to re-offend.

In 2014, two months after launching the deferred prosecution program, his office released an educational public service announcement on local radio. It was quickly pulled because some thought it was a campaign advertisement for the attorney general race. It was later picked up by the National Alliance to End Hitting Children.

He's also contended with people who question his authority in the first place, given that he was not elected by the people.

"I came into office appointed by the governor, not by the community," he says. "We were facing a host of criminal justice issues, along with budget cuts. I was trying to figure out how I can have an impact on racial justice and create restorative programs."

For reinforcement, Ozanne has reached out to the churches in the community, although only a few minsters responded with support for his program. The Reverend Everett D. Mitchell, senior pastor of Christ the Solid Rock Baptist Church, has led a number of community forums on this issue. He has helped white social service professionals to understand the historical roots and culture of black Christianity, and has made his own sanctuary a safe space where hitting children is prohibited.

While Ozanne has found difficulty in garnering support and trust from some black faith leaders and parents, he has faced similar opposition from whites, namely those who ran against him during the 2014 attorney general race. Those candidates and conservative writers claim that his plan lets abusers off the hook.

District Attorney Brad Schimel, a Republican from Waukesha County, said, "Wisconsin law already recognizes that parents have a right to use reasonable discipline in raising their children. But we shouldn't be bending over backward to excuse conduct that goes further than reasonable parental discipline."

Similarly, Susan Happ, the Jefferson County district attorney, issued a statement warning that, "Deferred prosecution agreements and
alternatives to incarceration programs can be of tremendous benefit
to offenders and to our communities, but they should be carefully
applied. When you are talking about violent offenses, public protection is paramount. This is especially true when you are talking about
offenders who have committed an act of violence against a helpless
child. It is up to those of us in law enforcement to ensure that all of
our children are safe and secure. I understand that there may be cultural differences that may contribute to these offenses, but we cannot
condone child abuse under any circumstance."

An online blog post titled "Ethnic Spanking," by Milwaukee community leader Gerald S. Glazer, is indicative of the criticism Ozanne's
program received. "Wisconsin permits parents to use reasonable discipline, so these are not cases of ordinary slapping or spanking with
an open hand. Unless abuse produces visible marks were injuries, it
is very unlikely to be reported to police at all. So these are parents
who have hurt their children enough to have drawn the attention of
teachers, counselors or social workers, who would have notified police
or the DA's office. Prosecutors have substantial discretion in pressing
charges, but what galls me about Ozanne's program is that it is designed for members of ethnic groups that approve of harsh corporal
punishment of children, but apparently not open to others."

Facts be dammed. Glazer's accusations are factually inaccurate, as
almost half of the program's participants are white.

Still, claims of reverse racism have anchored these discussions.
Brian Anderson, in an online post titled "Minorities Get Green Light
to Abuse Children in Wisconsin," called Ozanne an "activist Democrat" and the diversion program "affirmative action gone wrong." He
complained that the program

> looks to undo discrimination of the past by putting children at risk. . . .
> Instead of going to jail, minority parents accused of beating the crap
> out of their children will be inserted into a series of feel-good parenting
> classes. It doesn't matter if the abuse goes beyond simple spanking.
> The only conditions for this preferential treatment are: be a minority

and believe in corporal punishment. By implication, Whites will still be prosecuted to the fullest extent of the law.

Anderson said the program is racist and provides cover for parents to use violent discipline on their children, and he argued that black parents should not be excused from child abuse prosecution because of cultural differences: "Just because Blacks were treated horribly in the past doesn't mean they should get a free pass to beat the hell out of their children."

Echoing Anderson, conservative radio talk show host Dan O'Donnell wrote an opinion piece arguing that the district attorney

> believes it is perfectly acceptable (culturally acceptable, perhaps) to violate the very letter and spirit of the 14th Amendment of the Constitution, which provides that no state may "deny to any person within its jurisdiction the equal protection of the laws." At its most fundamental level, that means the law must apply equally to all people, regardless of their race, religion, gender, or, yes, what they believed to be "culturally acceptable."

Within Ozanne's program, parents are referred to parenting skills services, regardless of their ability to pay. They are enrolled in the Adults and Children Together (ACT) parenting curriculum, which was developed by the American Psychological Association. The purpose is to help parents understand developmentally appropriate behavior, the impact of child imitation and observation of caregiver behavior, and the impact of early experiences. The program teaches parents positive skills and strategies to use with and model for children, including:

- Dealing with children's difficult behaviors with developmentally appropriate responses
- Controlling their own anger
- Helping children control their anger
- Teaching children how to resolve conflicts without using violence
- Using positive discipline methods that fit the child's age
- Reducing the influence of media violence on children

As of May 2015, there were 61 defendants in the deferred prosecution program, with a total of 141 children residing in their households. As for race, 55 percent of the participants were persons of color and 44 percent were white. The average age was thirty-six, with an average of two children. Seventy percent had a post–high school education experience and 20 percent possessed a secondary degree. Most were unemployed; 63 percent had an annual income of less than $30,000; 22 percent from $30,000 to $50,000; and 15 percent had an income of $50,000 or more.

Parents enrolled in the program are asked why they used corporal punishment. More than half said it was because they were angry or frustrated, or because they were replicating approaches of their own parents. These same parents also spoke about a lack of awareness about the cultural norm against corporal punishment, and how they used "tough love" approaches to teach their children not to "act grown." The parents of color admitted that they felt pressure from family to use corporal punishment, and they were the only parents who said they whupped their children to deter them from prison.

While black folks in Dane County, like in other communities across the country, have a legitimate distrust of child protective services and the criminal justice system, there's also denial about the ugly realities of child abuse in our homes.

"Communities, ours included, struggle to define corporal punishment, and to reach a consensus on what is acceptable versus unacceptable physical punishment, or if any physical punishment is acceptable. This struggle between beliefs, culture, and research is what makes these conversations so important," Ozanne says.

In conversations with community members, he says he has heard varying perspectives—from certainty that physical punishment should never be an option, to certainty that it's the only and best option. "We've heard from people who believe that physical force has no place in parenting, while others believe it's the most effective way to get a child in line and find it difficult to abandon a method of parenting they believe is effective and that has been passed down through generations," he says.

At one community forum that I spoke at in 2014, a number of black mothers came up to me and declared that the state was unfairly punishing parents for disciplining their children. "The state is coming into our homes and taking our kids away just for disciplining them when they misbehave," one mother said to me.

Reviewing criminal complaints from 2008–2013, it was clear that many black families were being hurt through this process. The list of things that were done to children in the name of discipline included the following:

- Hitting with cell phone chargers
- Slapping the face
- Pushing and throwing across rooms
- Banging heads into walls
- Hitting with belt buckles and extension cords
- Bloodying noses
- Cutting eyes and face
- Wrapping belts around the fist and punching kids
- Punching in the face, back, and chest
- Whupping infants with belts and switches
- Pinching and bruising crying babies
- Choking and slamming children to the ground and kicking them
- Pulling chunks of hair out of the head
- Assaulting children, mostly stepchildren, when they got in the middle of parents fighting
- Pulling knives on children
- Hitting kids with ironing boards and other household furniture

Though there are hundreds of files similar to these examples, the black community is in deep denial about the impact and damages caused by spanking their children. They don't have a working definition of what constitutes "abuse." Parents are assaulting their children, in some cases as if they were full-grown adults, for perceived disrespect, failure to complete chores, bad grades, and toilet mishaps.

What keeps Ozanne and his staff going, what reassures them of the rightness of their cause, is that they have heard hundreds of children describe the pain they experience when they are spanked or beaten—how they cope with the pain and how it confuses them as it injures their bodies. These voices keep them motivated to work for positive change.

The biggest tragedy of all is that even if black folks in Dane County, in the state of Wisconsin, or in America writ large woke up tomorrow and decided to stop whupping their kids, it wouldn't cure the firmly entrenched racist systems that will keep them living in substandard housing, living below the poverty line, attending crumbling schools, and being locked up.

Not beating our kids won't protect them from a racist criminal justice system. So what do we have to gain by not beating them? We can decrease their risk for aggressive behavior, a lower IQ, and various types of delinquency that might lead to them getting suspended or ending up in foster care or jail in the first place. It will make our homes the one place that is a safe haven for our black children.

While Dane County District Attorney Ismael Ozanne continues to face an uphill battle to break the parent-to-prison pipeline in his jurisdiction, he was set to face a challenger for his job in August 2016—someone from within his own office. Former Kenosha County district attorney Bob Jambois, a white man who worked as an assistant DA in Dane County, has been critical of Ozanne for failing to be directly involved in jury trials.

"If you're going to be the chief prosecutor, you need to prosecute jury trials," Jambois said in an interview with the *Wisconsin State Journal.*

In another media interview, with WKOW, he portrayed Ozanne as an employee who doesn't come to work, has poor management skills, and hasn't "done anything" over the four years of his tenure.

"I'm going to file an open-records request with Dane County to get those card swipes—to see when he's showing up for work and when he's leaving," Jambois said, referring to Ozanne's access card to the Dane County Courthouse. "The staff in the Dane County DA's Office are demoralized. I think the office is dysfunctional, I think it's being improperly administered, I don't think the office is being properly led."

Jambois promised that he would try more cases, which meant that Ozanne's restorative justice initiatives—including the deferred prosecution program—would be axed if he lost the election. In my view, Jambois would probably never admit to it, but his complaint that Ozanne is trying few cases and diverting black bodies from the traditional prison is part of a worry law enforcement officials in other places have—job losses and deep deficits are happening because they are being deprived of the inmates needed to keep them afloat. While state government and private prisons are looking to boost their own revenue, sentencing, drug policy reforms, and diversion programs are bad for business.

Despite the many challenges that Ozanne faces, his diversion program has value. It should serve as a model for the country, providing parents with the tools they need to expand their disciplinary practices. This program gives parents and their children a better chance of surviving a system that is so clearly stacked against them.

While there is no guarantee that if black parents stop whupping their kids tomorrow, the parent-to-prison pipeline will magically disappear, that racism will disappear, or that the countless inequities and disparities will no longer exist. What is guaranteed is that there is ample science to demonstrate the many negative risks and outcomes of physical discipline on developing children.

There are also examples of innovative approaches to providing parents of color with the tools to become more effective disciplinarians, which, while not perfect, are a necessary start. Like his role model Geoffrey Canada of the Harlem Children's Zone, Ozanne sees the big picture—both the perils and the possibilities facing parents and children in his district. He is deeply committed to creating real-world solutions. They might not be perfect, but progress is never perfect. If he is reelected, his work will likely continue to face resistance.

"Throughout our conversations in the community, we've been energized by seeing leaders step up and become willing to explore this issue, review the research, learn the effects, and as a result challenge their own beliefs and encourage their friends, family, and communities to do the same," Ozanne says. "The research on corporal punishment, including some from our backyard, is helping people to better understand the short- and long-term effects of physical punishment, and in turn is influencing the way people view the use of physical punishment."

One thing that makes him especially hopeful is that young people, including pastors, are less likely to endorse the use of corporal punishment these days. The views are evolving, albeit slowly, and reflect the conclusions of available research.

Most importantly, he adds, the Dane County, Wisconsin, community is beginning to recognize the cost of corporal punishment on children, families, and the larger communities—particularly as it affects racial disparity in the criminal justice system. For these reasons, it is imperative that the conversations continue, and that our communities continue to challenge themselves to adopt safer, healthier, more effective ways of parenting.

Ozanne wants parents everywhere to think about the risks associated with continued use of corporal punishment as a parenting strategy. "Consider how endorsing physical punishment, or simply failing to address it, results in children whose brain chemistry has been altered to pair love with violence; and that those children grow up to be adults who also pair love with violence and therefore are more likely to engage in, or become victims of, violent, assaultive behavior in the name of love."

He hopes that along with concerns about throwing another parent into the "system" and thereby adding to the racial disparities in criminal justice and child welfare, people will also reflect on how their decisions impact the children who may continue to be mistreated without meaningful "system" involvement.

"I hope that people will reflect on those situations where we do not address the parent's behavior because of these fears and concerns, so salient in our communities right now, but that they'll also think about the child who continues to experience physical punishment, and will be more likely to engage in aggressive and antisocial behaviors in the future. According to research, this child is now more likely to become a part of the very systems we're trying to prevent their parents from encountering."

10

SPARING THE ROD

Testimonies of Black Parents Who Stopped
Hitting or Never Whupped

Whupping children is so deeply entrenched into black culture that folks often won't have a rational conversation or be receptive to new information about the potential physical and psychological harms of hitting children. That's because when we were children, being whupped was presented to us in the context of "love" and "protection." As such, many folks' opinions and feelings about whuppings are based on their repression or forgetting what it was like to be a child. They've either repressed or forgotten the betrayal, pain, bewilderment, fear, resentment, sadness, and anger they felt while being on the receiving end of an adult hitting their body. They've turned pain into a positive. So when they talk about whuppings, there appears to be a sharp disconnect between what they likely experienced as a child and their staunch adult defense of the harmful practice.

The popular belief within black communities is that parents must whup their kids because there is no other model for disciplining and protecting them as they grow. The prevailing cultural view is that whupping is essential to keep our children safe, out of jail, or from falling prey to the dangers of the streets. Then there's the fact that a parent's self-image, ego, loyalty to his or her own parents, and allegiance to their culture and religion are tied to the core belief that black children require whuppings to grow up responsibly. Most black adults endorse hitting kids, believing that the violence helped them survive the racist perils facing black communities. These beliefs and the scars from their own experiences often keep black parents from objectively evaluating their parenting practices or even recognizing that there are nonviolent alternatives.

All the data tell us that the majority of black people endorse hitting kids. As my previous chapters indicate, that ubiquitous message to whup is reinforced over and over again by celebrities, athletes, ministers, political figures, educators, radio hosts, and comedians. Sadly, far too many of our children have come to expect the whuppings, to normalize the pain, and to believe that they deserve to be hit at home and at school. What has been missing from the national and community conversations are black parents who used to hit their children but have stopped, and those who have successfully raised children without ever whupping them. When this group is mentioned, many folks are quick to emphasize that not spanking doesn't work for all kids. "Some kids need a good whupping, and some don't," retorts that parent who dismisses all the data. But that implies that some children are so inherently "bad" and their behavior is so uncontrollable that physical violence is the only solution.

But what about the parents who don't or never hit their kids? If the popular logic holds true, then most or all of their children who haven't been beaten should be victims of police violence, locked up for criminal offenses, and have no hope of being healthy, happy, contributing members of society.

As you know, I'm not a parent. But even if I were, I would have only my own individual and very subjective experience to rely upon. So I conducted a survey of black parents from different backgrounds in two categories: those who used to spank their children but, for various reasons, have chosen to stop and utilize other forms of discipline and punishment; and those who have never hit their children.

What do these parents, whose voices are often bullied into silence and completely missing from the national and community conversation, have to say about whupping children? How do they respond to the accusations that they are irresponsible, negligent, and/or parenting like white people? How do they respond to peer pressure from family and friends who try to convince them that physical punishment is the only way?

In my survey, I asked whether these parents were hit and if so, by whom, how often, for what kinds of infractions, and whether objects were used. I asked how they felt about being physically punished, and whether being hit changed their behavior for the better, for the worse, or not at all. And then I asked about their experiences as parents. For the group who used to hit their kids but stopped, I asked what changed their minds, and how that impacted their relationships with their children. I also asked about the nonhitting methods of discipline and punishment that they use instead, and how effective those are proving to be. For parents who have never whupped, I asked what went into making that decision, and how they discipline and punish their children without hitting.

I sent surveys to a total of 132 black parents and 105 responded— 84 female and 21 male. Eighty-eight are African American, two Haitian, four Nigerian, seven Jamaican, and four are biracial. Just more than a quarter are in their forties; twenty are in their thirties; nine are in their fifties; and five are under age thirty. Forty-nine of the respondents grew up in the South, thirty-one in the North, seven on the West Coast, seven in the West Indies, five in the Midwest, four in Nigeria, and two in Canada. They come from diverse religious backgrounds, ranging from atheist to Muslim.

In terms of education, thirty-two respondents hold a bachelor of arts degree; sixteen hold a bachelor of science degree; twenty-two hold a master's degree; two hold a doctoral degree; twenty-seven have "some college"; and six are high school graduates. Ninety-eight of the respondents are employed. Fifty are married, including five in a same-sex marriage; forty-eight are single; and seven are divorced. Two respondents are adoptees.

The vast majority—ninety-seven—of people who responded were hit as children, and eight were not. Of those who were physically punished, fifty-nine said it took place often; thirty-one were spanked rarely; nine were spanked occasionally; and six were hit only once. Just twenty-one were struck with objects other than a hand: mostly belts, shoes, extension cords, and switches, and a few with paddles, brooms, combs, and other household items. Eleven of the respondents reported being bruised or injured from the whuppings.

The parents surveyed reported that they had been spanked for talking back, not completing chores, not caring for younger siblings, "acting grown," being disobedient, swearing, questioning authority, skipping school, losing objects, sneaking a boy into the house, being "mouthy," having a bad attitude, lying, stealing, getting bad grades, rolling eyes, breaking household items, running up the phone bill, acting up in school, talking in class, and coming home late. After being whupped, they reported that they had felt sad, angry, frustrated, scared of their parent, mad, and embarrassed. Some said the whupping made them better at not getting caught.

As for the impact of spanking on their behavior, sixty-nine said it had no impact, twenty-five said it worsened their behavior, and eleven said their behavior was "changed." Eighty-nine of the respondents said they harbored negative feelings toward those who spanked them.

As parents, eighty-six of the respondents have one child; thirteen have two; three have three; two have four, and one has six. Fifty-eight of their children are girls and forty-seven are boys. Seventy-two of the respondents have spanked their child(ren)—forty-nine at least once, ten occasionally, nine rarely, and four often. Just eight parents have used an object, such as a belt or sandal, to spank a child. They hit their children for not listening, for hitting them first, for slamming a door in the parent's face, and for poor performance at school, lying, stealing, poor grades, and talking back. After hitting their children, respondents said they cried, felt guilt and extreme remorse, were angry, "felt like an asshole," felt like they'd lost control, and reminded themselves of the parent who had hit them.

Black Parents Who Are Sparing the Rod

Alicia Chymel Reid
Age forty-two
Dublin, Georgia

"I VOWED THAT DAY TO FIND ANOTHER WAY."
Alicia Chymel Reid is the single parent of a twenty-year-old daughter and a thirteen-year-old son. When her daughter slammed her bedroom door in Reid's face while she was still talking to her, she spanked her daughter with her hand.

"In my mind, I saw her cowering in the corner when I raised my hand to her—the very same hand I had used to wipe her tears after a scraped knee. That broke me. The look of betrayal I saw on my daughter's face made me stop, midstrike, and leave the room. I felt ashamed and petty. I was angry at myself for not being the adult in the situation. I was sad because I hurt my daughter, the very person I had sworn to lay down my life for, and that led to confusion and frustration. I vowed that day to find another way."

The hardest part about not hitting her daughter anymore was grappling with her own emotional response. "I had to face my own childhood and the demons that still lingered in that closet. My mother refused and still refuses to acknowledge the pain and won't answer the 'whys.' So it was a journey I traveled alone. I read books and research studies. And once I let go of the pain from my past, it was easier to focus on raising my daughter my way and not the way others thought I should."

When loved ones and others criticized her choice to stop spanking, Reid said she "tried to explain at first. But as my confidence grew, I chose to stay away from them." Since she stopped spanking, Reid and her daughter have become closer. She replaced spanking with taking things away and denying special privileges. Most importantly, "We always talked about the consequences of the choices we were making." As a result, Reid says that her son and daughter are both "happy, healthy, and thriving. They both talk to me about any- and everything."

When talking with parents who insist upon spanking their children, Reid says she "tries to explain the damage they are inflicting upon their children for generations to come, but to no avail." Her takeaway is that she has learned "more about relationships and how—good or bad—they form us into the adults we become."

Robert Ellington
Age forty-five
Charleston, South Carolina

"SOME OF THE MOST TROUBLED CHILDREN I'VE SEEN HAD PARENTS WHO 'DIDN'T PLAY.'"

Robert Ellington is married and has a seven-year-old son whom he has "popped on the bottom on at least three occasions." His change of heart was motivated by his professional observations of children who'd been traumatized by physical punishment.

"Some of the most troubled children I've seen had parents who 'didn't play,'" he says. "I realized that I could discipline my son by taking away things like his tablet or video game time, and his behavior would change for the better. We also have a written contract that he's signed, and we go over the details weekly. He understands what the consequences will be if he doesn't do what's required. It seems to be working."

Natalie Lamb
Age forty-three
Palmdale, California

"WHEN MY EMOTIONS ARE OUT OF CONTROL, NO ONE IS STRIKING ME."

Natalie Lamb is a single parent of two daughters, ages fifteen and sixteen. She works as a financial manager at her father's church and runs her own counseling businesses where she teaches classes and seminars on all types of relationships. Her father spanked her just once as a child. This made her feel frightened.

Lamb admits that she has "a high tolerance for kids trying to figure things out. I refuse to hold my children to a higher standard than myself. When my emotions are out of control I can throw a tantrum or act out, yet no one is striking me. So I am sure that I can allow a much smaller, inexperienced child to figure their way through emotions."

Because there wasn't much hitting in her childhood, Lamb says it was never something she had to accept or make sense of. "I truly believe that children are to respected, and how we treat them becomes how they feel about themselves and how they treat others."

What does she do with her daughters? "I think that there are so many more effective ways of teaching and training how to be amazing humans. Teaching that whatever you feel, you must control how you act it out." She admits that this approach isn't always easy. "It takes time and patience—two factors that many parents lack, which is why they rely so heavily on hitting."

With parents who insist that spanking is necessary, Lamb encourages them to open their minds to other more effective disciplinary methods. "What I have noticed is that people either think you're practicing permissive parenting where you let your kids just do whatever they want, or authoritative parenting where the parent is the absolute role. Many don't understand that there is a middle ground, and boundaries that can be instilled without violence.

"Those parents that are for violence often fail to see the lack of teaching they are doing, and they fail to see the amount of harm that is being done. They refuse to look in the mirror, so that stops them from being brave enough to venture out into positive, respectable parenting with the future in mind instead of always just focusing on the right now."

She thinks that for a shift to happen, "parenting must be looked at through a wider lens. If you put parenting under the microscope, the fine details make it too hard for others to move away from their favorite go-to discipline. You broaden the lens and they start seeing relationships in a greater context. This helps with the shift that needs to happen."

Alyson Richardson
Age forty-five
Silicon Valley, California

"I THINK THEY CAN LEARN A DIFFERENT WAY OF BEING."
Alyson Richardson is a married, stay-at-home mother of five daughters. She says that her childhood spankings did not change her behavior; they "just made me hide it better." She tried spanking her kids a few times, but found that it made her feel tired. "I stopped because it wasn't helping, and it was making them hit their younger siblings." It also made her think of how her children were feeling at the time that an incident occurred, "and work harder to get them to express anger without hitting."

Instead of spanking them, she has open discussions with her children about how they might be feeling. "If they don't want to talk, we encourage them to use art to express themselves. We also ask them to see the other person's perspective. Rather than focusing on the idea of discipline, she says they "consider life lessons. We say that one way or the other, you'll get the lesson, either now or later." It seems to be working; she says her older children are now more oriented toward problem solving and are working to help their younger siblings to do the same.

To parents who insist upon spanking, Richardson shares that "spanking hasn't worked for us, and it typically doesn't work for most children. It only makes them hide who they really are. I think they can learn a different way of being and possibly heal old childhood wounds from having been whupped themselves."

Sylett M. H. Strickland
Age fifty-three
Allen, Texas

"NOT HITTING AND DEEP COMMUNICATION HAVE LED US TO REALLY GOOD OUTCOMES."

Sylett Strickland has hit her seventeen-year-old daughter just once—after the daughter, then a toddler, hit her first. Strickland says she "felt horrible and cried while I did it, knowing in my heart that I was doing it because I was frustrated."

She recognized that she had lost her cool by seeing her daughter's behavior as "disrespectful and needing to be extinguished. The second I hit her, I knew I was not in control." They already had a timeout chair and a cool-down area in place, and Strickland finds that has been effective. "She is a well-behaved young woman who thinks for herself and expresses her conflicts in a healthy and appropriate way."

Strickland says her own mother gives mixed signals about the topic of spanking. "She says in one breath that she wishes she had not spanked, then tells me I needed to spank my child for certain behaviors." She says she doesn't talk to pro-spanking parents about their discipline methods unless she is asked. "I tell them that the methods of not hitting and deep communication with the child have led us to really good outcomes. And though it requires more work on the part of the parents, my child does not fear me and I know that the compliance and behavior I get is because she understands and believes in the good behavior, not just because she is trying to avoid punishment."

Nicole Keenon
Age forty-two
Chicago, Illinois

"I SHOULDN'T HAVE TO HIT HER FOR HER TO RESPECT ME."
Nicole Keenon is the single mother of a twelve-year-old daughter whom she describes as "strong-willed and petulant." Keenon remembers that the first time she was spanked by her own mother was for wearing her mother's good high heels outside. The second time, she was caught sneaking a boy into the house. Being hit made her feel remorseful for the high-heels incident.

"When I snuck the boy in, I was ashamed that I got caught 'doing nothing.' I felt like I had lost my mother's trust, and that she saw me differently." As a result, she never sneaked out of the house again, with or without her mother's shoes, but she did sneak more boys into the house. "I just didn't get caught again."

Keenon says she spanked her daughter three times with a belt, but stopped three years ago. While thinking, "'I hope this helps straighten her out,' I also felt powerless, like my only recourse was whupping. It made me feel like a failure as a parent. I shouldn't have to hit her for her to respect me."

She feels better about her decision not to spank anymore. "I honestly just don't want to do it. I want to be able to reason with her. I don't want her to think conflict is solved with violence. And I definitely don't want her to think that being hit is normal."

Sean Hines Sr.
Age forty-three
Slidell, Louisiana

"TAKING AWAY THEIR GAMING DEVICES AND TV TIME SEEMS TO BE MORE PAINFUL THAN A BELT."
Sean Hines Sr. is a divorced single father of a thirteen-year-old son and a ten-year-old daughter. He used to spank them but stopped because he felt he could get the same or better results with a nonviolent approach.

Giving up spanking "wasn't as difficult as I thought it would be," he says. "It was just a matter of breaking that reflex response, taking time to view the entire situation and decide on a suitable course of action."

Once Hines stopped spanking, he found that his children were "easier to talk to, less afraid. That made it easier for me to educate them. They became more forthcoming with the truth." Instead of hitting, he administers discipline according to the violation. "Taking away their gaming devices and TV time seems to be more painful for them than a belt."

He says he "makes sure to talk to them afterwards, to make sure they understand why they were being punished, and how to avoid making the same mistakes over and over," and says that this approach is very effective.

Sherice Monique Dunham
Age forty
Decatur, Georgia

"I REALIZED HE WAS DEALING WITH SOME ISSUES THAT INVOLVED THE ABSENCE OF HIS FATHER."

Sherice Monique Dunham is a single mother of a thirteen-year-old son, whom she has spanked for lying and stealing from her. "I was pissed. To have him stealing from me was the ultimate betrayal," she says. That was the last time she spanked him.

Now that her son is getting ready to start high school, Dunham says that instead of spanking, she tries to "talk to him more and explain that his actions aren't going to be beneficial to him in the long run, especially being a black male in today's volatile society."

The transition to other methods of discipline wasn't difficult, she says. "After the stealing incident, I realized that he was dealing with some issues that involved the absence of his father. I reached out to my friend who had experienced the same dilemma with her son when he was the same age. Whereas before she would beat him across the butt with a belt, "Now I just take all electronics away from him. He also plays baseball so I will make him run extra laps or sit him out for the first couple of innings. Baseball is his lifeline so taking that from him is like slitting his wrists!"

Dunham feels her new methods of discipline are working. "He recognizes that I am bat-shit crazy and have absolutely no problem embarrassing him wherever and whenever." She says she is still dealing with some lying and sneakiness on her son's part, which causes her to yell and curse at him more than she did when she was spanking him. "I keep telling him that there is nothing he can do in this house that I won't know about. I've tried to explain to him that it is imperative to always tell the truth, no matter if he thinks he's going to get in trouble or not."

Sherri Moore
Age forty-one
Philadelphia, Pennsylvania

"I KNOW HOW HARD IT IS TO BE A CHILD."
Sherri Moore is an academic dean and the married lesbian mother of a fourteen-year-old son and a twelve-year-old daughter. As a child, she hated being spanked to the point of having welts and a busted lip, and was upset that both her mom's boyfriend and her dad's wife were allowed to hit her and her siblings.

"Being spanked made me angry and made me hate the person who was spanking me, at least for the moment," she says. "I have a deep gut hatred for my mom's boyfriend, and I even disliked my dad's wife for a while."

Moore spanked her daughter for lying to her and her son for using her credit card to download games on his Xbox. "I'm sure there were other 'pops' along the way. Writing this just makes me sad because I can see how I have minimized it by saying 'pops,' even though hitting a child will always be hitting a child."

She says that spanking her children made her feel sad. She would cry before and after the spankings. About a year ago, she stopped the practice because she didn't see the added value of hitting. She never relied solely upon spanking and has always utilized other methods including timeouts; taking away their laptops, allowance, and television privileges; and verbal lessons. "It was easy to remove the physical punishment because I saw that it was truly ineffective for what the intended purpose was in my head, and extremely detrimental to the children. It invoked fear, and having been in an abusive relationship that my children observed, I knew that I didn't want to be a villain in my children's eyes."

Moore stopped spanking altogether when she "woke up and realized that it was detrimental and nonessential." The process wasn't difficult, since the spankings had been "very few and far between."

She endured heavy criticism for her choices. Many people viewed her children as "white" because they were given timeouts and never beaten. Her family criticized her when she didn't beat her daughter for drawing all over the walls of their home. "Insanity!" she says. "I don't entertain their opinions. I don't see the added value of beating children. Instead, I purchased chalkboard paint and repainted the house and allowed her to be as creative as she wanted to be. I believe in nurturing children and learning from them. I think people begin to fail their children by trying too hard to teach them 'how' to be. Raising kids is extremely difficult, but I also know how hard it is to be a child."

Moore thinks parents who insist upon spanking their children "need to understand the history of this form of abuse. They need to see that children like mine are still the same as they were before I made the decision not to hit them anymore. They are still good kids; beatings have no influence on who they become."

Apryl Felder
Age thirty-three
Atlanta, Georgia

"WHAT WORKS IS WHEN PEOPLE CAN SEE THE FRUIT OF YOUR LABOR."

Apryl Felder is the mother of two sons, ages ten and four. Growing up in South Carolina, she was spanked both at home and at school, where she was the only black student. "Paddling singled me out even further and was intensely humiliating," she says, especially since many of the other children's parents were nonspankers. She said that childhood spankings made her more compliant out of self-preservation. "I'm not entirely certain, as I wasn't a noncompliant child in the first place. In the long run I learned to avoid the pain of punishment by becoming a better storyteller and building strong but perhaps invisible walls between my mother and I, which were motivated by fear."

She says she was spanked mostly for issues related to communication, such as rationalizing behaviors aloud, rebutting adults, asking adults "uncomfortable questions," and lying. "In school, I was paddled for accidentally hitting a friend with a small woodchip and giggling about excrement in a nursing home. Occasionally, mediocre grades could land a spanking."

Felder says she spent years being upset with her mother, "not so much because she caused me intentional pain, but because it seemed to me as though she celebrated the pain and refused to validate my narrative." She describes her relationship with her mother as "strong, despite the spankings. Beyond the few angry years during which I regularly confronted her about the ethical treatment of children, we've been close friends. She has also come to understand my pain, and while she may never fully admit to it, I believe that she's mostly in agreement with me about spanking."

Felder whupped her own children due to experiencing "a loss of control and feeling threatened, coupled with intense frustration stemming from not knowing what else to do in the moment. Hundreds of parenting books and articles in, and I was still at a loss in those moments. Like many parents, I don't remember what my son was up to at the time," she remembers with a grimace.

Treating her children this way left Felder feeling "angry and deflated." Though in one case she had only smacked her son's hand, "I felt as though I'd violated his space and his body in a way I never wanted."

Her decision to stop hitting altogether was made before she became a mother. "But because hitting is deeply ingrained in my family's collective unconscious and socially acceptable—even encouraged—across the board, I struggled during my eldest son's toddlerhood. There were times of deep insecurity and loneliness and times when I wondered if the pro-spanking paradigms were true and if I was doing my son a disservice by not spanking."

Since both of Felder's parents and her in-laws "insisted that spanking was proper and necessary," she found that turning to other nonspanking parents for support was "key." And she has raised her children "to understand that spanking is wrong. And although he was young when I smacked his hand, my son was quick to call me out on my hypocrisy. I apologized both times and we rebonded over conversation about forgiveness, obedience, emotional control, and truthfulness." Today, she says, "most discipline in my home is centered around empathy, validation, communication, logical consequences, and reconciliation. Every now and then the Wii gets nabbed or someone ends up sitting it out for a few minutes."

Felder notes the ups and downs of her approach. "I'm proud of my boys. They're both highly intelligent and very well-behaved children. My eldest son's teachers have always considered him to be exceptionally empathetic, kind, and thoughtful. My youngest son is quite different in personality, but he's also exceptionally loving towards others and he places a very high value on social cohesion.

"The entire truth is, having no fear of your parents makes some children especially prone to brutal honesty in the form of unfiltered emotional displays and behaviors behind closed doors. It can be exhausting, even when your children who are generally compliant. Sometimes my kids have meltdowns that I never would have dreamed of having in front of my mother! Sometimes they say things, not altogether awful things but just mouthy things that would have had me fearing for my personal safety. So overall, nonpunitive discipline in my home has been largely effective, but setting strong boundaries in nontraditional, creative ways becomes all the more important."

When she encounters parents who spank, she says she is more inclined to want to help them than to tell them that they're wrong, which she found to be ineffective. "What works is when people can see the fruit of your labor. When they remark how well-behaved and loving your children are, which often leads to conversations around discipline, and then you tell them that you don't spank and never have. That's enormous. Even better, when you can offer parents working alternatives, most are willing to bite."

Felder notes that, "Although many people brag about hitting their children, spanking (giving and receiving) is loaded with complex emotions like shame and anxiety. Not spanking requires so much of a person: a willingness to break tradition, the emotional wherewithal to self-soothe in what feels like crisis, the intellectual ability to find

and implement alternative disciplinary practices, ethical commitment, emotional intelligence, sleep, a long-range vision for the overall
well-being of one's children, and most of all, social support."

———

Dawnnesha Wilcher Lasuncet
Age forty
Beaverton, Oregon

"NO BEAT THE BABIES. HUG THE BABIES!"
Dawnnesha Lasuncet has a fifteen-year-old son and six-year-old daughter. She spanked her son a few times but stopped in part because of
studies she'd read about how corporal punishment affects the brain.
"I watched my son's memory issues and ways that he dealt with adversity. My brother has memory issues and other anger indicators as an
adult, and I didn't want to perpetuate that," she says.

"I know it has to do with being spanked by my father. My own
resentments and anger issues are something that I don't want my
children to carry with them as they grow. I also don't want them to
correlate love with physical violence and it just doesn't make sense
to hit children to show them the 'right way.' We don't tolerate it in
adulthood."

At first, giving up spanking wasn't easy. Lasuncet said she has tried
"love and logic," but found that she began yelling more. "My daughter calls me 'Yellie Mom,' which I hate and don't want to be. My anger
issues are still there and have manifested themselves in verbally abusive ways now. I read more articles and books on child development so
that I can understand the impacts of my behavior management techniques and where my kids are cognitively.

"It's tough. But I have completely made the shift in terms of believing that hitting solves problems or teaches. It doesn't. My mother still
believes that she can 'pop' my daughter when she sees her. We disagree
often on this."

Lasuncet says she now uses such methods as "timeouts, evil eyes,
raised voice, and minimizing screen time or access to technology" instead of spanking. "My husband and I also like to be proactive now.
We engage with our kids in ways that let them know that we have the

right to be upset when they lie or disobey us, but we will celebrate when they do the right stuff often enough and that mistakes don't warrant big blowups."

She sees a change in her relationship with her son. "He seems more at ease at home. He is also having to learn to stand up for himself as a young man, something he couldn't do before. He has been bullied often, and I know now that it's because he was also being physically hurt at home and wasn't empowered in any space. That saddens me to know that my parenting toolbox was lean and I depended on something that really hurt his capacity to grow and strengthen himself."

Overall, she says that her children are responding well. "Even with grumblings in the background, this speaks volumes about what works for us. We have loving, happy, and charismatic kiddos. I like being around them and people enjoy having them around. I think it's been going well.

When her best friend, whom she describes as "incredibly religious, and her husband believes in the belt," threatened her youngest children with '. . . or else y'all are gonna get beat,'" Lasuncet said, 'No, no. No beat the babies. Hug the babies.' She laughed and we moved on. I find that dropping little gems rather than sweeping judgments . . . work best with her. I know if they both stopped and looked at their own children's development and personal struggles in school and with others, they might be open to hearing how spanking contributes to the problem. It's still a work in progress."

Abby Fernanda Dottin
Age forty-eight
Hollis, Queens, New York

"IT DOESN'T MAKE SENSE TO ME
THAT HITTING TEACHES LESSONS."

Abby Dottin has never felt the need to spank her fourteen-year-old daughter. "Beating a child sends a message that it's okay to hit and to be hit. Unfortunately, I've seen too many instances where black folks settled problems with their hands instead of using their brains to problem solve. I want my daughter to know and understand when to physically defend herself but also know that she has to be smart and intelligent to defend herself with 'snark,' at times."

Dottin was not spanked as a child. "When I would see a friend or family member spank, I would step in and stop them, and then pull the child aside for comfort and then speak to the adult. Sometimes I was met with a 'Mind yo business' response. Other times, they would calm down and 'seem' to understand my point of view."

Dottin says she tells pro-spanking parents "that you cannot expect a child to learn without talking to them and appealing to their need to understand why what they did was 'wrong.' Beating the child only makes them fear the parent and maybe teaches them not to do something as instructed, but only because they are in fear of the pain they will receive."

She is passionate about how she disciplines her daughter. "It is way more important for me to allow my child to articulate when she's feeling wronged or upset, and for me to explain why she isn't allowed to do something so that she understands. I am not trying to inflict bodily harm to my child, who is the most precious thing to me. I won't stand by and allow anyone else to, either. I can't wrap my head around, listening to my daughter maybe say a curse word and me swelling up her lip with a backhand. It doesn't make sense to me that hitting teaches lessons."

Monifa Colón
Age forty
Columbia, South Carolina

"WE SHOULDN'T BE TARNISHING THEIR GOOD NATURE WITH VIOLENCE."

Monifa Colón, a single mom of an eight-year-old girl and a five-year-old boy, suffered from being physically disciplined as a child "for just about anything—moving too fast, moving too slowly, talking too much, not talking enough, laughing too loudly, eating, not wanting the food I was served, spilling something, grumbling about doing some work that wasn't my responsibility. The boys in our family could make all the messes they wanted; the girls were expected to clean up after them. If we didn't? Beatings.

"My mom would hit me for any random reason under the sun. I think she'd still assault me if she thought she could win. She was most fond of accusing me of 'talking back,' then hitting me in the mouth or the face. When I got older, she would run at me with her forearm and try to hit me in the back of the neck or in the face."

As a result, she grew to distrust adults and "be fake around them or avoid being noticed entirely. It still makes me angry, and I still wish I could square up with my mom and her family," she says. "I'm glad some of them are dead so they can't hurt anyone else."

She spanked her daughter once, in an unusually stressful situation, and was "mortified. We had a long talk about how I was wrong and how I really needed a cooling-off period instead of going there." Making the change wasn't difficult, she says, but it required her to be more honest with her children. "I think it's more helpful for them to hear me tell them why I'm upset than striking them because I'm upset. I'm not here to terrorize them. They're smart kids and they can hear me when I talk to them. They know they frustrate me sometimes, and I frustrate them sometimes. We work on being emotionally honest. If they're not feeling me, they're allowed that space away from me. If I'm in a mood, they give me room. We try to respect boundaries and if any of us get angry, we give the angry person space to process how they're feeling so they can discuss it.

"It's not even a fair fight to hit a child so I get pretty disgusted at the idea of it. I'm blown away by how forgiving they are, but I also work hard at not doing things they have to forgive. I think the journey is really about acknowledging that they're little people who are learning and growing, and I don't have the right to do harm to them because I'm angry or frustrated. The world is hard enough. I have to be their safe space—even when they're saying or doing things that bother me. I have to be the adult."

Her approach to discipline requires her to "think about what works for each child. My daughter loves to read and draw. If she misbehaves, she loses her book or her art privileges. My son loves to be around people. Putting him in timeout sends the message to him that he really took things too far. When their punishments are done, we talk about what we can all do to not repeat the negative behavior. Sometimes they get in trouble because they're looking for attention from me, and

I don't have it to give. So, I'm working on structuring my time so that they get enough of me to feel secure. As their interests evolve, my hope is that they'll value the things they enjoy enough to model the behavior that allows them to continue enjoying those things."

She feels these methods of discipline work for her kids. "They seem okay with it." With those who might pressure her to spank, she makes it clear that there is a "hands-off" policy with her kids. "I also teach my children to assert themselves when it comes to people being in their personal space," she says. "There are some adults who really get angry that my children aren't fearful of adults. But they don't have to be. I don't want them to feel they have to respect any person who is being disrespectful to them."

As a community, Colón thinks that, "parents really need to challenge ourselves to be better than how we were raised. There's no lesson learned by being violent with children. I think parents who spank need to understand that children are resilient and forgiving and loving—but we shouldn't be tarnishing their good nature with violence. Those resentments manifest in a host of ways. I wonder sometimes whether I'd have chosen an abusive partner if I'd never equated some form of violence with love. What seems small to the person doing the spanking has a ripple effect that changes the trajectory of a child's life."

Tanisha Penn Moore
Age thirty-seven
Tulsa, Oklahoma

"WE TREAT KIDS LIKE THEY DON'T HAVE FEELINGS."
Tanisha Moore, who grew up in the projects in St. Thomas in the US Virgin Islands, is the mother of two boys, ages fifteen and eleven. She spanked her sons a few times but stopped entirely when the oldest was nine and he was diagnosed with dyslexia; the youngest was four at the time. She wanted to break the cycle of violence that she experienced as a child.

"I was hit in the head with the receiver from a rotary dial phone, a saucer, and a tree branch, not a switch. I was also beat with wire hangers and extension cords," she says. Her mother mostly punished her, but schoolteachers also hit her. "Teachers were brutal at my school. Wooden paddles were used on all parts of the body. Arms, legs, calves, back. . . . Once when I was ten, I stole twenty dollars from my mom. She beat me with a belt for what seemed like hours. I was unable to walk without pain for a few days. I had welts all over my body. That was the worst beating that I ever received."

That beating and the others didn't change her behavior, she says. "It just made me see my teachers and my mother as vicious, uncaring people."

So when she started hitting her sons, she realized that she was doing the same thing to them that was done to her. "I wanted to raise them differently. I knew spankings didn't work on me so chances are they wouldn't work on them."

Instead of hitting, Moore uses the following tactics: lecturing, making them spend time alone, taking away privileges, airing her concerns, making them write essays about their behavior, extra chores, and letting her sons tell her what they will do to rectify the situation. When conversations over whupping come up with other parents, she says, "I just tell folks that spanking doesn't help the situation. I believe black folks, American and Caribbean, want children to behave like adults. We treat kids like nonentities, like they don't have feelings. They only know one way to parent and to go against it means that they would have to admit that some parts of how they were parented weren't the best. To do this would mean that they would have to change their narrative of how they were treated as kids."

Evelyn Alvarez
Age forty
New York, New York

"WE DON'T RESPECT CHILDHOOD IN THIS COUNTRY."

Evelyn Alvarez, a trainer for a youth development organization and a doula who assists parents who have lost custody of their children and then become pregnant again, believes that spanking doesn't help. She is a single mom of an eleven-year-old son. Making the shift from hitting was somewhat of a challenge, she says.

"Before I had a kid, I worked in schools, and here are some things I told myself I wouldn't do when I became a parent. Then I fucked up and did them anyway, and really had to assess myself and my actions," she says. "The beatings started when I found myself a single mama, grieving my old relationship and feeling kind of hopeless. I was just so, so, so mad. So mad and sad and not really having support. The support I did have was old-school and not interested in letting kids be kids. Then I had a life-changing conversation with a friend who said to me, 'We don't respect childhood in this country.'"

That conversation was so powerful that it changed Alvarez's thinking. "I started to really aim to respect his childhood. Beating his ass for minor infractions did not fit in that space, so I stopped. It wasn't hard. What is hard is finding alternative ways to stop, to explain, to develop patience, to build relationships, to teach with peace."

Alvarez says she gets the "usual bullshit" from other parents who criticize her for not hitting her son. "Spare the rod . . . yada, yada, yada . . . ain't nobody here for that. My son, my rules. As a parent trainer, when I hear parents swear by whupping kids, I ask, 'How many here were whupped by parents?' Most will raise their hands. Then I ask, 'How many were whupped twice?' Most raise their hands. Then I say, "So then maybe it's not that effective. If it were, we'd only have to get beaten once to get the message.""

We have seen over and over again the devastating costs of centuries of abuse inside deeply wounded families and communities. But there is hope.

There are many black families who have decided to emancipate themselves from this legacy of violence and raise their children free of fear, pain, and intimidation. Their stories show that black children raised without whuppings and fear can flourish. Rooting out violence in all forms—from our families, schools, and communities—is an essential step to challenging racist devaluation.

The work will be hard work. It will try your patience. But as the parents in this chapter have shown, confronting the past and their painful childhood memories has helped transform their own child-rearing practices. They have taken the difficult step of breaking with an awful history and rejecting the popular lie that whupping our children will save black families and communities. Their stories show us that we don't have to be prisoners of our history. We can free ourselves one family, one child at a time. And when we exorcise the pain and rage, we will discover that other emotions and liberating possibilities will spring forward.

Acknowledgments

I was so blessed to have an endless stream of support during my nine-month journey writing this book.

The first person I need to thank is one of my "village mothers," Ta-Ressa Stovall. In late September 2014 she called me while I was at the airport waiting to catch a flight from New York City back to Washington, DC. I had just appeared on the *Melissa Harris-Perry* show and had an intense week of back-to-back radio and television appearances surrounding the Adrian Peterson child abuse controversy. I was tired and coming down with a case of bronchitis. My voice was literally starting to sound like Marlon Brando's in *The Godfather*. All I wanted to do was sleep.

"Just hear me out," TaRessa pleaded. "I've been watching all of your interviews and rereading many of the pieces you've written over the years on child abuse in black communities. You need to bring all of this together in a book!"

I gave my cell phone a side-eye and reminded her that I had already written a memoir about child abuse when I was in my twenties. Not to mention I was being cussed out and dragged through the Internet streets for my antispanking stance expressed during my media interviews. The thought of writing another book about violence against children made me feel weak. After about twenty minutes of pitching the idea, TaRessa finally convinced me that my work was not yet finished. So I put together a proposal but then set it aside because life got busy.

Flash-forward to July 2015.

My literary agent, Faith Childs, introduced me to Rakia Clark, a young, brilliant, and striving editor from Beacon Press who had been following my journalistic work over the years. During our initial conversation we reflected on how the urgency of this book was being pushed by the Adrian Peterson and "Baltimore Mom" stories and the growing movement for black lives, which was all being played out on a very public stage. Suddenly, in the national and international press and on social media, people were talking about the intersections between race and parenting in America.

The time was now. And so the journey of this book began.

I initially wanted to write a book that I wish someone would have given to my adoptive parents before I entered their home. But as I got deeper into the research, interviews, and writings it became clear to me that I needed to keep black children central to my mission. I wanted to write a book that could potentially save other children from the abuse I experienced. Even if just one child is saved then this journey will have been worth it.

I am extremely grateful to Rakia for finding me, for choosing me as a client, for acquiring this book, for bringing further clarity to the mission, for her humor, for letting me cry on the phone during her shopping trip to West Elm, for gracefully handling all of our intense debates over this hot-button issue, and for her patient guidance shepherding this heartfelt project to a worthy conclusion.

Writing this book was more challenging than I initially expected it to be. Not only because it brought up some painful emotions, but also because I was writing this as a journalist, historian, activist, and child-abuse survivor. I had to figure out how to synthesize all four of those perspectives with enough rigor to satisfy each: Emotionally satisfying for the survivor. Politically satisfying for the activist. Intellectually satisfying for the historian. And I needed enough viable data and flesh and blood stories to satisfy the journalist.

A number of people showed me love and intellectual support that pushed me to make nuanced arguments: David Leonard (my academic boo), Angela Jackson-Brown, Mark Naison, Dorothy Roberts, Kera Bolonik, Malkia Cyril, Toby Rollo, Kenneth Wright-Vazquez, Cynthia Liu, Deborah Hill, Nadine Bean, Lisa Fontes, Kirsten West-Savali (my brain's boo), Denene Millner, and Noliwe Rooks. I also need to pay homage to the work of Nell Irvin Painter, whose critical work "Soul Murder and Slavery" inspired me to ask deeper questions about the lasting psychological impact of slavery on African Americans, particularly abusive child-rearing practices.

I need to thank Audrey June-Williams for all the laughter and for the trove of "bourgie" chocolate that gave me fuel, Valerie Boyd for our random chats and her insightful lessons on empathy, and Dr. Tanya Greenfield for breathing life back into me each time the writing process got me down and for reminding me that joy matters!

I want to say thank you to my nearly thirty thousand Facebook followers who took this journey with me. They listened to my incessant rants over corporal punishment. They engaged in lively debates—"wig snatching"—on my page. I want to thank the folks who shared their personal testimonies and participated in my surveys and interviews. Thanks to those who sent me visual images, links to study after study on the negative impact of corporal punishment on children, and heart-wrenching videos of children being shamed and mistreated. It's not too often that writers get to bring thousands of people along with them as they begin and end a book journey. I certainly have never seen this happen through social media. It was quite a lively experiment.

I'd like to thank a few folks at Beacon Press: Helene Atwan, who was a big champion for the book early on. Ayla Zuraw-Friedland, who kept me on schedule and handled a lot of the important little things. My excellent publicist, Pamela MacColl. The production team: Marcy Barnes, Beth Collins, Susan Lumenello, and Daniel Barks. Tom Hallock in sales, Alyssa Hassan in marketing, and Bob Kosturko for designing a beautiful cover for this book.

And lastly, I need to acknowledge my adoptive mother. Though you have scarred my body for life, thankfully I am not devoted to being a victim. I now understand all the reasons why you hurt me. You may have dished out all those whuppings onto my body, but I know they did not originate with you. This does not create an excuse for the harm you caused. But without your cruel "loving" hands I would not have written this book. The eight years I spent in your home were part of an otherworldly spiritual agreement made between us long before we came to Earth. You did not kill me. And I grew up to do this work. For that, there is no more anger, and there is nothing to forgive.

Reader's Guide

1. *Spare the Kids* includes a lot of scientific research on the long-term, negative effects of whuppings on children (i.e., early puberty, low IQ, aggressive behavior and delinquency, depression, drug and alcohol abuse, obesity, diabetes, and even cancer). How does this information influence your opinion and approach to child-rearing? Will the science ever outweigh the cultural tradition?

2. The history of hitting black children links directly to American slavery and the practice of overseers beating slaves with a whip to get them to submit and obey orders. The whip evolved to the belt and later to household items like shoes, purse straps, hangers, and kitchen utensils. How does the origin story affect your outlook, if at all?

3. Many people argue that there's a difference between "spanking" and "abuse," and they often call hitting by different names: "pop," "whup," "beat," "spank," etc. Does the language change how you view the action? Do you believe a child can make a distinction? If so, how?

4. *Spare the Kids* centralizes the child as a victim of physical punishment inflicted by parents, guardians, and trusted caretakers. How does "centralizing the child" fit with your own ideas about the role of children in society? Are they to be seen and not heard?

5. Do children have any right to their own physical bodies? If so, at what age? And if not, to whom and in what spaces do they relinquish these rights?

6. If you were whupped as a child, what were your thoughts about your own experience while you read this book?

7. In your estimation, is any type of physical discipline of a child ever appropriate? Is it okay to remove a child from his or her home because he or she was hit?

8. Do you agree that the black church has played a significant role in promoting corporal punishment in black families? Is that role positive or negative? Is that role changing?

9. The overwhelming majority of Americans in prison received whuppings as children. How does that connect to the cultural mythology that whupping kids at home keeps them out of trouble?

10. Did anything you read in *Spare the Kids* change your opinion about the value of whupping children? If so, what changed your mind?

11. Did you strongly disagree with any parts of the book? If so, which parts?

12. Social media outlets have become a common place to see videos and images of children being chastised by their parents for misbehaving. Could this kind of punishment be considered a form of cyber-bullying?

13. Think about the most effective discipline you received from your parent as a child and the most effective discipline you've administered as a parent. How do they compare? What accounts for the differences, if any?

14. What tactics might be a good alternative to physical punishment?

———

For alternatives to physical discipline, please visit
www.sparethekids.com.

Notes

CHAPTER 1: A FAMILY CONVERSATION

1. W. E. B. Du Bois, "Of the Giving of Life," *Crisis* 4, no. 6 (October 1912): 287.

2. Candace Bond-Theriault, "Violence Against the Black Community Gives Me Fear About Becoming a Black Mom," *The Grio*, February 12, 2016, http://thegrio.com/2016/02/12/violence-against-black-community-fea r-becoming-black-mom/; Assita Camara, "I'm a Young Childless, Black Woman and I'm Afraid to Have a Black Son," *XOJane*, March 7, 2014, http://www.xojane.com/issues/im-a-young-childless-black-woman-and -im-afraid-to-have-a-black-son; Monica Simpson, "Considering Motherhood and Murdered Black Children," *Ebony*, August 18, 2015, http:// www.ebony.com/life/considering-motherhood-and-murdered-black -children-503#axzz4CdBvvFrj; Attica Scott, "A Mother's Fear for Her Black Son," *Courier-Journal* (Louisville, KY), August 11, 2014, http:// www.courier-journal.com/story/opinion/contributors/2014/08/11/mothers -fear-black-son/13905957/; Stereo Williams, "Sandra Bullock's Fear for Her Black Son," *The Daily Beast*, October 7, 2015, http://www .thedailybeast.com/articles/2015/10/07/sandra-bullock-s-fears-for-her -black-son.html; Michael Fitzgerald, "I'm a White Dad Afraid for My Black Sons," *Boston Globe*, August 11, 2015, https://www.bostonglobe .com/magazine/2015/08/11/parenting-while-white-afraid-for-black-sons /FFljQduvjNmesY51OR9eiN/story.html; Kera Bolonik, "White Mothers of Black Sons Are Terrified of Darren Wilson, Too," *DAME*, November 25, 2014, http://www.damemagazine.com/2014/11/25/white-mothers -black-sons-are-terrified-darren-wilson-too.fa.

3. US Department of Education Office for Civil Rights, Civil Rights Data Collection: Data Snapshot (School Discipline), March 21, 2014, http:// ocrdata.ed.gov/Downloads/CRDC-School-Discipline-Snapshot.pdf.

4. Phillip Atiba Goff et al., "The Essence of Innocence: Consequences of Dehumanizing Black Children," *Journal of Personality and Social Psychology* 106, no. 4 (2014): 526–45.

5. Tanzina Vega, "Schools' Discipline for Girls Differ by Race and Hue," *New York Times*, December 10, 2014, http://www.nytimes.com/2014 /12/11/us/school-discipline-to-girls-differs-between-and-within-races.html.

6. M. K. Goyal et al., "Racial Disparities in Pain Management of Children with Appendicitis in Emergency Departments," *JAMA Pediatrics* 169, no. 11 (2015): 996–1002, doi:10.1001/jamapediatrics.2015.1915; Matteo Forgiarini, Marcello Gallucci, and Angelo Maravita, "Racism and the Empathy for Pain on Our Skin," *Frontiers in Psychology* 2 (2011): 108, PMC, June 25, 2016.

7. Erin Schumaker, "Suicide Among Elementary-Age Black Children Is on the Rise," *Huffington Post*, May 20, 2015, http://www.huffingtonpost .com/2015/05/20/increased-suicide-among-black-children_n_7313720.html.

8. Joy DeGruy, *Post Traumatic Slave Syndrome: America's Legacy of Enduring Injury and Healing* (Portland, OR: Uptone Press, 2005).

9. Tori Rodriguez, "Descendants of Holocaust Survivors Have Altered Stress Hormones," *Scientific American*, March 1, 2015, http://www .scientificamerican.com/article/descendants-of-holocaust-survivors-have -altered-stress-hormones/.

10. Akemi Tomoda et al., "Reduced Prefrontal Cortical Gray Matter Volume in Young Adults Exposed to Harsh Corporal Punishment," *NeuroImage* 47, Suppl. 2 (2009): 66–71, PMC, June 3, 2016.

11. Elizabeth T. Gershoff, "Spanking and Child Development: We Know Enough Now to Stop Hitting Our Children," *Child Development Perspectives* 7, no. 3 (2013): 133–37, PMC, June 3, 2016; Fengling Ma et al., "To Lie or Not to Lie? The Influence of Parenting and Theory-of-Mind Understanding on Three-Year-Old Children's Honesty," *Journal of Moral Education* 44, no. 2 (2015): 198–212; Alan King, "Violent Experiences Questionnaire Predictors of Low Base-Rate Aggressive Acts," *Journal of Aggression, Maltreatment & Trauma* 23, no. 8 (2014): 804–22; Elizabeth T. Gershoff, "Should Parents' Physical Punishment of Children Be Considered a Source of Toxic Stress That Affects Brain Development?" *Family Relations* 65, no. 1 (2016): 151–62, doi: 65:10.1111/fare.2016.65.issue-1; Christina Barrasso-Catanzaro and Paul J. Eslinger, "Neurobiological Bases of Executive Function and Social-Emotional Development: Typical and Atypical Brain Changes," *Family Relations* 65, no. 1 (2016): 108–19, doi: 65:10.1111/ fare.2016.65.issue-1; Patrick J. Fowler et al., "Housing Mobility and Cognitive Development: Change in Verbal and Nonverbal Abilities," *Child Abuse & Neglect* 48 (2015): 104–18; Christopher J. Ferguson, "Spanking, Corporal Punishment, and Negative Long-Term Outcomes: A Meta-Analytic Review of Longitudinal Studies," *Clinical Psychology Review* 33 (2013): 196–208; Jennifer E. Lansford et al., "Forms of Spanking and Children's Externalizing Behaviors," *Family Relations* 61,

no. 2 (2012): 224–36, doi: 61:10.1111/fare.2012.61.issue-2; Victoria Talwar and Kang Lee, "A Punitive Environment Fosters Children's Dishonesty: A Natural Experiment," *Child Development* 82, no. 6 (2011): 1751–58, doi: 82:10.1111/cdev.2011.82.issue-6; Victoria Talwar, Stephanie M. Carlson, and Kang Lee, (2011) "Effects of a Punitive Environment on Children's Executive Functioning: A Natural Experiment," *Social Development* 20, no. 4 (2011): 805–24, 20:doi: 10.1111/sode.2011.20.issue-4, pages; M. J. MacKenzie et al., "Corporal Punishment and Child Behavioural and Cognitive Outcomes Through 5 Years of Age: Evidence from a Contemporary Urban Birth Cohort Study," *Infant Child Development* 21 (2012): 3–33.

12. US Department of Health and Human Services, Administration for Children and Families, Administration on Children, Youth, and Families, Children's Bureau, *The AFCARS Report: Preliminary Fiscal Year 2014 Estimates as of July 2014* (Washington, DC, July 2014).

13. Franklin Law Group, "Over-Medication of Psychotropic Drugs & African-American Girls in Foster Care," submission to the United Nations Convention Against Torture and Other Cruel, Inhumane or Degrading Treatment or Punishment, Fifty-Third Session, November 3–28, 2014.

14. Peter Breggin, "The Psychiatric Drugging of America's Foster Children," Citizens Commission on Human Rights International, May 28, 2014, http://www.cchrint.org/2014/05/29/psychiatric-drugging-of-americas-foster-children; Mark Abdelmalek et al., "New Study Shows US Government Fails to Oversee Treatment of Foster Children With Mind-Altering Drugs," ABC News, November 30, 2011, http://abcnews.go.com/US/study-shows-foster-children-high-rates-prescription-psychiatric/story?id=15058380; Brinda Adhikari, Joan Martelli, and Sarah Koch, "Doctors Put Foster Care Children at Risk With Mind-Altering Drugs," ABC News, December 1, 2011, http://abcnews.go.com/Health/doctors-put-foster-children-risk-mind-altering-drugs/story?id=15064560; "Foster Kids Prescribed Psychotropic Drugs," ABC News, December 2, 2011, http://abcnews.go.com/2020/video/foster-kids-prescribed-psychotropic-drugs-heavy-duty-drug-treatments-neglect-2020-15077792; "Efforts to Address Psychotropic Medications and Foster Youth in California Pick Up Speed," *National Center for Youth Law Newsletter* 31, no. 4 (October–December 2012), http://www.youthlaw.org/publications/efforts-to-address-psychotropic-medications-and-foster-youth-in-california-pick-up-speed/; Rick Nauert, "Child's Mental Health Diagnosis Influenced by Ethnicity," *PsychCentral*, May 20, 2008, http://psychcentral.com/news/2008/05/20/childs-mental-health-diagnosis-influenced-by-ethnicity/2317.html.

15. Peter J. Pecora et al., *Improving Family Foster Care: Findings from the Northwest Foster Care Alumni Study*, revised ed. (Seattle: Casey Family

Programs, March 14, 2005), http://www.casey.org/media/AlumniStudies
_NW_Report_FR.pdf; Mark E. Courtney et al., "Midwest Evaluation
of the Adult Functioning of Former Foster Youth: Outcomes at Age 19,"
working paper, Chapin Hall Center for Children, University of Chicago,
May 2005, 22, 61, https://www.chapinhall.org/sites/default/files
/ChapinHallDocument_4.pdf; Mark E. Courtney, Jennifer L. Hook, and
Jung-Sook Lee, "Distinct Subgroups of Former Foster Youth During the
Transition to Adulthood: Implications for Policy and Practice," working
paper, Chapin Hall Center for Children, University of Chicago, 2005.

16. Elizabeth T. Gershoff, *Report on Physical Punishment in the United
States: What Research Tells Us About Its Effects on Children* (Columbus, OH: Center for Effective Discipline, 2008).

17. On racial and ethnic variations on the use of spanking by race, see the
following: K. Deater-Deckard et al., "Physical Discipline Among African
American and European American Mothers: Links to Children's Externalizing Behaviors," *Developmental Psychology* 32 (1996): 1065–72; E.
T. Gershoff et al., "Longitudinal Links Between Spanking and Children's
Externalizing Behaviors in a National Sample of White, Black, Hispanic,
and Asian American Families," *Child Development* 83, no. 3 (May–June
2012): 838–43; L. J. Berlin et al., "Correlates and Consequences of
Spanking and Verbal Punishment for Low-Income White, African Amer-
ican, and Mexican American Toddlers," *Child Development* 80, no. 5
(September–October 2009): 1403–20.

18. L. R. Knost, *Jesus, the Gentle Parent: Positive, Practical, Effective Discipline* (Little Hearts Books, 2014), 102–4.

19. Sarah Carr, "Why Are Black Students Being Paddled More in the Public
Schools?" *Hechinger Report*, April 14, 2014, http://hechingerreport.org
/controversy-corporal-punishment-public-schools-painful-racial-subtext/.

CHAPTER 2: "A LOVE WHUPPING"

1. John Amato, "NFL's Adrian Peterson Indicted for Child Abuse," *Crooks
and Liars*, September 13, 2014, http://crooksandliars.com/2014/09/nfls
-adrian-peterson-indicted-child-abuse.

2. Sam Farmer and James Queally, "Adrian Peterson Indicted on Child
Abuse Charges; Deactivated for Game," *Los Angeles Times*, September
12, 2014, http://www.latimes.com/sports/sportsnow/la-sp-sn-adrian
-peterson-indicted-child-abuse-20140912-story.html.

3. Stacey Patton, "What It Really Means to Hit a Child," *Al Jazeera*,
September 24, 2014. See, also, the Gundersen National Child Protection
Training Center, *Corporal Punishment State Statute Analysis*, http://
www.gundersenhealth.org/ncptc/center-for-effective-discipline/discipline
-and-the-law/state-laws.

4. See, for example, Stephanie Siek, "Researchers: African-Americans Most Likely to Use Physical Punishment," CNN, November 10, 2011, http:// inamerica.blogs.cnn.com/2011/11/10/researchers-african-americans-most -likely-to-use-physical-punishment/; Lisa J. Berlin et al., "Correlates and Consequences of Spanking and Verbal Punishment for Low-Income White, African American, and Mexican American Toddlers," *Child Development* 80, no. 5 (2009): 1403–20; and Jennifer E. Lansford et al., "Ethnic Differences in the Link Between Physical Discipline and Later Adolescent Externalizing Behaviors," *Journal of Child Psychology and Psychiatry, and Allied Disciplines* 45, no. 4 (2004): 801–12.

5. Child Trends Databank, "Attitudes Toward Spanking," 2015, http:// www.childtrends.org/?indicators=attitudes-toward-spanking.

6. Tamar Lewin, "Black Students Face More Discipline, Data Suggests," *New York Times*, March 6, 2012, http://www.nytimes.com/2012/03 /06/education/black-students-face-more-harsh-discipline-data-shows .html.

7. Libby Nelson, "The Hidden Racism of School Discipline, In 7 Charts," *Vox*, October 31, 2015, http://www.vox.com/2015/10/31/9646504 /discipline-race-charts.

8. "State Survey of California Prisoners—What Percentage of the State's Polled Prison Inmates Were Once Foster Care Children?," *Policy Matters*, December 2011, http://sor.senate.ca.gov/sites/sor.senate.ca.gov/files /State%20Survey%20of%20California%20Prisoners.pdf; "Striking Back in Anger: Delinquency and Crime in Foster Care," *Adoption in Child Time*, 2012–14, http://adoptioninchildtime.org/bondingbook /striking-back-in-anger-delinquency-and-crime-in-foster-children?page=1.

9. Child abuse and fatality statistics from the US Department of Health and Human Services, Administration for Children and Families, Children's Bureau, Child Maltreatment (2003–13). Foster care data from the Adoption and Foster Care Analysis and Reporting System made available through the National Data Archive on Child Abuse and Neglect.

10. Pew Research Center, *Parenting in America: Outlook, Worries, Aspirations Are Strongly Linked to Financial Situation* (Washington, DC: Pew Research Center, December 17, 2015), http://www.pewsocialtrends.org /files/2015/12/2015-12-17_parenting-in-america_FINAL.pdf.

11. Sam Brodey and Jenna McLaughlin, "Eyewitnesses: The Baltimore Riots Didn't Start the Way You Think," *Mother Jones*, April 28, 2015, http:// www.motherjones.com/politics/2015/04/how-baltimore-riots-began -mondawmin-purge.

12. Tom Scocca, "Those Kids Were Set Up," *Gawker*, April 28, 2015, http://gawker.com/those-kids-were-set-up-1700716306.

13. Justin Fenton and Erica L. Green, "Baltimore Rioting Kicked Off with Rumors of a 'Purge,'" *Baltimore Sun*, April 27, 2015, http://www.baltimoresun.com/news/maryland/freddie-gray/bs-md-ci-freddie-gray-violence-chronology-20150427-story.html.

14. Julia Rose, "The Obamas 'Don't Spank,'" CNN, April 25, 2009, http://ireport.cnn.com/docs/DOC-249854.

CHAPTER 3: EXTENDING THE MASTER'S LASH

1. Lloyd DeMause, "The Evolution of Childhood," in Lloyd DeMause, ed., *The History of Childhood* (New York: Harper & Row, 1975), 1.

2. See, for example, Richard C. Trexler, "Infanticide in Florence: New Sources and First Results," *History of Childhood Quarterly* 1, no. 1 (1973): 98–116; Richard C. Trexler, "The Foundlings of Florence, 1395–1455," *History of Childhood Quarterly* 1, no. 2 (1973): 259–84; Emily Coleman, "Medieval Marriage Characteristics: A Neglected Factor in the History of Medieval Serfdom," *Journal of Interdisciplinary History* 2 (1971): 207–15; S. Ryan Johansson, "Centuries of Childhood/ Centuries of Parenting: Philippe Aries and the Modernization of Privileged Infancy," *Journal of Family History* 12 (1987): 355; L. DeMause, "The Formation of the American Personality Through Psychospeciation: Appendix: On the Demography of Filicide," *Journal of Psychohistory* 4 (1976): 1–30; Barbara A. Kellum, "Infanticide in England in the Later Middle Ages," *History of Childhood Quarterly* 1 (Winter 1974): 367–88; R. H. Helmholz, "Infanticide in the Province of Canterbury During the Fifteenth Century," *History of Childhood Quarterly* 1 (Winter 1974): 379–90.

3. On child sacrifice, see Peter Warren, "Knossos: New Excavations and Discoveries," *Archaeology* (July/August 1984): 47–55.

4. Karen J. Taylor, "Venereal Disease in Nineteenth Century Children," *Journal of Psychohistory* 12 (1985): 431–63.

5. Linda Pollack, *Forgotten Children: Parent-Child Relations from 1500 to 1900* (Cambridge, UK: Cambridge University Press, 1983); *A Lasting Relationship: Parents and Children over Three Centuries* (Hanover, NH: University Press of New England, 1987); and Marilyn Brown, ed., *Picturing Children: Constructions of Childhood Between Rousseau and Freud* (Burlington, VT: Ashgate, 2002).

6. DeMause, *The Evolution of Childhood*, 17.

7. Elizabeth Fleck, *Domestic Tyranny: The Making of American Social Policy Against Family Violence from Colonial Times to the Present* (New York: Oxford University Press, 1987), 205.

8. Archer B. Hulbert and William N. Schwarze, eds., "David Zeisberger's History of the North American Indians," *Ohio Archaeological and Historical Quarterly* 19 (1910): 16.

9. Benjamin Wadsworth, "The Nature of Piety," in *Sermons on Early Piety; By Eight Ministers Who Carry on the Thursday Lecture in Boston* (Boston: S. Kneeland, 1721), 10.

10. Alice Earle, *Child Life in Colonial Days* (New York: Macmillan Company, 1899), 191–92.

11. Benjamin Wadsworth, *A Course of Sermons on Early Piety*, as cited in Edmund S. Morgan, *The Puritan Family: Religion and Domestic Relations in Seventeenth-Century New England*, rev. ed. (1944; New York: Harper & Row, 1966), 93.

12. Monica L. McCoy and Stefanie M. Keen, *Child Abuse and Neglect*, 2nd ed. (2009; New York: Psychology Press, 2014), 7–8.

13. Joseph Hawes, *Children in Urban Society: Juvenile Delinquency in Nineteenth-Century America* (New York: Oxford University Press, 1971), 19; LaMar Empey, *American Delinquency: Its Meaning and Construction* (Homewood, IL: Dorsey Press, 1978).

14. C. Ashley Ellefson, *The Private Punishment of Servants and Slaves in Eighteenth-Century Maryland* (2010), http://aomol.msa.maryland.gov/megafile/msa/speccol/sc2900/sc2908/000001/000822/pdf/am822.pdf (accessed December 17, 2015).

15. Kenneth Blackemore and Brian Cooksey, *A Sociology of Education for Africa* (London: George Allen and Unwin, 1981); Mark Bray, David Stephens, and Peter B. Clarke, eds., *Education and Society in Africa* (London: Edward Arnold, 1982).

16. Melville J. Herskovits, *The Myth of the Negro Past* (1941; Boston: Beacon Press, 1990), 196–98.

17. Alma Gottlieb, *The Afterlife Is Where We Come From: The Culture of Infancy in West Africa* (Chicago: University of Chicago Press, 2004); John E. E. Njoku, *The Igbos of Nigeria: Ancient Rites, Changes and Survival* (New York: Edwin Mellen Press, 1990).

18. Elisha P. Renne and M. L. Bastian, "Reviewing Twinship in Africa," *Ethnology* 40, no. 1 (2001): 1–11.

19. See, for example, Robin Law and Paul E. Lovejoy, eds., *The Biography of Mahommah Gardo Baquaqua: His Passage from Slavery to Freedom in Africa and America*, 2nd rev. ed. (2001; Princeton, NJ: Markus Wiener Publishers, 2007); and Mohammad Ali Sa'id, *The Autobiography of Nicholas Said, a Native of Bornou, Eastern Soudan, Central Africa* (Memphis: Shotwell & Co., 1873).

20. Venture Smith, *A Narrative of the Life and Adventures of Venture, a Native of Africa, but Resident Above Sixty Years in the United States of America. Related by Himself* (New London, CT, 1798); and Olaudah Equinao, *The Interesting Narrative of the Life of Olaudah Equiano, or Gustavus Vass, the African, Written by Himself*, vol. 1 (New York: W. Duell, 1791).

21. Paul E. Lovejoy, "The Children of Slavery—The Trans-Atlantic Phase," *Slavery & Abolition* 27, no. 2 (August 2006): 197–217; and Audra A. Diptee, "African Children in the British Slave Trade During the Late Eighteenth Century," *Slavery & Abolition* 27, no. 2 (August 2006) 183–96.

22. Colleen A. Vasconcellos, "Children in the Slave Trade," *Children & Youth in History*, item 141, http://chnm.gmu.edu/cyh/case-studies/141 (accessed July 17, 2016).

23. Robert Hamlett Bremner, *Children and Youth in America: A Documentary History*, vol. 1, *1600–1865* (Cambridge, MA: Harvard University Press, 1970), 22; and Wilma King, *Stolen Childhood: Slave Youth in Nineteenth-Century America* (Bloomington: Indiana University Press, 1995), 15.

24. Delia Garlic, interviewed in *The American Slave: A Composite Autobiography*, George P. Rawick, vol. 6 (Westport, CT: Greenwood Publishing, 1972), 130–31; Brenda E. Stevenson, *Life in Black and White: Family and Community in the Slave South* (New York: Oxford University Press, 1996), 250; Bruce Levine, *Half Slave and Half Free: The Roots of Civil War*, rev. ed. (1992; New York: Hill & Wang, 2005), 106.

25. As quoted in King, *Stolen Childhood*, 92.

26. Ibid., 70.

27. Marie Jenkins Schwartz, *Born in Bondage: Growing Up Enslaved in the Antebellum South* (Cambridge, MA: Harvard University Press, 2000), 112.

28. In *American Slavery, as It Is: Testimony of a Thousand Witnesses* (New York: American Anti-Slavery Society, 1839), 20.

CHAPTER 4: WOULD JESUS WHUP A CHILD?

1. King James Version, Matthew 7:9, 18:3–4; Mark 10:13–16; Luke 11:7, 11:11; and John 16:21.

2. James Dobson, "Protect Your Kids from Tyrant Obama," *WND*, May 30, 2016, http://www.wnd.com/2016/05/protect-your-kids-from-tyrant-obama/.

3. See Knost, *Jesus, the Gentle Parent*, 12–13, 29, 49–51.

4. Erik Eckholm, "Preaching Virtue of Spanking, Even as Deaths Fuel Debate," *New York Times*, November 6, 2011, http://www.nytimes.com/2011/11/07/us/deaths-put-focus-on-pastors-advocacy-of-spanking.html?_r=0.

5. Alan Judd, "Inside the House of Prayer," *Atlanta Journal-Constitution*, October 28, 2013, http://www.ajc.com/news/news/local/inside-the-house-of-prayer/nbbKN/.

6. Alan Judd, "Church Joyful as Kids Return: They're Not Going to Tell Us How to Raise Our Children," *Atlanta Journal-Constitution*, May 28,

2001, https://culteducation.com/group/978-house-of-prayer/9856-church-joyful-as-kids-return.html.

7. David Firestone, "Child Abuse at Church Creates a Stir in Atlanta," *New York Times*, March 30, 2011, http://www.nytimes.com/2001/03/30/us/child-abuse-at-a-church-creates-a-stir-in-atlanta.html.

8. Libby Copeland, "Creflo Dollar and Believing Our Girls," *Slate*, June 18, 2014, http://www.slate.com/blogs/xx_factor/2012/06/18/the_creflo_dollar_abuse_scandal_and_why_so_many_assume_his_daughter_is_lying.html.

9. Libor Jany, "Black Church, Civic Leaders Decry 'Inconsistent' Treatment of Adrian Peterson," *Star Tribune* (Minneapolis and St. Paul, MN), November 24, 2014, http://www.startribune.com/black-church-civic-leaders-decry-inconsistent-treatment-of-adrian-peterson/283757721/.

10. Toby Rollo, "Feral Children: Settler Colonialism, Progress, and the Figure of the Child," *Settler Colonial Studies* (June 29, 2016): 8.

11. On the Christianizing of slaves, see Barry Hankins, *The Second Great Awakening and the Transcendentalists* (Westport, CT: Greenwood Press, 2004); Raphael G. Warnock, *The Divided Mind of the Black Church: Theology, Piety & Public Witness* (New York: New York University Press, 2014); Anthony B. Pinn, *The African American Religious Experience in America* (Westport, CT: Greenwood Press, 2005).

12. As cited in Joseph R. Conlin, *The American Past: A Survey of American History, Enhanced Edition, Volume 1: To 1877* (Boston: Wadsworth Publishing, 2009), 97.

13. Amy Kate Bailey and Stewart E. Tolnay, *Lynched: The Victims of Southern Mob Violence* (Chapel Hill: University of North Carolina Press, 2015), 66.

CHAPTER 5: "YOU ALWAYS WERE A BLACK QUEEN, MAMA"

1. The reality is that the poverty affecting black communities makes them more at risk regarding child abuse and various violence. See Brett Drake et al., "Racial Bias in Child Protection? A Comparison of Competing Explanations Using National Data," *Pediatrics* 127, no.3 (2011): 471–78.

2. Ralph Ellison, "Richard Wright's Blues," in *Shadow and Act* (New York: American Library, 1966), 91.

3. Reginald Robinson, "Gangsta Rap Lyrics and Early Childhood Cruelties: Are These Artists Searching for Enlightened Witnesses and Seeking to Reveal the Real Truth of Black Mother-Son Love?" *Journal of Research in Gender Studies* 5, no. 1 (2015): 73–92.

4. William C. Holmes and Mary D. Sammel, "Brief Communication: Physical Abuse of Boys and Possible Associations with Poor Adult Outcomes," *Annals of Internal Medicine* 143, no. 8 (2005): 581–86.

5. Ibid.

6. US Department of Health and Human Services, Administration on Children, Youth and Families, *Child Maltreatment 2000* (Washington, DC: US Government Printing Office, 2002).

7. Robinson, "Gangsta Rap Lyrics and Early Childhood Cruelties," 73.

8. It is well established that suffering maltreatment as a child leads to various neurological changes in the brain, including reasoning skills and emotional regulation. See Dana M. Hagele, "The Impact of Maltreatment on the Developing Child," *North Carolina Medical Journal* 66. no. 5 (2005): 256–59; and Danya Glaser, "The Effects of Child Maltreatment on the Developing Brain," *Medico-Legal Journal* 82, no. 3 (2014): 97–111.

9. Charles M. Blow, "Black Dads Are Doing Best of All," *New York Times*, June 8, 2015, http://www.nytimes.com/2015/06/08/opinion/charles-blow-black-dads-are-doing-the-best-of-all.html?_r=0.

10. Holmes and Sammel, "Brief Communication," 585.

11. Jean M. Ipsa and Linda Halgunseth, "Talking about Corporal Punishment: Nine Low Income African American Mothers Talk Punishment," *Early Childhood Research Quarterly* 19 (2004): 463–84, 477.

12. Joe Coscarelli, "Dr. Dre Apologizes to the 'Women I've Hurt,'" *New York Times*, August 21, 2015, http://www.nytimes.com/2015/08/22/arts/music/dr-dre-apologizes-to-the-women-ive-hurt.html?_r=0.

13. Jennifer E. Lansford, "The Special Problem of Cultural Differences in Effects of Corporal Punishment," *Law and Contemporary Problems* 73 (2010): 89–106, 96–99.

14. US Department of Health and Human Services, Administration on Children, Youth, and Families, *Child Maltreatment 2014* (Washington, DC: Child Bureau, 2016), 64.

15. Ibid., 22.

16. Ibid.

17. Ibid., 52.

18. Katherine Elliot and Anthony Urquiza, "Ethnicity, Culture, and Child Maltreatment," *Journal of Social Issues* 62, no. 4 (2006): 787–809, 792.

CHAPTER 6: "TALK TO THE WOOD OR GO TO THE 'HOOD"

1. Jessie P. Guzman and W. Hardin Hughes, *Lynching—Crime: Negro Year Book: A Review of Events Affecting Negro Life, 1944–1946* (Pasadena, CA: Tuskegee Institute, 1947).

2. Ralph Ellison, *Shadow and Act* (New York: Random House, 1964), 90.

3. Ingraham v. Wright, 430 US 651, 661 (1977), case transcript available at https://supreme.justia.com/cases/federal/us/430/651/case.html.

4. See, for example, Advancement Project, *Test, Punish, and Push Out: How Zero Tolerance and High-Stakes Testing Funnel Youth into the School to Prison Pipeline* (Washington, DC, Civil Rights Project/

Advancement Project, June 15–16, 2000); Advancement Project, *Opportunities Suspended: The Devastating Consequences of Zero Tolerance and School Discipline Policies*, paper presented at the National Summit on Zero Tolerance, Washington, DC, 2000; Matt Cregor and Damon Hewitt, "Dismantling the School-to-Prison Pipeline: A Survey from the Field," *Poverty & Race* 20 (2011): 223–37; Linda M. Raffaela Mendez, "Predictors of Suspension and Negative School Outcomes: A Longitudinal Investigation," *New Directions for Youth Development* 99 (2003): 17–33; Katherine Masyn Hanno et al., "Who Is Most at Risk for School Removal? A Multilevel Discrete-Time Survival Analysis of Individual-and-Context-Level Influences," *Journal of Educational Psychology* 103 (2011): 223–37; and Donna St. George, "More Schools Rethinking Zero-Tolerance Discipline Stand," *Washington Post*, June 1, 2011, http:// www.washingtonpost.com/local/education/more-schools -are-rethinking-zero-tolerance/2011/05/26/AGSIKmGH_story.html (accessed June 10, 2011).

5. Sarah Carr, "Why Are Black Children Facing Corporal Punishment in Public Schools?," *Nation*, April 28, 2014, http://www.thenation.com /article/why-are-black-students-facing-corporal-punishment-public -schools/.

6. Mike Denison, "Video: Girl Held Down by Boys, Paddled in School," *Palm Beach Post*, March 11, 2015, http://www.palmbeachpost.com/news /news/education/video-girl-held-down-boys-paddled-school/nkSnw/.

7. Forrest Wickman, "Paddling: A History," *Slate*, October 5, 2012, http:// www.slate.com/blogs/browbeat/2012/10/05/who_invented_paddling _the_history_of_spanking_people_s_butts_with_paddles_.html; James Glass Bertram, *Flagellation and the Flagellants: A History of the Rod in All Countries from the Earliest Period to the Present Time* (London: John Camden Hotten, 1869), 304; Darius Rejali, *Torture and Democracy* (Princeton, NJ: Princeton University Press, 2007); George Ryley Scott, *The History of Corporal Punishment: A Survey of Flagellation in Its Historical, Anthropological, and Sociological Aspects* (London: Werner Laurie, 1938).

8. For examples of school discipline that resulted in injuries to students, see Eli Ross, "Waco-Area School Principal Charged with Injury to A Child," KWTX-TV, February 10, 2010, http://www.kwtx.com/home/headlines /83842062.html; Sonja Garza, "Student Sues Charter School Over Paddling-Related Injuries," *Express-News* (San Antonio), January 12, 2005, http://www.nospank.net/n-n87r.htm; Brooke Kelley, "Parent: School Went Too Far with Paddling," WTOC-TV, November 20, 2009; Marie Leeh, "Mom Sues Birmingham Schools, Says Son Beaten at Barrett Elementary," *Birmingham News*, December 9, 2010, http://blog .al.com/spotnews/2010/12/mom_sues_birmingham_schools_sa.html;

Madeleine Davies, "Texas Teen 'Covered in Bruises' Following Paddling by Her Male Vice Principal," *Jezebel*, September 24, 2012, http://jezebel.com/5945837/texas-teen-covered-in-bruises-following-paddling-by-her-male-vice-principal; Ed Doney, "Parents Gave Permission, School Spanking Left Bruises," KFOR-TV, http://kfor.com/2012/09/10/school-spanking-of-6th-grader-being-investigated/; Mark Rice, "Mom Says Daughter Was Bruised by School Paddling; Muscogee County Considers Banning Corporal Punishment," *Ledger-Enquirer* (Columbus, GA), April 13, 2013.

9. MS Code § 37-11-57 (2013), http://law.justia.com/codes/mississippi/2013/title-37/chapter-11/section-37-11-57.

10. Debbie Elliott, "Tackling Obesity amid Poverty in a Mississippi County," *All Things Considered*, National Public Radio, August 9, 2011, http://www.npr.org/2011/08/09/139238924/tackling-obesity-amid-poverty-in-a-mississippi-county.

11. Ibid.

12. Alan Huffman, "How White Flight Ravaged the Mississippi Delta," *Atlantic*, January 6, 2015, http://www.theatlantic.com/business/archive/2015/01/how-white-flight-ruined-the-mississippi-delta/384227/.

13. Sarah Carr, "Why Are Black Children Facing Corporal Punishment?"

14. The Office of Civil Rights collected data from all US public schools. The data used here are aggregated to the state and national level by the Office of Civil Rights and can be found at http://ocrdata.ed.gov/StateNationalEstimations/Estimations_2011_12.

15. Anya Kamenetz, "The Untold Stories of Black Girls," *NPREd*, National Public Radio, March 23, 2016, http://www.npr.org/sections/ed/2016/03/23/471267584/the-untold-stories-of-black-girls.

16. Tracey Michae'l Lewis-Giggetts, "When Did Black Folks Stop Loving Our Children?" *DAME*, November 3, 2015.

17. Southern Education Foundation, *A New Majority: Low Income Students Now a Majority in the Nation's Public Schools*, January, 2015, http://www.southerneducation.org/getattachment/4ac62e27-5260-47a5-9d02-14896ec3a531/A-New-Majority-2015-Update-Low-Income-Students-Now.aspx.

18. Chico Harlan, "In This Part of the United States, Principals Still Legally Hit Students," *Washington Post*, October 19, 2015, https://www.washingtonpost.com/news/wonk/wp/2015/10/19/in-this-part-of-the-united-states-principals-still-legally-hit-students/.

19. "Paddling Okay Again at Marion Schools: Misbehaving Students May Be Struck with Paddle," WESH-TV, April 24, 2013, http://www.wesh.com/news/central-florida/paddling-ok-again-at-marion-schools/19872376. See, also, Human Rights Watch and the ACLU, *A Violent Education: Corporal Punishment in US Public Schools*, 2008, https://www.hrw.org/report

/2008/08/19/violent-education/corporal-punishment-children-us
-public-schools.

20. "Corporal Punishment in Schools and Its Effect on Academic Success," joint statement by Human Rights Watch and the American Civil Liberties Union for the hearing before the House Education and Labor Subcommittee on Healthy Families and Communities, April 15, 2010, https://www.hrw.org/news/2010/04/15/corporal-punishment-schools-and -its-effect-academic-success-joint-hrw/aclu-statement.

21. Holbrook Mohr, "Lawsuit Seeks Ban on Paddling in Mississippi," Associated Press, February 23, 2010, http://djournal.com/news/lawsuit-seeks -ban-on-paddling-in-mississippi/.

22. Alison Bath, "Despite Opposition, Paddling Students Allowed in 19 States," *USA Today*, April 23, 2012, http://usatoday30.usatoday.com/news /nation/story/2012–04–22/school-corporal-punishment/54475676/1.

23. Carr, "Why Are Black Children Facing Corporal Punishment?"

24. Valerie Strauss, "Why Hedge Funds Love Charter Schools," *Washington Post*, June 4, 2014, https://www.washingtonpost.com/news/answer -sheet/wp/2014/06/04/why-hedge-funds-love-charter-schools/.

25. See, for example, a 2013 national study on charter school quality by Stanford University's Center for Research on Education Outcomes (CREDO) found that academic growth in 37 percent of charter schools is significantly worse than in traditional public schools. In addition, 46 percent of charter schools have the same academic results as traditional public schools. The report can be accessed at http://credo.stanford.edu.

26. Ronald Smothers, "Jailed for Paddling the Paddler," *New York Times*, November 13, 1987, http://www.nytimes.com/1987/11/13/us/jailed-for -paddling-the-paddler.html.

27. "Corporal Punishment in Schools and Its Effect on Academic Success," Hearing before the Subcommittee on Healthy Families and Communities, US House of Representatives, Washington, DC, April 15, 2010.

28. Ibid.

CHAPTER 7: "I'LL BUST YOU IN THE HEAD TILL THE WHITE MEAT SHOWS!"

1. Randal D. Day, Gary W. Peterson, and Coleen McCracken, "Predicting Spanking of Younger and Older Children by Mothers and Fathers," *Marriage and Family* 60 (1998): 79–94; J. Giles-Sims et al., "Child, Maternal, and Family Characteristics Associated with Spanking," *Family Relations* 44 (1995): 170–76; M. A. Straus and J. H. Stewart, "Corporal Punishment by American Parents: National Data on Prevalence, Chronicity, Severity, and Duration, in Relation to Child and Family Characteristics," *Clinical Child Family Psychology Review* 2 (1999): 55–70; E. E. Pinderhughes et al., "Discipline Responses: Influences of Parents' Socioeconomic Status, Ethnicity, Beliefs About Parenting, Stress, and

Cognitive-Emotional Processes," *Journal of Family Psychology* 14 (2000): 380–40.

2. Elizabeth White, "'Bernie Mac,' Tough Love, Tougher Laughs," *Media Life*, November 14, 2011, http://www.medialifemagazine.com:8080 /news2001/nov01/nov12/3_wed/news2wednesday.html.

3. Sevonna Brown and Esperanza Dodge, "Breastfeeding on This Side of Trauma," *Rewire*, April 8, 2016, https://rewire.news/article/2016/04/08 /breastfeeding-side-trauma/.

4. Simon McCormack, "Harvard Researchers: Every 64 Days There's a Mass Shooting," *Huffington Post*, October 15, 2014; the Gun Violence Archives can be accessed at http://www.gunviolencearchive.org.

5. Mikhail Lyubansky, "Robin Williams and the Mask of Humor," *Psychology Today*, August 11, 2014, https://www.psychologytoday.com /blog/between-the-lines/201408/robin-williams-and-the-mask-humor.

6. Alice M. Solomon, "The Paradox of Holocaust Humor: Comedy That Illuminates Tragedy," PhD diss., City University of New York, 2011.

CHAPTER 8: "DON'T BE A FAST GIRL"

1. See Louise Greenspan and Julianna Deardorff, "What Causes Girls to Enter Puberty Early?," *New York Times*, February 5, 2015, http://www .nytimes.com/2015/02/05/opinion/what-causes-girls-to-enter-puberty -early.html/. These researchers tracked more than 1,200 girls and found that by the age of seven, 23 percent of black girls, 15 percent of Hispanic girls, and 10 percent of white girls had started to develop breasts. See, also, Elizabeth Weilmarch, "Puberty Before Age 10: A New 'Normal?,'" *New York Times*, March 30, 2012, http://www.nytimes.com /2012/04/01/magazine/puberty-before-age-10-a-new-normal.html. There has been a long debate in the pediatrics profession, dating to the late nineteenth century, about the timing of puberty in girls. Much of this discussion, especially the explanation for why the age of onset of puberty has declined, has been racialized. Scientists have provided a number of explanations, including exposure to chemicals in plastic and household products. Family stress and obesity appear to be the biggest culprits. Girls who grow up in homes without their biological fathers have found to be twice as likely to go into puberty at an earlier age than girls who grow up with both parents. Perhaps mothers without a partner are more likely to be poor, even when working two or more jobs. Those working hours also contribute to stress for the women and children, as child care is expensive, difficult to find, and unpredictable. Children adopted from poorer countries who have experienced significant early-childhood stress have also been found to experience early puberty once they're adopted into Western families. It has also been speculated that growth hormones, particularly in commercial cows' milk, could

play a role in early puberty. Growth hormones used in factory-farmed animals, including fish, are designed specifically to make the animals reach physical maturity faster. As such, those hormones can be passed on to the young children who consume the animals' meat and milk.

2. M. V. Flinn et al., "Evolutionary Functions of Early Social Modulation of Hypothalamic-Pituitary-Adrenal Axis Development in Humans," *Neuroscience and Biobehavioral Reviews* 35, no. 7 (2011): 1611–29.

3. M. E. Hyland et al., "Beating and Insulting Children as a Risk for Adult Cancer, Cardiac Disease and Asthma," *Journal of Behavioral Medicine* 36, no. 6 (December 2013): 632–40.

4. Dante Cicchetti and Fred Rogosch, "Diverse Patterns of Neuroendocrine Activity in Maltreated Children," *Developmental Psychopathology* 13 (2001): 677–93; Cicchetti and Rogosch, "The Impact of Child Maltreatment and Psychopathology on Neuroendocrine Functioning," *Developmental Psychopathology* 13 (2001) 783–804; D. Glaser, "Child Abuse and Neglect and the Brain—A Review," *Child Psychology Psychiatry, and Allied Disciplines* 41 (2000): 97–116; J. Hart et al., "Altered Neuroendocrine Activity in Maltreated Children Related to Depression," *Developmental Psychopathology* 8 (1995): 201–14; R. M. Sapolsky, "Why Stress Is Bad for Your Brain," *Science* 273 (1996): 749–50; M. B. Stein et al., "Hippocampal Volume in Women Victimized by Childhood Sexual Abuse," *Psychological Medicine* 27 (1997): 951–59; Akemi Tomoda et al., "Reduced Prefrontal Cortical Gray Matter Volume in Young Adults Exposed to Harsh Corporal Punishment," *NeuroImage* 47, Suppl. 2 (2009): T66–T71, *PMC*, July 23, 2016.

5. Z. Strassberg et al., "Spanking in the Home and Children's Subsequent Aggression Toward Kindergarten Peers," *Development and Psychopathology* 6 (1994): 445–61; D. A. Granger et al., "Preschoolers' Behavioral and Neuroendocrine Responses to Social Challenge," *Merrill-Palmer Quarterly* 40 (1994): 20–41.

6. Akemi Tomoda et al., "Reduced Prefrontal Cortical Gray Matter Volume in Young Adults Exposed to Harsh Corporal Punishment," *NeuroImage* 47, Suppl. 2 (2009): T66–T71, *PMC*, September 16, 2016; Y. S. Sheu et al., "Harsh Corporal Punishment Is Associated with Increased T2 Relaxation Time in Dopamine-Rich Regions," *NeuroImage* 53, no. 2 (2010), doi:10.1016/j.neuroimage.2010.06.043; Akemi Tomoda et al., "Exposure to Parental Verbal Abuse Is Associated with Increased Gray Matter Volume in Superior Temporal Gyrus," *NeuroImage* 54, Suppl. 1 (2011): S280–S286, *PMC*, September 16, 2016.

7. Stacey Patton, "Is Being Pro-Spanking a Sign of Brain Damage?" *Daily Dose*, May 18, 2015, http://www.damemagazine.com/2015/05/18/being -pro-spanking-sign-brain-damage.

8. Marcia E. Herman-Giddens et al., "Secondary Sexual Characteristics and Menses in Young Girls Seen in Office Practice: A Study from the Pediatric Research in Office Settings Network," *Pediatrics* 99, no. 4 (April 1997): 505–12; B. Ellis et al., "Quality of Early Family Relationships and the Timing and Tempo of Puberty," *Development and Psychopathology* 23 (2011): 85–99; T. E. Moffitt et al., "Childhood Experience and the Onset of Menarche: A Test of a Sociobiological Model," *Child Development* 63 (1992): 47–58; J. Belsky et al., "Family Rearing Antecedents of Pubertal Timing," *Child Development* 78 (2007): 1302–21; L. Wise et al., "Child Abuse and Early Menarche: Findings from the Black Women's Health Study," *American Journal of Public Health* 99 (2009): S460–S466; J. M. Vigil, D. C. Geary, and J. Byrd-Craven, "A Life History Assessment of Early Childhood Sexual Abuse in Women," *Developmental Psychology* 41, no. 3 (2005): 553–61; P. K. Trickett, J. G. Noll, and F. W. Putnam, "The Impact of Sexual Abuse on Female Development: Lessons from a Multigenerational, Longitudinal Research Study," *Development and Psychopathology* 23, no. 2 (2011): 453–76; Jane Mendle et al., "Associations Between Early Life Stress, Child Maltreatment, and Pubertal Development Among Girls in Foster Care," Research on Adolescence 21, no. 4, (2011): 871–80; C. Heim et al., "Pituitary-Adrenal and Autonomic Responses to Stress in Women After Sexual and Physical Abuse in Childhood, *JAMA* (2000): 2, 284, 592–597; R. Boynton-Jarrett and E. W. Harville, "A Prospective Study of Childhood Social Hardships and Age at Menarche," *Annals of Epidemiology* 10 (2012): 731–37, doi: 10.1016/j.annepidem.2012.08.005.
9. Kevin Geary, "The Viral Popularity of Child Abuse," *Revolutionary Parent*, April 20, 2016, http://revolutionaryparent.com/author/kgeary/.
10. Schwartz, *Born in Bondage*.
11. Marie Jenkins Schwartz, *Birthing a Slave: Motherhood and Medicine in the Antebellum South* (Cambridge, MA: Harvard University Press, 2006), 80.
12. Schwartz, *Born in Bondage*, 173.
13. Testimony of Ferdie Walker in William H. Chafe, Raymond Gavins, and Robert Korstad, eds., *Remembering Jim Crow: African Americans Tell About Life in the Segregated South* (New York: New Press, 2003), 9–10.
14. Danielle McGuire, *At the Dark End of the Street: Black Women, Rape, and Resistance—A New History of the Civil Rights Movement from Rosa Parks to the Rise of Black Power* (New York: Knopf, 2010), 64, 66, 86, 191.
15. M. A. Straus and J. H. Stewart, "Corporal Punishment by American Parents: National Data on Prevalence, Chronicity, Severity, and

Duration, in Relation to Child and Family Characteristics," *Clinical Child and Family Psychology Review* 2 (1999): 55–70.

16. See Sigmund Freud, *Three Essays on the Theory of Sexuality*, trans. James Strachey (London: Hogarth Press, 1953); "A Child Is Being Beaten: A Contribution to the Study of the Origin of Sexual Perversion" (1919), reprinted in the standard edition of the *Complete Psychological Works of Sigmund Freud*.

17. Oskar Pfister, *Love in Children and Its Aberrations* (London: Dodd, Mead, 1924), 401.

18. John F. Oliven, *Clinical Sexuality: A Manual for the Physician and the Professions*, 3rd ed. (Philadelphia: Lippincott, 1974), 65.

19. Shere Hite, *The Hite Report on the Family: Growing Up Under Patriarchy* (New York: Grove Press, 1995), 42.

20. Haim G. Ginott, *Between Parent and Child: New Solutions to Old Problems* (New York: MacMillan, 1965).

CHAPTER 9: THE PARENT-TO-PRISON PIPELINE

1. Lateshia Beachum, "'I Decided to Be a Parent and I'm the Bad Guy': Mom Charged for Whipping Kids She Says Burglarized Neighbor," *Washington Post*, June 24, 2016, https://www.washingtonpost.com/news/morning-mix/wp/2016/06/24/i-decided-to-be-a-parent-and-im-the-bad-guy-mom-charged-for-whipping-kids-she-says-burglarized-neighbor/.

2. Maya Lau and David Mitchell, "Baton Rouge Mom Wants '6 Pack Back Under One Roof' After Arrest for Whipping Sons Over Alleged Burglary," *Advocate* (New Orleans), June 22, 2016.

3. M. A. Straus and C. L. Yodanis, "Corporal Punishment in Adolescence and Physical Assaults on Spouses Later in Life: What Accounts for the Link?," *Journal of Marriage and Family* 58 (1996): 825–41.

4. D. A. Simons and S. K. Wurtele, "Relationships Between Parents' Use of Corporal Punishment and Their Children's Endorsement of Spanking and Hitting Other Children," *Child Abuse & Neglect* 34 (2010): 639–46.

5. Child Welfare Information Gateway, *Long-Term Consequences of Child Abuse and Neglect* (Washington, DC: US Department of Health and Human Services, 2006), http://www.childwelfare.gov/pubs/factsheets/long_term_consequences.cfm.

About the Author

Dr. Stacey Patton is an adoptee, child abuse survivor, and former foster youth turned award-winning journalist, child advocate, and assistant professor of multimedia journalism at Morgan State University. Dr. Patton was formerly a senior enterprise reporter with the *Chronicle of Higher Education*, where she covered graduate education, faculty life and research, and race and diversity issues. She writes frequently about race and child welfare issues for the *Washington Post*, *Al Jazeera*, *BBC News*, and The Root.com, and she is a weekly columnist for *DAME Magazine*. She has appeared on *Democracy Now*, *CBS News*, and programs on Fox News, MSNBC, CNN, Al Jazeera, and the BBC. Dr. Patton has won journalism awards from the National Association of Black Journalists, Scripps Howard Foundation, William Randolph Hearst Foundation, and the National Education Writers Association, and, in 2015, she was the recipient of the Vernon Jarrett Medal for Journalistic Excellence in reporting on race. In addition to her work as a journalist, Dr. Patton is the author of a memoir, *That Mean Old Yesterday*, published in 2008 by Simon & Schuster. Dr. Patton also travels the United States delivering keynote addresses and conducting cultural competency trainings for child welfare and juvenile justice professionals. In 2016, she received an award from the American Professional Society on the Abuse of Children for her service and advancement of cultural competency in child maltreatment prevention and intervention. Dr. Patton is also the creator of www .sparethekids.com, a web portal that offers education on child development issues and positive discipline techniques as alternatives to the physical punishment of children.